Experience Clay

Experience
CLAY

Maureen Mackey

Davis Publications, Inc.
Worcester, Massachusetts

Front Cover: Tom Coleman, *Untitled.* Cone 6 glaze, oxidation atmosphere, 20" (50.8 cm) high. Courtesy of the artist.

Half-title page: Paul A. Menchhofer, *Primal,* 2002. Raku fired, multiple firings, 29" (73.7 cm) high. Courtesy of the artist.

Frontispiece: Aurore Chabot, *If You Cracked Open a Football While Sleeping,* 1995. Earthenware, 6 x 10½ x 17½" (15.2 x 26.7 x 44.4 cm). Courtesy of the artist. Photo by Balfour Walker.

Senior Art Education Consultants:

Jennifer Childress, The College of St. Rose, Albany, NY
Lynn Hickey, Los Angeles Unified School District, Los Angeles, CA
Naomi Keller, Omaha North High School, Omaha, NE
Ellen Kong, art educator, author, and clay artist, Durham, NC

Educational Consultants:

Suzanne Andleton, Virginia Beach, VA; Dale Baker, Austin, TX; Nancy Brancheau, Edmonds, WA; Carol Carmack, Virginia Beach, VA; Diane Chisdak, Fleetwood, PA; Sal Digeralando, Newark, NJ; Tim Hunt, Garland, TX; Bob Keller, Bellevue, NE; Sallye Mahan-Cox, Alexandria, VA; Cathy Opfer, Virginia Beach, VA; Mariana Palmer, Havertown, PA; Sara Reich, Virginia Beach, VA; Sharon Seim, Bellevue, NE; Nancy Skullerud, Shoreline, WA; Angela Sweigart, Havertown, PA; Kathy Thompson, Paris, TN; Paula Valenti, Englewood, NJ; David Vukelich, Virginia Beach, VA; Dave Wegener, Olympia, WA; Sharon Williams-Welch, Haverhill, MA; Anne Wolcott, Virginia Beach, VA.

Publisher: Wyatt Wade
Editor-in-Chief: Helen Ronan
Developmental/Production Editor: Carol Harley
Editorial Assistance and Photo Acquisitions: Jillian Johnstone
Educational Content Specialist: Kaye Passmore
Copyediting: Deborah Sosin
Manufacturing: Georgiana Rock
Design: Douglass Scott, Cara Joslin, WGBH Design
Layout/Production: Carolyn Kasper and Dede Cummings, DCDESIGN

Printed in the United States of America
Library of Congress Control Number: 2002110717
ISBN 10: 0-87192-598-2
ISBN 13: 978-0-87192-598-5
10 9 8 7

Acknowledgments

This book could not have been completed without the capable guidance, help, and ideas of Carol Harley, Helen Ronan, and the staff of Davis Publications—thank you! Special thanks go to the students who participated in this undertaking and their artist-teachers who responded with enthusiasm to requests for claywork: Jane A. Archambeau, Graham Hay, Diane Levinson, Timothy Ludwig, Kim Megginson, Marti Osonwitz, Ann Perry, Robert Putnam, Clay Sewell, Nancy Skullerud, and Kevin Tunstall. Their remarkable examples are special highlights for the book. I am also grateful to Kathy Roberson; associates, instructors, and students from the Tucson Parks and Recreation clay program, especially Randy O'Brien for the wonderful documentation and organization of the SA-KU firing; and Cassie Gonzales who always seemed to appear when I needed help. One of the delightful outcomes of this book has been the opportunity to work with Jerry Vaughan and learn new ideas for old firing techniques. Thanks to Paul Menchhofer for sharing information and providing exciting photographs of his raku firings, as well as Eddie Dominguez, Barbara Grygutis, Heeseung Lee, Diane Levinson, and Charles Smith who shared insights and inspiration about their careers in clay. Thanks also to the many clay artists who provided illustrations, photographs, and assistance, and to Karen Durlach who photographed the glaze and firing defects. I particularly want to thank University of Arizona professors W. Dwaine Greer, whose advice helped me combine my interests in clay with the concepts of discipline-based art education, and Maurice Grossman, who always challenges me to delve deeper into clay history.

Finally personal and very special thanks go to my family. They were always there to offer kindness and encouragement when I really needed it; especially Heather Mackey whose moral support and professional expertise were indispensable, Eric Mackey who provided ideas and insights, and Kristina Mackey who always managed to save me with her technical skills. Thanks also to Paul for his patience, subtle guidance, and awesome sense of humor.

Contents

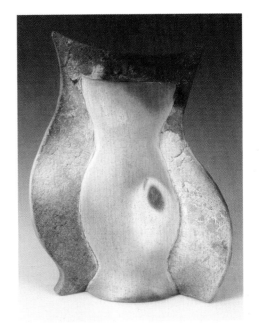

3 **Chapter 1**

Introduction to Clay

4   **Earth, Water, Fire**
5   **Origins of Ceramics**
6   **Early Techniques**
6   Production
7   Preparation
9   Forming Clay
10   **Elements of Design:** Shape and Form
10   Drying Clay
11   Decorating
12   Glazing
12   **Principles of Design:** Contrast
14   Firing
16   **Art History:** Narratives on Clay: A Global Interest
18   **Studio:** Superhero Narratives
20   **Career Profile:** Diane Levinson
21   Chapter Review

Drew Blass, *Rock Series #1*. Slab form, saggar fired, 16 x 10" (40.6 x 25.4 cm). Spruce Creek High School, Port Orange, FL. Photo by Timothy Ludwig.

Courtney Teschner, *Untitled*. Slab sculpture, press mold, cone 4 saggar fired, 14 x 10" (35.5 x 25.4 cm). Spruce Creek High School, Port Orange, FL.

Jenni McDonough, *Pitcher*. Slab formed pitcher, soda fired, 8 x 16" (20.3 x 40.6 cm). Spruce Creek High School, Port Orange, FL.

Students throwing. Photo by Randy O'Brien.

Timothy Ludwig, *Tulip Jar*. Low fire with slips and mason stains, fired to cone 04 oxidation, 16 x 17 x 17" (40.6 x 43.2 x 43.2 cm). Courtesy of the artist.

Richard Koong, *Dragon*. Hand-built, slipped and incised. Bellarmine College Preparatory, San Jose, CA. Photo by Diane Levinson.

23 **Chapter 2**

Working with Clay

24   **Clay Properties**
24   Plasticity
24   Shrinkage
25   Texture
25   **Elements of Design:** Texture
26   **Art History:** Casas Grandes Revival
27   Moisture
27   Handling Clay
28   **Preparing the Clay**
29   **Principles of Design:** Emphasis
30   Kneading
31   Wedging
31   Spiral
32   Ram's Head Spiral
32   **Tools: Physical and Verbal**
32   Physical Tools
33   Verbal Tools
35   Steps in Aesthetic Scanning
38   **Studio:** Build a Paperclay Structure
40   **Career Profile:** Eddie Dominguez
41   Chapter Review

43 Chapter 3

Hand-Built Forms

44 Pinching
45 Practice: Pinch Pot
47 How to Join Two Pieces of Clay
48 Variations on the Basic Pinch Pot
50 Making a Rattle
51 **Art History:** Tea and Its Influence on Ceramics

52 Coiling
52 Making a Coiled Pot
54 How to Extrude Clay
58 **Art History:** Discovering Jomon Ware

59 Slabs, Molds, and Tiles
59 How to Make Slabs
61 Soft Slabs
62 Using Molds
67 Stiff Slabs
68 Practice: Making a Clay Box
71 Tile Making
74 Relief
74 **Principles of Design:** Unity
74 Practice: Relief Panels

76 Sculpture
76 Using Supports and Braces
77 Making a Solid Structure
78 Mixed-Media Sculpture
78 **Elements of Design:** Space
79 Clay Sculpture: Horses
80 **Studio:** Sculpting a Fantasy Animal
82 **Career Profile:** Barbara Grygutis
83 Chapter Review

85 Chapter 4

Thrown Forms

86 The Wheel
88 Centering and Coning
90 Opening the Dome
92 Throwing the Cylinder
94 **Principles of Design:** Balance
95 **Art History:** Rookwood Pottery
96 Trimming

98 Thrown Tableware
98 Throwing the Bowl
100 Throwing the Plate

103 Lids and Spouts
104 Throwing a Flat Lid with a Knob
105 Throwing a Flat Lid with a Flange
105 Throwing a Dome Lid
106 Pouring Lips and Spouts
108 How to Make a Spout

109 Handles
109 Making a Pulled Handle
110 Making Lug Handles
111 Making Thrown Handles
111 Attaching the Handle

111 Teapots
111 Planning Your Teapot
112 **Elements of Design:** Line
113 Making a Teapot
114 **Studio:** Mixed-Media Sculpture
116 **Career Profile:** Charles Smith
117 Chapter Review

119 Chapter 5
Surface Decoration

120 Texture
121 Impressing
121 Incising
122 Appliqué
122 Piercing
123 **Elements of Design:** Value
123 Burnishing

124 Color
124 Colored Clay
125 Inlaying
125 Oxides and Carbonates
126 Colored Slips
127 **Art History:** Blue-and-White Ware
128 Underglaze
128 Techniques for Color
133 Printing Techniques
134 **Principles of Design:** Pattern

136 Glazes
137 Types of Glazes

142 Applying Glazes
143 Dipping
144 Pouring
145 Brushing
145 Spraying
146 How to Spray Glazes
147 Glazing Problems and Solutions
148 **Studio:** Incised Design:
       Mishima and Sgraffito
150 **Career Profile:** Heeseung Lee
151 Chapter Review

153 Chapter 6
The Firing Process

154 Common Kiln Types
154 Electric Kilns
155 Gas Kilns

156 Variables in Firing
157 Atmosphere
158 **Elements of Design:** Color
159 Temperature

161 Stages of Firing
161 Bisque Firing
163 Glaze Firing
165 **Principles of Design:** Movement and Rhythm
166 Works in a Series
167 Finding Inspiration
169 **Art History:** Peter Voulkos and the Birth of Ceramic Art
170 Firing Problems and Solutions

171 Additional Firing Techniques
171 Bonfire
172 Pit Firing
173 How to Do a Pit Firing
174 Sawdust Firing
174 Wood Firing
175 Saggar Firing
176 Raku Firing
178 **Studio:** SA-KU Firing
180 **Career Profile:** Paul Menchhofer
181 Chapter Review

182 Appendix

189 Bibliography

190 Glossary

196 Index

Owner's Manual
for *Experience Clay*

To get the most out of any tool it is valuable to understand its key features and intended uses. In detailing the unique design and features in this textbook, the following will help make *Experience Clay* the most valuable tool in your clay studio.

These opening pages **introduce a topic with a visual and verbal overview** of the concepts and ideas in the chapter.

Build your clay vocabulary.
Key terms are highlighted and defined the first time they appear. *These and other terms are also defined in the Glossary.*

These headings which divide large ideas into **manageable, easy-to-follow concepts** are ideal for quick reference and review.

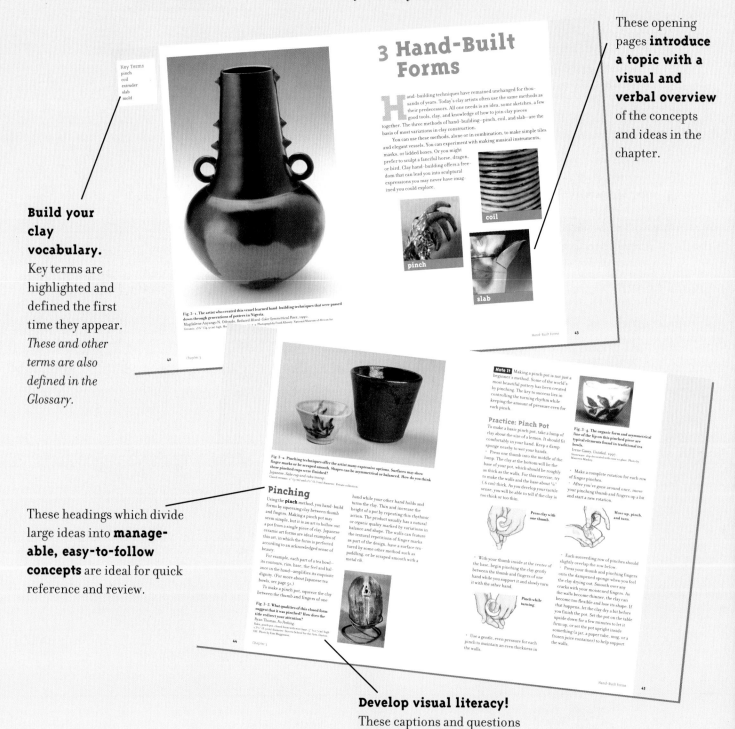

Develop visual literacy!
These captions and questions help you to look deeper at the artwork

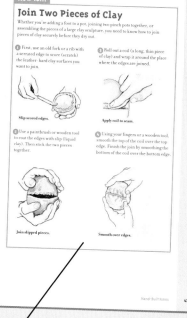

Interviews with professional artists dispel the myth of "the poor starving artist" and set a course for a career in art.

Art is not made in a vacuum. These in-depth profiles **highlight the historical and cultural influences** that have shaped a work of art.

These illustrated, step-by-step studio guides will help you **master fundamental techniques and skills**.

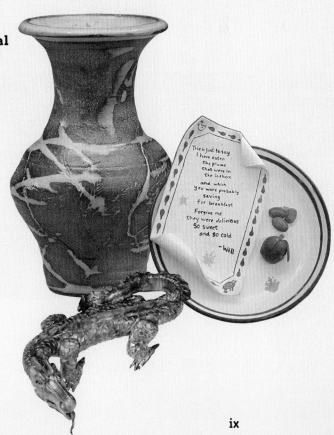

Samples of student art in each studio-rich chapter encourage peer sharing and critique.

Don't miss the **ceramics timeline, glossary**, and the **technical support** in the appendix

Fig. 1–1. This ancient clay form speaks with an elegant power. Can you imagine the life of the Nile Valley artist who sculpted this bird-headed spirit?
Egypt, *Female Figurine*, from Ma'mariya Predynastic Period, Naqada 11, c. 3650–3300 BC.
Terracotta, 11½" (29.3 cm) high. Brooklyn Museum of Art, Museum Collection Fund, 07.447.505.

1 Introduction to Clay

Most of you have experienced at one time or another how it feels to make something in clay, usually at an early age. This kinship with one of the most naturally occurring substances on the planet is as old as human life and has been repeated throughout history. Whose hand can resist tracing a picture or design on the ground, modeling moist natural earth to make a figure, or building a castle in the sand?

Many techniques used to make pottery were developed thousands of years ago, yet they are still practiced today. Methods of preparing, forming, and decorating pottery used in prehistoric times are still employed by folk artists and artisan potters around the world. Clay is an especially versatile medium.

Pottery and spaceship panels are both examples of **ceramics**—things made from clay, the basic material for all ceramic creations. But what is clay exactly, and what separates it from mere mud?

earth, water, fire

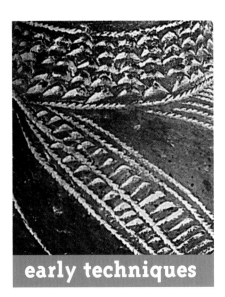

early techniques

origins

Fig. 1–2. From humble cooking pots to artistic sculpture to high-tech products like artificial hips, the range of forms and purposes people have devised for clay is almost infinite. This vessel was made with a press mold, drilled, sandblasted, then sprayed with low-fire glazes.
Randy O'Brien, *Erose*, 2001.
Clay with perlite, 6 x 14 x 14" (15.2 x 35.5 x 35.5 cm). Courtesy of the artist. Photo by Clemens Roether.

Earth, Water, Fire

Clay is created as a result of the decomposition of igneous rock, which makes up the entire earth's crust. Igneous rock is produced when rock that is melted by volcanic heat cools and hardens. This action began when the earth was formed millions of years ago and happens each time a volcano erupts and spews magma, or molten rock, from inside the earth onto the surface. Granite, the rock that makes up the earth's crust, is produced from this volcanic activity. An essential element of granite, feldspathic rock, or feldspar, is the geological basis for clay.

Over time, exposure to weathering causes these materials to break down into smaller and smaller elements. The gradual movement of ice, water, wind, and tree roots pulverize the earth's mantle, grinding boulders to rocks, rocks to pebbles, and, ultimately, pebbles to the finest grains of minerals that comprise clay.

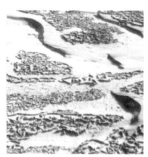

Fig. 1–3. Clay, deposited by a flood, dries in the sun.
Photo by Maureen Mackey.

Note It Clay minerals have microscopic compositions and platelets, or crystallographic structures. Platelets are flat and slide back and forth over one another when moistened. Moisture also helps them cling together. The ability to hold together while being shaped gives clay its **plastic** quality. In its plastic state, it can be formed into different shapes. Fire or heat makes the shape permanent and returns the clay to its rocklike state.

Everything you will do with clay involves the interplay of these three variables: moisture, plasticity, and heat. A delicate porcelain cup and a rough prehistoric cooking pot are still the products of clay (earth), water, and fire. But the porcelain cup is made of a different type of clay and fired (heated) at a vastly

Fig. 1–4. What might have been the inspiration for this low-fire slab form?
Drew Blass, *Rock Series* #4.
16 x 10" (40.6 x 25.4 cm). Spruce Creek High School, Port Orange, FL. Photo by Timothy Ludwig.

different temperature from the earthenware pot. The history of ceramics, then, reveals how people in various places and times discovered new ways to work with these basic materials.

Origins of Ceramics

Of all the arts, ceramics has perhaps the longest history, dating back to when people first learned to control fire. From clues discovered at Stone Age sites, anthropologists have pieced together theories about the origins of ceramics.

One theory suggests that people first began to model clay as a diversion. They may have formed clay animals and human images to embellish a story or to use in a religious ritual. Some of the clay pieces may have been tossed into a communal fire.

When clay is heated quickly, the water trapped inside expands and turns to steam. This rapid expansion happens with such a powerful force that the clay explodes and shatters. Some anthropologists speculate that people thought these explosions were a magical wonder, something like fireworks, and they most likely repeated the process just for the excitement.

But some clay figurines may have dried before they were put into the fire. Instead of exploding, they were transformed by the heat into ceramic figures. Another marvel! Mud turned into stone! Such ancient ceramic effigies or images have been found in many parts of the world.

Sometimes clay was used for practical purposes. When people began cultivating crops, they needed containers to cook in, hold water and food, and store seeds. They shaped clay into vessels by pinching, coiling, or pressing it over round stones and gourds. They also pressed clay

Fig. 1–5. The multi-strand belt and "miniskirt" on this terracotta figurine are typical of those found on other figurines from the Indus Valley culture, which flourished around 2500 BC in present-day western India and Pakistan. What do you think the figure's headgear signifies?

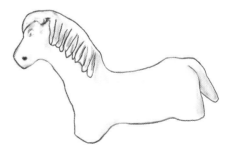

Fig. 1–6. Some of the first clay objects may have been made as a form of entertainment. This fired clay horse from 2300 BC was found in Syria.

into woven baskets, using the basket shape as a kind of mold. Most likely, these people baked clay pots in the same fires that they used for cooking. Cooking fires don't get very hot, so the combination of low-temperature firings and impurities in the clay caused this primitive pottery to be extremely fragile and porous.

As populations increased, people wanted stronger vessels in greater quantities. Clay slabs were used to construct huge vessels and granaries (bins) for crop storage. To keep track of what was in

Fig. 1–7. This large vessel from Marajo Island is an example of the river island culture's complex geometric pottery. Can you find the faces and figures?
Brazil, *Funerary Urn*, 1000–1200 AD.
Ceramic, 42" (106 cm) high. Brooklyn Museum of Art, Museum Expedition 1933. Purchased with funds given by Jesse Metcalf, 33.675.

storage, people marked symbols on clay. Scholars believe that this was probably the beginning of writing.

Cuneiform script, one of the first writing systems, developed in ancient Mesopotamia to record inventories and accounts, and was later used on clay tablets. Surviving clay tablets include detailed information on laws, historical events, and harvests, and offer rare insights into the nature and concerns of ancient societies.

But ceramic objects weren't used just for everyday purposes. They also had religious and mystical uses. Excavations of prehistoric burial grounds show that pots were widely used as funereal objects. Some contained food meant to accompany the dead on their journey to the spirit world. Others held bodies of infants and small children. Later tombs held not only pottery jars filled with food but also ceramic figures and animals placed there with the intention of protecting the deceased.

Early Techniques
Production

Early potters developed a wide range of production techniques. They passed on information and skills from generation to generation, including:

- knowing where to dig the best clay
- deciding which type of clay was best suited to a particular use
- transporting the clay
- removing any impurities
- blending in other materials to strengthen or improve clay
- forming the desired shape
- adding design elements
- drying the work
- firing the work
- glazing
- developing systems of distribution for ceramics

Note It Over time, potters discovered ways to improve each step of the process. Sometimes, the improvements were so revolutionary, potters from another region or society tried desperately to copy them. The delicate blue-and-white glaze that the Chinese developed in the fourteenth century, for instance (see page 127), set off a worldwide craze for pottery of this style. Some potters failed to successfully imitate the blue-and-white glazes, but their attempts led to new discoveries. In this way, technological and artistic innovations leapfrogged from country to country and from era to era.

Innovations continue to press ceramic art forward, but the early techniques endure. Folk artists and artisans still work in traditional ways and use many of the techniques described below.

Preparation

The clay that you work with in a studio has typically been processed and prepared to some degree. Early potters dug their raw material out of the ground, and it often contained impurities such as pebbles or plant matter. To remove impurities from the clay before use, some early potters dried their clay in the sun, crushed it into smaller lumps, and picked out unwanted material. Then they rehydrated or slaked the dry clay to make it workable. This method was fine for making only a few pots, but it was difficult and time-consuming.

Eventually, potters discovered that it was much easier and faster to separate impurities by adding water to the clay and then pouring the liquid clay (or **slip**) from one container to another. This process, known as decanting, causes the coarser materials to settle on the bottom.

Another traditional method for removing impurities is known as *levigation*. Here, the clay is prepared as a slip and allowed to flow slowly down a gently sloping channel. Finer particles flow over a lip at the end of the channel, while the coarser particles settle behind the lip.

Fig. 1–8. Bowls such as this one have been found in ancient tombs in the land now known as Iran. Pottery-making was widespread throughout the Near East, and this type of bowl may have been one of the first vessels to be produced on an early stone potter's wheel.

Iranian, Chalcolithic, *Conical Bowl with Leopard Design*, 3500–3000 BC.

Ceramic, 3½" (9 cm) high, 5½" (14 cm) diameter. The Detroit Institute of Arts, Founders Society Purchase, Henry Ford II Fund, the Catherine Ogdin Estate Fund, Hill Memorial Fund, and the Cleo and Lester Gruber Fund. Photo © The Detroit Institute of Arts, 2000.

Fig. 1–9. The Moche people believed the stirrup shape on this type of vessel was a link to their sacred ancestors. What do you think the falcons on this man's headdress tell about his social status?
Peru, Moche IV, *Portrait Head*, 450–550 AD. Ceramic, 12½" (31.7 cm) high, 8¾" (22.5 cm) diameter. Museo Arqueologico Rafael Larco Herrera XXC-000-012.

Try It Become a clay prospector. Pay attention to the landscape where you live. Cracking patterns on the earth signal sedimentary clay. When you find earth you think may be clay, test a sample:
- Form it into a small ball.
- Add a few drops of water.
- Rub it on the palm of your hand with your fingers.
- It is clay if it feels sticky and greasy.

Remove the impurities from the clay, and use it to make a pinch or coil pot. With adult supervision, fire your work with the ancient pit firing method described on pages 172–173.

Clay that is suitable for producing pottery needs to be plastic (able to be formed into shapes) but not so plastic that it will lose its shape or collapse under the pressure of its own weight. After removing impurities from their clay, early potters also added stabilizing materials to the clay to make it more workable and to decrease its chances of deforming or cracking.

Early potters often mixed additives (such as sand or tiny bits of straw) into large batches of clay by kneading it in with their feet, in much the same way people stomped grapes to make wine. First, they moistened the clay until it was soft. Then, they spread it over a flat area of hard-packed ground. They scattered the additives on the surface and then tramped all over it, systematically kicking down material from the top to mix with the clay at the bottom. Finally, when the clay was the proper consistency, it was allowed to age. Aging improves the quality of the clay and makes it easier to shape. It was not unusual for potters to store their clay in caves for years. In fact, potters from the same family often used clay processed and stored by their grandparents or great-grandparents.

If clay had been stored for a long time, it had to be wedged to get rid of air pockets and to ensure that the moisture and the additives were evenly distributed. The technique for wedging involves using the hands to rotate or roll the clay evenly. A potter usually repeats this rhythmic cycle until the clay seems ready for the forming process. To learn about wedging, see pages 28-32.

Fig. 1–10. **In ancient China, a potter discovered a way to pinch "legs" onto a cooking vessel. This three-legged pot could stand in the fire as a means of heating food efficiently.**
China, Early Shang Dynasty, *Tripod type Li cooking pot*, 16th–13th century BC.
Photo by Yar Petryszn.

potters keep the coils visible in their pots or even use them as decoration. Others use their hands or a paddle and anvil to smooth them out.

Most early storage and cooking vessels required some form of pinching or coiling. Sometimes only a ceramics expert can identify the exact technique used to make a pot. Coils may be laid on a pinched base or supported by pinched feet (like the cooking vessel in Fig. 1–10). Coils may also be used to decorate a finished pot. For instance, the Jomon potters of ancient Japan adorned their pots with fanciful swirls and jags of coiled clay, creating pots whose strange and exotic appearance delights us to this day. (See page 58.)

Forming Clay

As you work with clay, you'll learn a variety of ways to form it into the desired shape. Even the earliest and simplest methods are still used today by potters to fashion beautiful and inspiring ceramic works, including:

- *pinching*
- *coiling*
- *slab building*
- *molding*

These methods are described in Chapter 3.

Potters of ancient times made drinking and cooking vessels by pinching pots out of clay. Some ornamental and religious pottery was formed into shapes of animals and sacred creatures. In ancient Egypt, for example, a potter joined two pinch pots to form a hippopotamus. In ancient Iran, ceremonial wine and water vessels were pinched into the shape of revered animals like bulls and birds.

Potters often use pinching in conjunction with coiling. In the coil technique, the potter rolls out long, ropelike sections of clay and then coils them on top of a base, adding new coils to build up the walls. The potter can squeeze and pull the clay upward, refining the walls. Some

Fig. 1–11. **Women made impressed designs on these West African pots by using their bracelets, which they pressed into the clay and rolled along its surface. Can you tell whether the clay forms were created by pinching or coiling?**
Liberia, Mano, *Storage pots*, c. 1930–50.
White clay hand-rubbed with powdered charcoal, beeswax, and palm oil, 6½" (16.5 cm) and 4½" (11.4 cm) high. Private collection. Photo by T. Fiorelli.

To build anything very large in clay—like a statue of a king or a bin for storing the year's grain harvest—potters preferred to work with big pieces. In slab building, early potters formed large solid cubes of clay and used a bowlike device with a taut string to quickly slice off large slabs. The clay slabs were then pressed or smeared together. This technique produced very large vessels in a short time. For smaller pieces, potters flattened clay with their hands or rolled it out using a smooth tree branch as a roller.

Clay slabs could be used to make rectangular shapes like boxes, or draped over or pressed into molds. A mold could be as simple as a smooth rock or gourd, or as complicated as a clay cast of someone's face. Potters soon learned that they could decorate the surface of their molds with textures like incised or impressed designs, which transferred to the clay cast. For more about molds, see page 62.

Drying Clay

Potters must know how to control the rate at which clay dries. Clay shrinks as it dries and, if it shrinks too rapidly, it can crack. Not all types of clay shrink at the same rate due to their chemical composition. Even some parts of the same work—such as handles—can shrink more rapidly than others due to uneven moisture loss. As you learn to work with clay, you'll need to monitor the drying process to prevent cracking and breaking.

A potter in ancient times had to consider what type of clay to use, the thickness of the vessel's walls, and the local climate—among other variables. If the climate was hot and dry, vessels would have to be sheltered from the sun to slow the process. If the climate was damp and cool, the potter might place the work near a heat source.

An experienced potter also knows that moisture affects how clay can be shaped.

Elements of Design

Shape and Form

The terms "shape" and "form" are often used interchangeably. When referring to design elements, however, shape is a two-dimensional element such as a silhouette or outline. It has height and width, but no depth. Shapes may be drawn upon the surface of a pot as decoration. When you view the profile of a pot in silhouette, you view its shape.

The element of form is three-dimensional and includes an object's depth. Working with clay is about working with three-dimensional forms, although sometimes clay forms such as tiles can be very flat and take on the characteristics of two-dimensional artworks. Shapes and forms may be geometric or organic, curved or angular, positive or negative, static or dynamic.

Fig. 1–12. How would you describe the shapes and forms in this photograph of a clay sculpture? The artist used a slab construction technique, shaping the clay around balloons. Alfred McCloud, *Evolution*.
Stoneware, cone 10 reduction, 12½" (31.7 cm) high. Stivers School for the Arts, Dayton, OH. Photo by Don Clark.

As clay begins to dry, it loses its plastic properties. Some ceramic pieces must be built in stages, after some of the clay hardens. For example, a coiled pot can be refined with a paddle when the clay stiffens. The upper sections of a large coiled pot can be added only when the lower sections have dried enough to support the weight of additional coils.

Clay that has dried to this point is in the *leather-hard* stage; when pressure is applied to the clay, the form will not easily distort. The potter may scrape the surface of a piece to smooth the walls. Early potters used scraping tools such as shells and sharp-edged stones. After removing bumps and flaws, potters may add finishing touches like handles and decoration.

Decorating

For as long as people have been making pots, they've been decorating their surfaces. Some decorative techniques also serve a practical purpose—burnishing makes the clay watertight, for instance.

Early potters used a range of techniques to decorate their clay:

- *Incising* involves carving or cutting the surface with a sharp tool.
- *Impressing* uses an object to press or stamp a design into the clay.
- *Combing* marks the surface of the clay with uniform lines (as if you dragged a comb across it).
- *Burnishing* involves rubbing and polishing the surface with a smooth stone or piece of hard wood.

Modern techniques for surface decoration and glazing are explored in Chapter 5.

Note It Burnishing helps to press the clay particles closer together. Because clay fired at a low temperature remains porous, early pottery could be made waterproof by burnishing ware before it was fired. Coating a pot with pine pitch after firing was another waterproofing technique.

Beautification of the human form is one of the oldest artistic impulses. From early times, people used colorants, such as iron (red) and manganese or carbon (black), to decorate themselves and paint designs and images on cave walls. Painting designs on clay pots was a natural extension of the artists' individual creativity—decoration could enhance the clay's beauty, tell a story, or communicate religious beliefs.

Fig. 1—13. The texture of the incised appliqué creates a rough organic surface on the body of this bottle, which contrasts with the burnished smoothness of the stirrup spout.
Peru, Cupisnique, *Bottle Decorated with Appliqué Nubbins*, 1200—200 BC.
Ceramic, 9¼ x 6¼" (23.5 x 15.5 cm). Museo Arqueologico Rafael Larco Herrera, XXC-00-044.

Fig. 1–14. These sculptures from West Mexico show the fascinating details that pre-Columbian ceramic artists incorporated into their works.

Nayarit, *Male and Female Figures*, 100 BC–400 AD. The Detroit Institute of Arts, Founders Society Purchase, Henry Ford Fund, Benson and Edith Ford Fund, Mr. and Mrs. Walter Buhl Ford II Fund, Alan, Marianne, and Marc Schwartz Fund, with funds from Lois and Avern Cohn, Robert B. Jacobs, Milford Nemer, Margaret Demant, and Mr. and Mrs. William L. Kahn. Photo © Detroit Institute of Arts, 1998.

When vessels were completely dried, they could be decorated with a range of metallic elements. A very fine slip wiped over the surface of a pot gave it a smoother, more uniform texture that helped to make the pot less porous. If a potter added color to the slip, the pot became even more special. A design could be painted on a bone-dry pot using a metallic oxide mixed with water. The dry clay quickly absorbed the water while the clear, crisp lines of the color remained on the surface. When the pot was fired, a change in the range of color could happen depending on the temperature and the atmosphere (oxygen level) of the firing.

Glazing

Glazing makes pots watertight and easy to clean, and enhances their aesthetic qualities. Before glazes were discovered, potters made their work watertight by coating it with animal fats and plant resins.

Think of **glaze** as a thin coat of glass you give your pot. You must fire the pot at a high enough temperature for the glaze to melt and become glasslike. The glaze fuses to the surface of the clay as it cools and hardens. The beautiful, rich colors and textures of glazes are determined by the chemical composition of the glaze.

Principles of Design

Contrast

Contrast is a term used to describe noticeable differences within a design. Contrast adds interest to a work of art. A potter might use contrasting colors, values, textures, sizes, or shapes to get the viewer's attention. A dramatic contrast in colors, for example, can be achieved by positioning dark blue and light yellow glazes next to each other. A subtle (less dramatic) contrast in value might be achieved by burnishing some areas of a pot to a deeper black than the unburnished areas. See Fig. 5-12 on page 123.

Different materials can be used in combination with clay for a contrasting effect. See page 78 for examples. An artist might even use different styles within the same artwork to provide contrast, perhaps to send a message.

Fig. 1–15. Where do you see the principle of contrast used in this design? Did the artist use dramatic contrasts or subtle contrasts? Krissy Dutridge, *Springtime*.
Platter with relief and textures. Whitmer High School, Toledo, OH. Photo by Corey Gray.

Ancient glazes were formulated by trial and error over long periods of time. Most potters tried to keep the composition of their successful glazes a secret. They often added some needless intricate process to the recipe just to confuse their competitors.

The four main glaze types used in early ceramics were alkaline, ash, lead, and salt. The first alkaline glaze appeared around 4000 BC in the Middle East and was mainly a mixture of sand and ash from burned desert plants, the same materials used to develop glassmaking at that time. These transparent and shiny glazes were used with a wide range of *underglazes*.

In the Far East, potters used the ashes of trees and plants to promote the glass-making qualities of high-temperature glazes. Later, feldspar minerals were used. These glazes were thin, but hard and watertight. Although the use of ash glazes was limited to China, Japan, Korea, and Thailand until the 1700s, it became more common in the West when people in the Far East increased their contact with Europe.

Lead glazes developed independently in many regions as a result of the preva-lence of lead ores in the earth. Lead glazes bind to most clays and mature at low fir-ing temperatures. However, they can be poisonous under certain conditions. When tin oxide is added to a lead glaze, it fires to a white, opaque surface. Islamic potters painted elaborate decorations and designs on these glaze surfaces and, later, the technique spread to Europe.

Salt glazes are a high-temperature form of alkaline glaze that originated in the twelfth century. When firing reaches a particular temperature, salt is thrown into the kiln. The vaporized salt joins with silica in the clay body to form a thin, hard, durable surface. German potters discovered this glaze inadvertently, while trying to achieve the high temperatures that Chinese potters had reached for their stoneware and porcelain firings.

Fig. 1–16. Celadon (light green) glazes of China and Korea were developed to duplicate the color of jade. These glazes use wood ash in combination with feldspar and other ingredients including iron oxide, which gives a color range of greens to blues depending on the amount of reduction or oxidation in the firing.
Korea, *Tortoise-shaped wine pot*, 12th century.
Glazed stoneware. Courtesy of Davis Art Slides.

Fig. 1–18. **Stacking pots in a bonfire is a simple open firing method.**

Firing

The earliest pottery was fired in open fires or cooking hearths. Firing at temperatures ranging between 500° and 800°F changes the physical state of clay mineral crystals into a hard, stable medium. When clays are heated above these minimum temperatures, they become ceramics. Early firing methods are still used in Asia, South America, North America, Africa, and other areas.

The main methods of firing clay are open firing, in which the vessels and fuels are set together, and **kiln** firing, in which the vessels and fuels are separated.

Open Firing

The earliest pottery was most likely fired in open cooking fires, which required limited structure and upkeep. Variations of the open firing method evolved as potters developed better control of the operation. A potter could control or restrict firing temperatures by setting some fuel beneath the vessels to allow for the rise of the heat, by leaving gaps between the pieces of fuel to facilitate air flow, or by taking advantage of wind to increase combustion.

Using different fuel offered the potter even more control. If a gradual rise in temperature was desired, animal dung, which burns slowly and uniformly, could be used. Cooking vessels would be fired with a slow-burning fuel. Storage vessels tempered with grog (an additive, typically crushed pottery, that makes the clay more stable) or straw could be placed in a fire that would rapidly rise in temperature, using twigs, straw, and grasses as a fast-burning fuel.

Potters modified this simple procedure by placing the vessels and fuel on stones spaced far enough apart to allow for air flow. They covered the vessels and fuel with shards (pieces of broken pottery), mud, or wet grass to insulate and capture more heat in the firing. They also placed holes in the covering to act as chimneys that would draw the air up through the setting or stacking pattern.

Eventually, potters placed the vessels and fuel in a pit or depression. Then they used more permanent structures in which to pile their vessels. Some enclosures had circular walls or were three- or four-sided.

Kiln Firing

A kiln is an enclosed structure like an oven or a furnace designed to withstand very high temperatures for firing ceramics. Early kilns were made of stone plastered with clay. Later, they were constructed of brick or adobe. Two types of kilns emerged in the ancient world, the updraft and the downdraft. Such kilns are still in use today.

The *updraft kiln* consists of a firebox with a chamber directly above it. Ancient Greek, Roman, Mediterranean, and Islamic pottery was fired in updraft kilns.

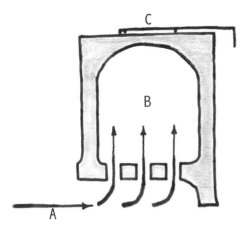

Fig. 1–19. Updraft kiln. Fuel is burned in the firebox (A) and the heat flows through the chamber (B), leaving the kiln through flues, or openings at the top of the chamber (C).

The *downdraft kiln* is more complex, and enabled artisans to be more productive. Potters in China and Japan set large kilns into hillsides with several interconnected downdraft chambers. These kilns made efficient use of the heat produced in the firing and accommodated great quantities of pottery. The earth surrounding the chambers was a natural insulator and very high temperatures could be achieved in these firings.

Note It Using kilns instead of cooking fires, potters were able to achieve new and greater effects by controlling the rate of heating, the maximum temperature, and the atmosphere of the firing.

Fig. 1–20. Downdraft kiln. From a firebox (A) the heat flows upward over a bagwall (B) and downward into the firing chamber (C). From there, the heat passes through holes at the bottom to a chimney (D), where it exits the kiln.

Early potters learned that:
- Controlling the rate of heating allowed enough time for chemical reactions to take place within the clay crystals. If the rate was too slow, a lot of fuel was used up unnecessarily. If the rate was too fast, the pieces could explode as a result of the rapid expansion of water in the clay.
- Controlling the maximum temperature allowed for chemical reactions to take place at the ideal temperature. If a firing temperature was higher than optimum, it could cause warping or cracking.
- Controlling the atmosphere allowed the potter to create different decorative effects. The atmosphere refers to the amount of air supplied to burn the fuel.

By learning to control the firing atmosphere of the kiln, potters held the final key to the outcome of their labor. Now the range of available colors increased dramatically. This led to a demand for pottery that was more than functional. With the command of design—combined with forming, decorating, and firing skills—potters could create distinctive pieces that were valued for their beauty.

Throughout the history of ceramics, high points of skill and beauty converged at various times in different cultures.

For Your Sketchbook
Research kilns worldwide and sketch at least three different basic kiln structures. Include views of both interior and exterior. Which one would you like to build? Which one would you like to use? Why?

Advances in firing techniques were key to such achievements.

What are some of these highlights? The narrative pottery of ancient Greece is renowned for its graceful forms and detailed compositional style (see Figs. 1–21 and 1–22). Other cultures focused on sculpting figures in clay. Etruscans crafted full-sized human figures from terracotta in the fifth century BC. In Africa, Nok full-sized terracotta heads

Fig. 1–21. By reducing the amount of air in the firing chamber, potters in ancient Greece were able to cause their pots to change colors, producing dramatic black-figure ware.
Greek, Archaic Period, *Amphora*, c. 500 BC.
Black-figure terracotta, 12⅝" (32 cm) high. The Cleveland Museum of Art. Purchase from the J.H. Wade Fund, 1929.979.

Narratives on Clay: A Global Interest

Narrative art tells a story, and the Greeks were the first to paint on clay pots as a way of telling stories. They painted action scenes featuring the human figure as early as the Bronze Age (around 2900–2000 BC).

Art that represents a form or the human figure is called "figurative." During the Greek classical period, figurative imagery reached a high point. Ceramic artists painted elegant pots with monsters, heroes, and mythological figures. In early classical narratives (seventh century BC), black figures were crafted on the pot's natural red background. (See Fig. 1-21.) Lines showing facial features, musculature, or clothing were laboriously incised. Later works (fifth century BC) featured the red-figure style—the background is painted black and the figure remains in red. (See Fig. 1-22.) Artists began to paint

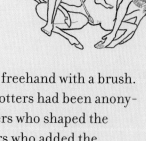

Fig. 1–23. Narrative from a red-figured kylix illustrating the myth of Lapith and the Centaur.

lines and details freehand with a brush. Until this time potters had been anonymous. Now potters who shaped the form and painters who added the details typically signed their pieces.

Narrative art also flourished in the ancient Americas. About 500 years after the Greeks first developed black-figure technique, the Moche, a people on Peru's north coast, were chronicling their beliefs and history on intricately painted pots. The Moche, who flourished from about AD 50 to 800, had no writing system. But scholars compare their ceramics to a library, because the and figures date from fifth century BC to second century AD. In China around 220 BC, armies of full sized terracotta human figures and horses were made to accompany the emperor in his tomb. Consider looking at books, in museums, and on the Internet for examples of these artworks. How were the works fired? Firing techniques and kilns are explored in greater depth in Chapter 6.

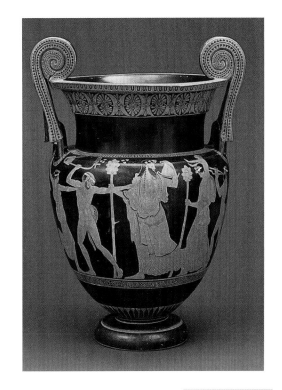

Fig. 1–22. By adding air to the firing chamber, potters were able to create the bright, clear colors we see on red-figure vases.
Greek, Attica, Methyse Painter (attr.), *Athenian Red-figure Volute Krater*, 460–450 BC.
Slip-glazed earthenware, 23½ x 13¾" (60 x 35 cm). The Minneapolis Institute of Arts, Gift of Mr. and Mrs. Donald C. Dayton.

Moche recorded so much on their pots. Moche artists applied fine lines to the pot with a clay slip, a technique known as slip painting.

North of the Moche people, the Maya—in the region now occupied by Belize, Guatemala, and Mexico's Yucatan province—created another great civilization. The Mayan classical period (AD 250–850) was marked by multicolor painted ceramics that detailed religious themes, rituals, and history. Mayan artists used basic shapes and relied heavily on lines as an expressive feature. Like the Moche, the Maya

Fig. 1–25. Two Moche warriors in battle gear.

used slip painting to create their designs, which were fired at a low temperature. Artists personalized the pots with their names, the names of patrons, and sometimes the workshop where the vessel was created.

Artists in all three cultures—Greek, Moche, and Mayan—mastered the difficult art of painting a narrative scene on the outside of a round pot. Wrapping a composition around a pot requires careful planning, because artists can see and work on only a small portion of the pot's surface at one time.

Fig. 1–24. Mayan figure in elaborate costume drinking from a bowl. Mayan artists usually painted the face and figure in profile and also used hieroglyphics (picture writing) as a design element.

Superhero Narratives

You will tell a story in a slip-painted format similar to that of a classical narrative work. In ceramics, classical style uses figurative imagery to tell a story. The artist uses line drawings for the wrap-around design and also writes on the piece.

The ceramic artists of the Greek, Moche, and Mayan classical periods decorated their pots with narrative (storytelling) themes that often featured superheroes or mythological creatures. Pots also were used to record special events such as weddings, funerals, festivals, and battles. Often, these classical works were high-status serving vessels used for rituals or awarded as regal gifts. They signified political power and social prestige.

Before You Begin

• Consider the narrative form as it exists today. What artistic devices do we use to visually tell our stories?

• Think about a story you would like to tell. This could be inspired by a superhero in popular culture, a story passed down through your family or culture, or an incident in the life of someone you admire. You might also choose to show a special event that has affected your life.

• Develop a narrative design that dramatizes the story.

• Sketch the story in sequence. Make a few sketches and choose the ones that best show the story.

• Use the human figure in your narrative. Your figures can be realistic, cartoonish, or stylized.

• In your design, include at least two decorative elements that follow the classical style: line drawings, face and body shown in profile, and pictorial field balanced by writing and/or symbols.

• Decide whether you want to portray the narrative on a plate, bowl, or other vessel. Contour lines can be incised or slip-painted.

You will need:
· sketches of your narrative design
· plate, bowl, or vessel (damp but fairly stiff)
· colored slip
· paintbrush to apply slip
· tools for carving or incising

Create It

1 Paint a band of slip around the surface of your piece. It should be wide enough to contain your narrative.

2 Working from your sketches, plan and draw your narrative on the slip-painted clay.

Fig. 1–26. Sarah Dawson adds a band using slip.

3 Incise (carve) contour lines through the band of slip. Slip-paint additional lines on the surface, as desired.

4 Use writing or symbols to balance each segment of your design.

5 Sign your work.

6 Bisque fire.

7 Apply clear glaze.

8 Complete final glaze firing.

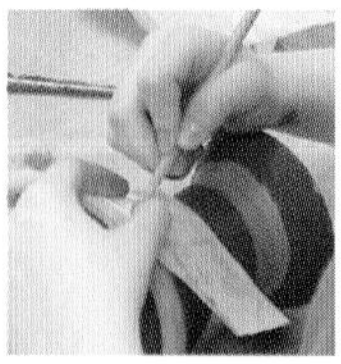

Fig. 1–27. Melissa Williams transfers her design onto her pot.

Check It Were you able to tell a story in the available space? Who do the figures represent? Explain why you chose them. Do they correspond to mythological fig-

Fig. 1–28. Ryan Anderson carves garbage collectors.

Fig. 1–29. Joelene Jackson incising lines.

ures, such as monsters or superheroes? Why or why not? Did you make your figures look real? Or did you make them look exaggerated or cartoonish? How successful were you? Point out at least two characteristics of your composition that represent the classical style. Explain how you balanced the design. Why did you choose the design elements you did? How does each fit with the story? Can you think of other ways you could use this narrative theme in clay?

Sketchbook Connection

Think of your sketchbook as a companion on your creative journey. Make one section for writing thoughts and ideas about your dreams, experiences, interests, and feelings. Draw to expand upon those themes. Make another section where you document the different stages of your creative process. Explain the decorative techniques you experimented with, and include glazing and firing information. Note the results and why you consider them successful or not. Finally, keep a section for notes, pictures, or articles about historical images and various clay artists whose works appeal to you.

Fig. 1–30. "The woman on my pottery represents Sioned with her royal circlet on. The large crests are my interpretation of what a family crest for Sioned's family would look like."
Jen Hansen, *Heroic Greek*, 2002. 7½" (19 cm) high.

Rubric: Studio Assessment

	4	3	2	1
Idea Communication • Sequential treatment of narrative • Additional symbols/writing • Realistic, cartoonish, or stylized	Figurative narrative is highly detailed and sequentially readable. Meaningful symbolic designs/figures help tell story. Stylistic approach beneficial. Detailed, meaningful story	Figurative narrative is detailed and sequentially readable, combines symbols and designs. Stylistic approach appropriate. Satisfying story	1 of these: Narrative lacks figurative emphasis; sequential readability needs development; stylistic approach inappropriate or inconsistent. Developing story	2-3 of these: Narrative lacks figurative emphasis; sequential readability lacks development; stylistic approach inappropriate or inconsistent. Underdeveloped story
Decorative Elements • Elements: line and color • Profile view • Balanced pictorial field • Location of narrative band	Lively use of line/color add variety, continuity. Figures in profile view; interact and flow with other elements. Balanced action on entire pictorial field. Location works with clay form. Unusual, engaging, integrated	Line/color add variety to narrative band. Some profile views; figures interact with other elements to balance majority of pictorial field. Location works with clay form. Effective, complete	1-2 of these: lack of variety in line use and color; few figures in profile view; pictorial field neglected in some areas; location needs much more consideration. Needs additions or edits	3-4 of these: lack of variety in line use and color; few figures in profile view; pictorial field neglected in significant areas; location needs much more consideration. Significant gaps, awkward
Media Use • Symmetrical clay form • Painted slip band • Incised lines • Clear glaze	No apparent mistakes in symmetry of clay form, slip or glaze application; incised lines do not puncture form. Skillful, controlled	Few apparent mistakes in symmetry of clay form, slip or glaze application; incised lines do not puncture form. Competent	Some noticeable mistakes in symmetry of clay form, slip or glaze application; incised lines may have punctured form. More practice indicated	Many noticeable mistakes in media use; detracts significantly from effect OR work very incomplete. Rudimentary difficulties
Work Process • Brainstorming • Sketches • Reflection/Evaluation	Thorough documentation; goes above and beyond assignment expectations. Thoughtful, thorough, independent	Complete documentation; meets assignment expectations. Meets expectations	Documentation is somewhat haphazard or incomplete. Incomplete, hit and miss	Documentation is minimal or very disorganized. Very incomplete

Career Profile:
Diane Levinson

Growing up in New York City, Diane Levinson attended the art school of the Museum of Modern Art. She moved to California in the 1970s and received her Master of Fine Arts degree in 1987. Today, Levinson has found the perfect way to balance her creative interests with a viable career in ceramics. As a teacher, she is not bound by the need to sell her clayworks but is free to create objects that fulfill her own artistic vision.

When did you discover ceramics?
Diane: I've been making art since kindergarten but didn't work with ceramics until I studied sculpture in college. Clay was used only to make molds for sculptures in other materials. I started to like making the molds and devoted my last year of college to working with clay.

Why did you become a teacher?
Diane: I had decided long ago not to be exclusively a studio potter because I wanted my time in the studio to be my own, which teaching allows. I love the interaction of teaching; I learn so much from the students—they are so ambitious and willing to try new things.

How do you motivate your students?
Diane: I start by saying, "Everyone is afraid of creativity; we're all art-phobic." I reassure them that it's fine if the piece doesn't look as good as they had hoped.

It's very humbling to work with clay. I try to teach them not to be afraid to take chances, and hopefully I can bring out their creativity.

What is your least favorite part of teaching?
Diane: Grading, because everyone should make their best piece because they want to make their best piece, not for a grade. But I grade every piece on craftsmanship and creativity, equating craftsmanship with effort. If the student puts in the effort, the piece usually looks well crafted.

Do you ever see a time that you would not teach?
Diane: Even if I won the lottery (which I don't play), I would still teach part time because I love the interaction, and I learn so much from the students because they are so ambitious and try new things.

Fig. 1–31. First I use the wheel to throw a base of about twenty-five pounds. Then I build up the pot with coils and wrap extruded clay ribbons around it. I never make anything to sell—I only trade or give away my pieces. It gives me a better feeling.
Diane Levinson, *Basket #4*, 2001.
Ceramic, glazed cone 6, 27 x 22 x 22" (68.6 x 56 x 56 cm). Courtesy of the artist.

Chapter Review

Recall List four basic techniques for forming clay.

Understand Explain why it is important for potters to control the temperature and rate of heating when firing a claywork.

Apply Use three pieces of clay of different thicknesses to form the same simple form (for example, a pinched pot, slab, or coil). Note the rate at which each form dries. At what point is each form too dry to be workable?

Analyze Study the image of the stirrup vessel on page 8. Describe how the form and decoration might have been constructed.

Synthesize How are comic books similar to the painted scenes of classical Greek, Moche, and Mayan pottery?

Evaluate Consider the processes of Greek black-figure and red-figure painting. Which method would you choose for decorating a pot? Explain.

Writing about Art

Research the ceramic work of an ancient culture from any part of the world. Write an essay that describes the types and purposes of ceramics produced, and the methods and materials used to create them. After carefully examining the examples of clay artwork from the culture, conclude your essay with a description of what ideas these artworks communicate about the culture. How are the messages they communicate today different from what they communicated in their time and place of origin? How are they similar?

Fig. 1–32. This organic form with a diagonal surface design of impressed lines is an appealing asymmetric and geometric combination. What qualities of the surface textures are repeated in the work's small rugged base?
Sherman Edwards, *Tornado Series 2.*
Slab sculpture, stain, terra sigillata, low fired, 16 x 7" (40.6 x 18 cm). Spruce Creek High School, Port Orange, FL. Photo by Timothy Ludwig.

For Your Portfolio

A portfolio gives a broad picture of your accomplishments in clay art. It should contain slides or photographs of your completed pieces, as well as organized notes on the glazing and firing processes used. Be sure to document each object's dimensions. You can also show examples of works you may have collaborated on. Include statements expressing your ideas, objectives, and sources of inspiration. Your portfolio might also hold research papers you've written relating to ceramics, clay artists, and historical periods.

Key Terms
traditional
  pottery
grog
wedging
kneading
aesthetics

Fig. 2–1. Ken Ferguson plays with the viewer by placing the hare in unlikely arrangements on functional ware. How many hares can you find on this piece? How does his placement of the tortoise symbolize the outcome of a well-known fable?

Ken Ferguson, *Hare Casserole with Turtle Lid*, 1998.

Stoneware with incised decoration, 18" (45.7 cm) high, 17" (43.2 cm) diameter. Arkansas Arts Center Foundation Collection. Purchased with a gift from the Vineyard-in-the-Park, 1998, 98.035.

2 Working with Clay

What kind of clay will you work with? Different types of clay (or clay bodies) have unique qualities that make them suitable for different uses. You might use one clay body to make a large sculptural work and another to make fine teacups. Clay is a material that constantly challenges the artist.

As a potter, you must get to know your clay because each clay has a distinct personality. The better you know your clay, the more successful your work. The key factors to learn about are plasticity (how easy or hard a clay is to shape), shrinkage, texture, and moisture.

tools

properties

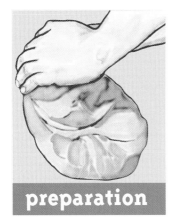

preparation

Fig. 2–3. **This work by a ninth-grade student combines organic and geometric forms. Which part of the sculpture relies most on the plastic quality of clay?**
Cannan Good, *Choreographed Temple.*
Raku, slab construction, 15" (38 cm) high. Stivers School for the Arts, Dayton, OH. Photo by Kim Megginson.

Clay Properties

Plasticity

Most beginners use highly plastic clay, or one that can easily take different shapes. A good plastic clay for beginners is earthenware, which stands up well to a lot of handling and can be used to form a variety of objects.

Numerous factors can make clay more plastic. For instance, you can mix in some ball clay to make your clay easier to shape. Ball clays are highly plastic. They are not used alone because of their high *shrinkage* rate—instead, they are used as an additive. Algae and bacteria also make clay easier to handle as they grow in aging clay. Some artists store bags of clay that look slimy and old. Experienced potters prize this clay because it is so good to work with.

Shrinkage

All clays shrink as they dry. Clay can crack when it shrinks if the potter doesn't carefully monitor the drying process. When the dried clay is fired, it will shrink again.

It's frustrating to spend a lot of time creating an artwork only to have it crack. You can minimize the number of pieces you lose if you familiarize yourself with how your clay shrinks, at what rate, and what you can do to affect the process. See page 186 for a test to help you determine how much your clay will shrink.

Fig. 2–4. How did this artist need to plan for clay shrinkage as he developed this tall sculpture?

Bill Stewart, *Frog Foot*, 1999.

Hand-built terracotta with slips and glazes, multiple firings, cone 05, 74 x 23 x 14" (188 x 58 x 35.5 cm). Courtesy of the artist. Photo by Bruce Miller.

Note It Shrinkage is part of experiencing clay. If you make a clay sculpture that includes pieces of different thickness, remember that the thin pieces will shrink more rapidly than the thick ones. Unless you slow down the drying process for the thin pieces, the work may crack or break. Wrapping thin sections in plastic or painting them with wax resist (see page 131) will help to slow the drying process.

Texture

The texture of a clay body can range from coarse to smooth. Much studio clay contains additives that modify it, making it easier to shape or stabilizing it so that it shrinks more uniformly when drying. The quantity and type of additives affect a clay's texture.

Fig. 2–5. How would you describe the texture of these hand-built slab vessels? Imagine how they might look if there was a strong light shining up from under them.

Jan Bell, *Palma Colorada*, 2001. Stoneware, 15" (38 cm) high. Courtesy of the artist.

Elements of Design

Texture

The texture of a clay body is how it feels to the touch—coarse, medium, or smooth. Texture is also the physical surface structure of the finished clay piece—such as pebbly, ridged, satiny, or grooved—and this surface structure can create diverse effects. When light hits an object, it strongly defines the texture of that object. If an object is in shadow or dim light, the surface texture may be reduced or become imperceptible. When the light is bright, depending upon its position, the texture becomes active or even dominant.

Casas Grandes Revival

Pottery that has been formed by hand, painted with natural pigments, and fired with an organic fuel (like wood or dung) is referred to as **traditional pottery**. Pottery-making traditions handed down through the ages still survive relatively unchanged in some areas of Africa, Asia, Mexico, and South America.

During the first to the late thirteenth century AD, pottery was made in the city of Paquime in northern Mexico's Casas Grandes valley. It became an important commodity on a network of trade routes. The pottery was remarkable both for its high quality and for its designs.

The original Casas Grandes pottery tradition died out in the fourteenth century when Paquime was destroyed by fire. Over time, new settlements arose in the area—small villages where farming and cattle were more significant than trade and crafts.

Today, hundreds of years after Paquime disappeared, the style of its pottery is once again thriving. An extraordinary example of how a traditional style can live again is seen in the revival of the Casas Grandes style by contemporary Mexican potters.

This revival began in the late 1970s thanks to Juan Quezada, a lifelong resident of Mata Ortiz in the Casas Grandes valley. As a young boy during the 1950s, Quezada gathered firewood in the mountains near his village. He often found and admired 700-year-old pieces of Casas Grandes pottery. Determined to discover how Paquime's people achieved such perfection in their ceramics, he experimented with clay, natural pigments, and firing techniques for twenty years. Through trial and error, he gradually mastered the ceramic art that had flourished centuries ago. He shared his skill with his family, and, ultimately, with the other people in his community.

Quezada's fascination with the Casas Grandes pottery style eventually transformed not only his life but that of his village. Quezada continues to teach, while his pottery is sought after by museums and collectors worldwide. A second generation of potters has now emerged to continue the legacy.

Fig. 2–6. From roughly the first to the late thirteenth century AD, **the area that is now northern Mexico and the southwestern U.S. was home to several flourishing cultures: the Casas Grandes, Hohokam, Mogollon, and Anasazi.**
Casas Grande, Arizona, *Hohokam Vessel*, 300 AD. Red on buff jar. Courtesy of the Heard Museum, Phoenix, AZ, NA-SW-HN-A4-18.

Fig. 2–7. How is the design of this Casas Grande revival pot similar to the traditional pot shown in Fig. 2–6?
Jose Silviera, *Mata Ortiz pot*, 2000. Courtesy of the artist.

Coarse clay contains sand or grog, and is best for large, thick-walled pieces. Medium-coarse clay can be used for hand-built slab work, tiles, and large coiled vessels or figures. A smooth-textured or fine-grained clay is good for throwing pottery, bead making, and other delicate work.

Moisture

It is important to learn how water affects the clay you work with. All clays contain water. You can add water to clay to make it more workable or plastic. Add too much water, however, and the clay loses plasticity—it won't hold any shape at all.

Clay begins to dehydrate, or lose moisture, when it is exposed to air. As you work on a clay project, you will occasionally need to rehydrate, or put water back into the clay, to keep it moist. Mist it with water from a spray bottle or dampen it with a wet sponge. When you're not working, cover the piece with plastic to keep it from overdrying.

Some water remains in the clay no matter how dry it seems. This water is driven out only when the clay is fired. Clay that looks dry but feels cold still contains water and should dry out further before it is fired.

A thick piece of clay can contain trapped moisture. This moisture will turn to steam when the clay is fired and can even cause the piece to explode during the firing process. Artists who build large pieces or pieces with thick walls typically add **grog** (crushed ceramics) or an organic material like sawdust to the clay to make it more porous.

Once the clay is fired, it becomes permanently harder, stronger, and less likely to break. It can never become plastic again.

Fig. 2–8. **Any piece of clay that is more than 1" thick must be hollowed and pierced to allow hidden moisture to escape. Clay that is more porous enables trapped moisture to exit more easily.**
Jane A. Archambeau, *Fall From Grace and the Angel Protects You*.
Earthenware, press-molded with commercial underglaze, pencils, 16 x 10 x 10" (40.6 x 25.4 x 25.4 cm). Courtesy of the artist. Photo by Corey Gray.

Handling Clay

Now that you're aware of the different factors that affect clay, it's time to familiarize yourself with the actual raw material. Developing your sense of touch will make it easier to work with clay. When you handle clay, pay attention to how the clay feels and try to take in as much tactile information as possible.

Flatten a lump of clay on your workspace. Smooth the surface with your fingers. Roughen the surface by digging into it, poking it, or scratching it. Use a damp sponge to smooth the surface again. How does the clay surface react when you add water and pressure?

Try It Cut a lump of clay in half. Roll one piece into a ball. Take the other piece and roll it into a short cylinder (like a short, squat candle). Stand the cylinder up on your workspace. Place the ball on top of the cylinder so that it stays balanced there. Does the shape look symmetrical—do its opposite sides match? Does the weight of the ball affect the cylinder? How far to the side can you move the ball before it falls? If you roughen the surface, will the ball stay in place?

Fig. 2–9. Students wedge clay.
Photo by Ann Perry.

Preparing the Clay

Before you make anything with clay, you'll need to prepare it. Whether your clay is premixed or you add water to a dry mix, the clay should always be *de-aired* before you begin. Air pockets in the clay can throw a wheel-thrown pot off-center or distort the shape of a hand-built slab. The time you spend working the clay at the wedging table can save you a lot of time and frustration later.

Kneading or **wedging** eliminates air bubbles and keeps the internal structure of clay more cohesive and consistent. You can use several methods to achieve this. Find the one that works best or feels most comfortable, and make it your own.

Do your wedging on a canvas-covered board or plaster slab, which absorb any extra moisture. Work on a surface slightly lower than table height. In this way, you can use your upper-body strength as leverage.

Fig. 2–10. Clay recycling.

Note It You can recycle your clay scraps by mixing them with water and pouring the soft mix on a plaster slab. Leave the clay uncovered. The water on the surface will evaporate into the air at the same time moisture is absorbed by the plaster. The clay can then be wedged or kneaded back into a workable consistency.

Safety Note Little bits of clay that end up on the surface of your worktable are harmless. However, when they are brushed onto the floor these crumbs break down into smaller and smaller particles which then scatter into the air you breathe and can cause lung damage.

Practice these simple actions to help limit your exposure to clay dust:
- **Wear protective clothing.** Put on an apron or smock when you begin work and take it off when you leave the studio. When it gets messy and grubby—and it will after a week or two—take a few minutes before the end of class to wash it out in soapy water, rinse, and hang it up to dry.
- **Capture clay dust with water.** Use a wet sponge to clean tables, tools, wheels, and sinks. Clean spills on the floor with a wet mop. Brooms and brushes only make more dust—avoid using them.
- **Don't eat while in the studio.** Ingesting clay dust can be harmful.
- **Wear a respirator or dust mask.** When sanding, scraping, or mixing dry clay, wear a dust mask or respirator.

Fig. 2–11. In order to produce a successful ceramic vessel, artists throughout history have begun their process by thoroughly preparing their clay.
Korea, *Bottle*, 16th century.
Stoneware. Courtesy of Davis Art Slides.

Premixed clay comes in 25-pound bags. Drop the bag on the floor a few times to soften and compress the clay particles before wedging. Choose one of the following techniques and practice it using two pieces of clay, one white and one dark, each about the size of an orange. Use a wire tool to cut the clay into pieces from time to time during the process to check for air pockets, which you can easily see. Slap the pieces together and continue kneading or wedging until clay is uniform in color. You'll be able to hear air bubbles pop as you do this—it sounds like someone chewing gum!

The method you choose is a matter of individual preference—there is no right or wrong choice. Some prefer kneading—the movement is similar to kneading bread dough. Other potters hate to knead and prefer to wedge. Try both methods to discover your own preference.

How much time does it take to eliminate the air pockets and blend the two colors into one? Plan to use that same amount of time whenever you prepare your clay.

Emphasis

Emphasis is the significance, or importance, that you give to something. A potter might decide to emphasize a particular area of the clay form by creating a special design in that area using design elements such as line, texture, color, or shape. Or, the entire form might be elegant in its simplicity, in which case the potter has emphasized the form itself. Find and describe an area of the work shown in Fig. 2–12 where you think the potter used emphasis.

Fig. 2–12. What are the areas of emphasis on this object? Which is dominant? Why?
Errienne Flodin, *Untitled*.
Painted terracotta, candle, 3" to 10½" (7.6 to 26.7 cm) high. Cone 04 electric. Blue Valley High School, Stilwell, KS. Photo by Janet Ryan.

Kneading

This method is best suited to small- or medium-sized pieces of clay. Both hands work together doing the same action side by side.

• Take a lump of clay and form it into a loaf shape, using the palms of both hands.

Form a loaf shape.

• Continue to press down hard with your palms to force the clay into a longer roll. Slam it down onto the work table to make the loaf more compact.

Fig. 2–13. How do the sensory qualities of the appliqué design convey unity, rhythm, and balance on this thrown platter?
Robert Putnam, *Untitled*.
Stoneware, cone 9 reduction, 19" (48.3 cm) diameter.
Courtesy of the artist. Photo by Janet Ryan.

• Cut the loaf in half down the center (you can use a wire cutter or tear it apart with your hands). Look for any air pockets.

Tear or cut in half. Check for air pockets.

• Forcefully slam the two pieces of clay together to make one lump.

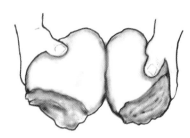

Slam back together.

• Pick up the flattened clay and stand it on edge.
• Push the clay down with both hands so that it forms a single lump.

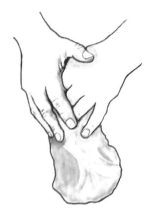

Stand on edge; push down.

• Repeat the process from the beginning about 20–30 times to rid the clay of air pockets.

Wedging

In wedging, the potter's left and right hands work opposite to each other. The left hand turns the clay and the right hand pushes down. Wedging works well with large pieces of clay—an experienced potter can wedge a large amount of clay very quickly. A good wedger at work is something to see. Other people in the studio will stop what they're doing to watch the performance of the rhythmic movement, and the way the clay responds.

The traditional wedging technique is the "Spiral." It requires some upper-body strength and can be hard on your wrists. An alternative wedging technique, the "Ram's Head Spiral," is gentler and generally works better with smaller pieces of clay. Experiment with both and find the one you like best.

Spiral

Begin with a lump of clay. Place one hand against the base of the clay with your thumb pointing up. This will be your lifting and turning hand. Put your other hand on top of the clay lump on the opposite side, palm down. This will be your pressing-down hand.

One hand lifts and turns, the other presses down.

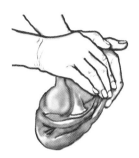

- Lift the clay with your lifting hand, and press it down with the other hand. Use your lifting hand to turn the clay lump a quarter-turn to the right. As you do this, push the clay on the opposite side of the wedge down with your pressing-down hand.
- Get into a turn-and-push rhythm.

Lift, rotate ¼, press down onto opposite side.

- Cut the wedge with a wire tool and examine the halves for air pockets.
- Slam one half down on the table.
- Slam the other half on top of it.
- Push the pieces together into a vertical cylinder.
- Start the process again.

Repeat several times until you don't see any air pockets.

Safety Note As you work with clay, notice that different processes require particular effort and endurance. Physical ergonomics is the science of adjusting the workplace to help reduce the risk of bodily strain and injury. Follow these ergonomic principles when wedging your clay:

- The surface of the wedging table should be at knuckle height when your arms are relaxed at your sides. This way, you use the big muscles in your shoulders to push and pull rather than the small muscles in your arms, wrists, and hands. If the wedging table is too high, stand on a stool or platform.
- Drop your bag of clay on the floor a few times to soften it before you begin to wedge. This helps to compress the clay molecules and shortens the time spent wedging.

The repetitive twisting motion of wedging can be hard on your wrists. When pressing down on the clay with the heel of your hands, release some pressure as you approach the movement's completion. This helps relieves your wrists from the full resistance they would encounter if they continued pushing hard into the table.

Ram's Head Spiral

- Begin with a lump of clay the size of a large grapefruit and put your hands on each side of it.

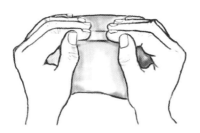

Position of hands.

- Grasp the clay with both hands and start turning it toward you, almost as if you were turning two doorknobs (one on either side of the clay lump).

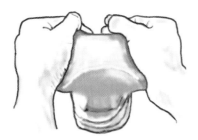

Turn top of clay, pull with fingers.

- Use the weight of your body to push the clay down and away. With your fingers, pull the clay toward you. Use your fingers to make sure the clay doesn't spread outward, but stays compact. Use very slight movements to turn the clay over and inward upon itself. Handling large amounts of clay can trap air.

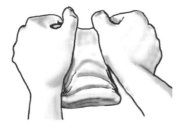

Push clay away with body weight while turning clay inward.

- When the clay feels like it has a more even consistency, pick it up, shape it into a ball, and start again.
- Repeat several times.

Note It Use light pressure to turn the clay onto itself. This brings trapped air to the surface. Heavy pressure tends to push the air inward and traps it deeper.

Tools: Physical and Verbal
Physical Tools

In the studio you will discover there is a wide array of tools for every possible need. Some people would be lost without their personal toolbox full of equipment. Others are content with a few basics like a rib, wire, a pointed wooden stick and needle tool. You can purchase your tools from an art supply store, fashion them from discarded kitchen utensils, or improvise and make your own. Since a tool merely adds strength, range, and extension to your fingers you will find that certain ones will become your favorites as you continue working with clay.

Fig. 2–14. Hand-building tools.

Fig. 2–15. Basic clay-building techniques can produce striking results. These pots, whose forms were inspired by calabash gourds, are typical of those found at the royal court.
Uganda, *Graphite-glazed pots (ensumbi)*, from the Ganda people, 19th cent.
Clay, graphite, tallest is 13½" (34 cm) high. © The British Museum.

Another kind of tool is a sketchbook to try out your ideas on paper before you begin different projects. In addition, you can keep a binder for slides or photographs of your pieces. Note the title, dimensions, and date completed on each one. This record shows how your ideas have developed and how your work has progressed.

Verbal Tools

In addition to basic physical tools, verbal tools will enable you to discuss the clay medium, your own work, and the works of others. Words are powerful—they can help you describe what you're trying to do and give you a common vocabulary to use with other artists. They can also enhance your own ideas and perceptions about ceramic art.

Throughout history people have tried to express their emotional response to an encounter with a thing of beauty. Writing, thinking, and discussion about what is beautiful, tasteful, or pleasing is all part of **aesthetics**, a branch of philosophy that deals with beauty. The word aesthetics

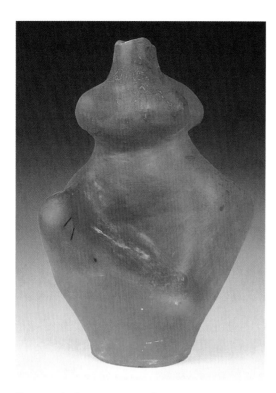

Fig. 2–16. Can you easily find the shoulder, neck, and belly of this vessel?
Kristin Shore, *Bold Woman*, 1998.
Red slip, wood fired, 15" (38 cm) high. Courtesy of the artist.

comes from the Greek *aesthetikos,* or sense perception. The language of aesthetics, therefore, applies to anything that can be perceived by the senses: a painting, a poem, the human form, a landscape, or a ceramic piece.

The word aesthetics can also mean the principles that define a taste or fashion. In the next chapter, for example, you'll read about the aesthetics of Japanese tea bowls. When used in this sense, aesthetics refers to the artistic ideal of a particular culture and art form.

When you describe works of art, the words you use should describe those qualities your senses respond to, or the aesthetic and sensory qualities of the object. As you become aware of these qualities, you can develop a framework to describe the character of ceramic works. Using words in this manner is referred to as criticism.

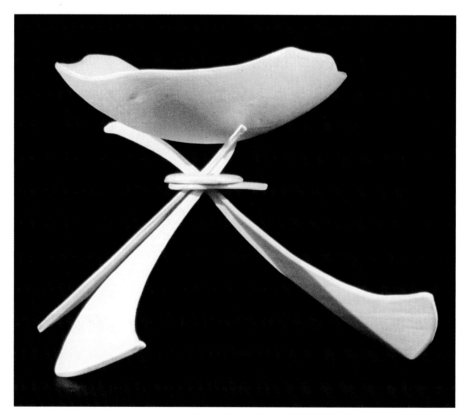

Fig. 2–17. The title of this piece defines its expressive qualities. What sensory and formal qualities add to the feeling of lightness and movement?
Kim Megginson, *Free Flight*, 1993.
Porcelain, cone 6, 11" (28 cm) high x 14" (35.5 cm) diameter. Courtesy of the artist.

Discuss It Analogies between the pot and the human form have always existed. Their parts even have common names—foot, belly, shoulder, neck, lip, and so on. When you look at the pot in Fig. 2–16, which part first catches your eye? Do the other sections have similar or contrasting characteristics? Explain how the sections relate. What do you see? Do the parts flow together or are they disjointed? How would the surface feel? Is it smooth or rough?

Steps in Aesthetic Scanning

Use these steps to scan—make a visual inventory of—your impressions of a ceramic work. After identifying the object's external characteristics and seeing how they are organized, you can look for deeper meaning in the work.

1. Note the object's sensory qualities. Sensory qualities refer to the design elements of shape and form, line, color, space, and texture.
• Shape and Form—As you look at a pot's profile or silhouette, how would you describe it as a two-dimensional shape? Is it geometric (square, rectangle, triangle, oval), organic, or a combination of both? Now look at the pot's three-dimensional form. Is it a cube, a pyramid, a cylinder, or a combination of forms? Is it open, closed, or free-form? Now look at the parts (foot, body, neck). How would you describe their forms? How do they relate to one another?
• Line—Lines can be described according to their width (thick, thin, tapering), length, and characteristics (sharp, fuzzy, continuous, or broken). Do the lines of the pot suggest movement (circulating, flowing) and direction (curving, horizontal, vertical, diagonal, parallel)? Do they have boundaries or edges?
• Color—How would you describe the color of the clay body itself (warm, dark,

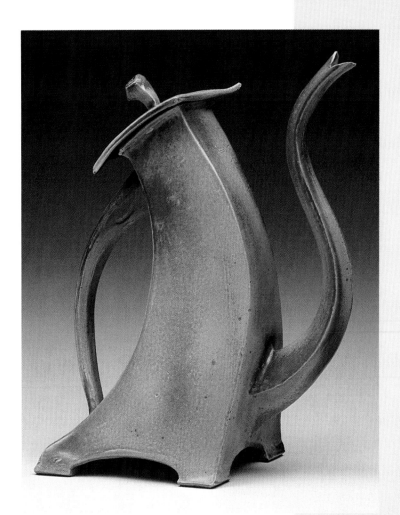

Fig. 2–18. Name the sensory and formal qualities of this work.
Robert Putnam, *Ewer.*
Stoneware, slab built cone 9 reduction, 13" (33 cm) high.
Courtesy of the artist. Photo by Janet Ryan.

rich, pale)? How would you describe the glaze color? Consider words like *hue, value, intensity, shade, transparent, opaque, monochrome,* and *polychrome.*
• Space—Is the space between the walls of the pot enclosed or open, deep or shallow? Can you locate areas of positive and negative space? (An example of negative space is the empty space enclosed within the handle of a cup.)
• Texture—How would you describe the surface (rough or smooth, ridged, pebbly, or grooved)? If the surface shows relief, is it high, low, or sunken? Are shadows part of the textural surface? Is light reflected or diffused? Does the texture vary in different areas of the work?

2. Note the object's formal qualities. Formal qualities are grouped according to design principles such as balance, unity, proportion and size, movement and rhythm, emphasis, and pattern.

• Balance—Review your list of the pot's sensory qualities. How are they organized to achieve balance? For example, imagine a vertical line through the center of the pot. Are the sides balanced? How do shape, color, line, texture, and other design elements contribute to the balance? Would you describe the piece as symmetrical (left and right sides are mirror images of each other) or asymmetrical (sides appear different)? Now imagine a line through the horizontal center of the piece. How would you describe the balance between the top and bottom?

• Unity—How do the forms of the parts (foot, body, neck, shoulder) contribute to the overall form of the pot? How does the surface decoration of the pot, including texture, color, and shape, work to make the pot seem whole? Are the parts harmonious?

• Proportion and Size—What words would you use to describe the size of the object? Consider words like *length*, *height*, *width*, *volume*, *weight*, *thickness*. Does the work have typical proportions for a functional object (for example, could you easily drink coffee out of a cup like this, by holding its handle), or is it more of a sculptural form (a miniature cup or a giant cup) because of its unusual proportions?

• Movement and Rhythm—Locate and describe any repeated sensory qualities, themes, or designs. Are they repeated in the same way each time or are they varied? Elaborate. Any repeated element contributes to the visual flow and rhythm in each area of the piece. For example, when using lines, a series of cross-hatchings on the body of a pot could slow down visual movement, whereas a horizontal line around the body could increase its speed. Locate any slow or fast areas on the pot. Describe them and explain why you think they are slow or fast. What rhythms do they create?

• Emphasis—Sometimes one area grabs your attention more than another—a design, some textural relief, an area of color, or even a major theme that tells a story. Find and describe dominant area(s) in the example and tell how the artist organized the sensory qualities to achieve that emphasis. Emphasis can also be achieved through the use of simplicity.

• Pattern—Are patterns in this work random or planned? Are they the result of

Fig. 2–19. Can you tell how this clay object was made? What clues does this photograph show that would help you determine the work's technical qualities?
Courtney Teschner, *Untitled*.
14 x 10" (35.5 x 25.4 cm). Spruce Creek High School, Port Orange, FL.

repeated colors, lines, shapes, or textures? How would you describe the patterns and where they appear? Consider words like *radial, grid, alternating, border* or *band.* What contrasts are formed by the use of pattern?

3. Note the object's expressive qualities. Unlike sensory and formal qualities, which are external observations, expressive qualities require a further step to determine how the external characteristics contribute to an expression or feeling that comes from within the work. Some examples are:

• Mood—How can you describe the feeling you get from looking at the clay work? Base your answer on the sensory and formal qualities you discovered. Think about mood words like *happy, witty, whimsical, playful, clumsy, mysterious, reflective, austere, calm, quiet.*

• Tension—How do the sensory and formal qualities you've noted give a sense of the clay work's energy? Describe that state. Consider words like *tranquil, dynamic, powerful, lumpish, relaxed, conflicting, stonelike, heavy.*

• Ideals—Sometimes a work seems to express an ideal. Some words that signify those qualities are *heroic, majestic, noble, humble, authoritative, regal.*

4. Note the object's technical qualities. Technical qualities relate to how the clay work was created. What materials and techniques did an artist use to make the finished object? These include the clay, forming process, surface treatment, and firing. Understanding these qualities can be challenging at first. As you continue to learn about the many aspects of clay you will find that solving technical puzzles can be a stimulating pursuit.

• Clay—What type of clay body (earthenware, stoneware, porcelain) is the object made from?

Fig. 2–20. How would you describe the expressive qualities of this work?
Ann Perry, *Alicante.*
Porcelain with cone 04 patina. Courtesy of the artist.

• Process—How was the object formed? Explain the method of construction (slab, pinch, coil, thrown, combination).
• Decoration—What decorative technique was used on the clay work's surface? Use words like *incise, carve, paint, wax resist, burnish, inlay.* Comment on the use of color (*slip, stain, underglaze*). Identify the type of glaze treatment (*crystalline, luster, enamel, multiple application*).
• Firing—Describe and comment on how the piece was fired (*reduction, oxidation, raku, primitive, wood, salt*).

Try It Look at the piece shown in Fig. 2–20. Identify the sensory qualities. Write as many comments as you can (at least two) for each design element. As you outline the object's sensory qualities, notice how they are organized. Their organization will be the basis for how you discover its formal qualities.

For Your Sketchbook
Use your sketchbook as a place to record your impressions about the work of other artists. List the artist's name, date and title of work, and media and firing technique. Then write your observations, using the steps of aesthetic scanning as a guide.

Studio Experience
Build a Paperclay Structure

Paperclay—a specially-prepared mixture of paper, clay, and water—is very strong and versatile, and has low shrinkage. You will build a structure with paperclay that shows a particular architectural style. Your construction can be based on a historical style or an imagined future style. Plan to use at least two geometric forms in your piece.

The first cities of the world—Harappa (Indus Valley, 2500 BC) and Sumer (Mesopotamia, 2400 BC)—were made of fired clay bricks. Architecture has been an essential part of every culture's development. Buildings echo the cultural style and social, economic, ritual, and mythic character of the time in which they were created.

Fig. 2–21. This building was made from dry paperclay slabs.
Jules Xavier, *Untitled.* Paperclay, stains, slip, 12½" (31.7 cm) high. Photo by Maureen Mackey.

Before You Begin

• Look at architectural styles from the past as well as contemporary buildings designed by Antonio Gaudi, Frank Lloyd Wright, R. Buckminster Fuller, or Paolo Soleri. What types of structures appeal to your aesthetic sense? What geometric forms can you see in the different examples? Can you tell the purpose of a building by looking at its structure? If you came from a different time in history or cultural background would you be able to identify the building's purpose?
• Mix paperclay using dry or recycled clay, shredded paper, and water. Spread into slabs.

• Consider the design of your structure. Will it display an architectural style from a certain time period or will you invent a future style? Will it be a shelter—a place you'd want to live in—or will it serve some other function? Will it be short, wide, tall, narrow? Will it demonstrate symmetry (balance) or asymmetry (imbalance)?

Fig. 2–22. Spreading the just-mixed paperclay evenly on a hard, smooth surface.

• Make sketches of your ideas. Select one and expand it. Will your structure appear bold and strong, or fragile and delicate? What geometric forms will you incorporate? Will the surface be smooth or textured?

You will need:
- slabs of paperclay
- paperclay slip
- hand-building tools—fettling knife, needle tool, sponge
- ware board to set your piece on
- round mold (optional)

Create It

1 Cut shapes for your piece out of paperclay slabs. Pyramids and cubes will need a front, back, and sides. You can make cylinders from rolled rectangles. Make a base for your building.
2 Make dome shapes by draping a slab into (or over) a round mold. For a sphere, slip and join two dome shapes of the same size.
3 For added texture, layer on paperclay slip at any time (damp or dry). Smear it on with a brush, your fingers, or a rib tool.
4 Seal seams with paperclay slip.
5 Poke a hole in any hollow or enclosed section to allow gases to escape during firing.

6 When your structure is dry it can be bisque fired. Fire slowly until smoking stops (500–900°F), then continue at the normal rate to cone 05.

Safety Note Make sure the kiln area is well ventilated. Smoke and fumes will emerge as the paper burns away.

7 Once your piece has been bisqued you can proceed with surface decoration and glaze application. See Chapter 5 for ideas. Plan your glaze firing for the clay type (earthenware, stoneware, or porcelain) you used in your paperclay mixture.

Check It Does your structure show a particular architectural style? Were you able to incorporate at least two geometric forms? How did you balance your piece? Does your form appear bold or delicate? Explain how you were able to achieve this look. Describe what you learned from this exercise.

Fig. 2–23. Summer Ahearn makes geometric forms as the basis for her structure.

Fig. 2–24. Can you see where the artist used a cube, a pyramid, cylinders, and spheres in this structure? What architectural style inspired her? Summer Ahearn, *Untitled.* Paperclay, stains, slip, cone 04. Photo by Misty Ahearn.

Sketchbook Connection

What other ways can you include architectural themes in a sculptural piece? Keep a record of interesting architectural models in your sketchbook. Use them as a starting place for sketching new ideas. Refer to them for inspiration before you begin new work.

Rubric: Studio Assessment

4	3	2	1
Idea Communication • Specific culture or function (real or imaginary) • Match between intentions and realization			
Structural form/surface attention clearly relate to specific function, yield strong cultural clues. Some supplementary information may be needed. Convincing, meaningful	Structural form/surface attention indicate specific function, yield sufficient cultural clues. Some supplementary information may be needed. Believable, satisfactory	Specific function and/or culture vague, much supplementary information needed; OR some mismatch between intentions and final form. Some gaps, vague	Specific function and/or culture very obscure even with explanation, OR broad mismatch between intentions and final form. Large gaps, obscure
Design Choices • At least two geometric forms • Symmetry/Asymmetry • Texture/other decorative elements			
At least two readily identifiable geometric forms present, symmetry choice adds striking effect. Specific texture(s) and/or other elements add unity and interest. Engaging, integrated	At least two noticeable geometric forms present, symmetry or asymmetry used to good effect. Specific texture(s) and/or other elements add unity and interest. All aspects considered	1 of these: Structural design utilizes only one geometric form; symmetry or asymmetry detracts significantly from overall effect; weak use of texture or other design elements. Needs additions or edits	2–3 of the factors listed in level 2. Monotonous, unfinished
Media Use • Paperclay use • Structural craftsmanship • Glaze application			
No apparent mistakes in paperclay use and construction of clay form. Very successful glaze application. Polished finish	Few apparent mistakes in paperclay use and construction of clay form. Successful glaze application. Competent finish	Some noticeable mistakes in media use. Glaze application may yield an uneven finish. More care indicated	Many noticeable, significant mistakes in media use. Rudimentary difficulties
Work Process • Research • Sketches • Reflection/Evaluation			
Thorough documentation; goes above and beyond assignment expectations. Thoughtful, thorough, independent	Complete documentation; meets assignment expectations. Meets expectations	Documentation is somewhat haphazard or incomplete. Incomplete, hit and miss	Documentation is minimal or very disorganized. Very incomplete

Web Links

Visit the New York State College of Ceramics at Alfred University to learn about the school and its associated ceramics museum, the Schein-Joseph International Museum of Ceramic Art.

http://nysccc.alfred.edu

What is an Artist-in-Residence Program all about? Find out about the program associated with the Roswell Museum and Art Center at

http://www.rair.org

Career Profile:
Eddie Dominguez

Eddie Dominguez believes strongly in building communities. He has worked with racially diverse populations from all age groups. Dominguez is also an assistant professor at the University of Nebraska, Lincoln. A native of New Mexico, he studied at the Cleveland Institute of Art followed by graduate work at New York State College of Ceramics at Alfred University. He has received many grants and two National Endowment for the Arts awards. In 2002 he was selected as an artist-in-residence at the Roswell Museum and Art Center in Roswell, New Mexico.

How did you become involved with ceramics?
Eddie: At first I thought of painting as the most popular art form. Then I discovered clay, and it opened up a whole new world for me. I like the "community" of it. It's a wonderful medium.

Describe some of your community work.
Eddie: I enjoy doing public artwork, especially when I can involve the community in the process. One of my earliest

Photo: Larry Gawel.

projects was designing a stage set for a dance company comprised of dancers with disabilities. Another artwork was a large-scale wind chime for an elementary school in Albuquerque, New Mexico, in which I worked with more than 500 students. One of my largest public artworks is a 25-by-55-foot wall mosaic on the exterior of the Martin Luther King apartment complex in Tucson, Arizona. Called *A Show of Hands*, the project involved more than 800 elementary school students, artists, senior center residents, and college students.

What positive outcomes of your community projects have you noticed?
Eddie: I particularly notice the strong sense of ownership that the community feels for the finished work. Such pride of ownership is certainly the result of the direct, intense community involvement.

Please share your advice for a young artist.
Eddie: Art may be something you were *born* to do, but it can also be something you can *learn* to do. Education is so valuable, and there are all types of art programs. Just follow your instincts and practice, because that is evidence to everyone around you that you are serious about what you do.

Fig. 2–25. This ceramic dinnerware set for twelve was inspired by a floral bouquet the artist received when his son Anton was born. Eddie Dominguez, *Anton's Flowers*, 1997. Collection of the Renwick Gallery of the National Museum of American Art at the Smithsonian Institution, Washington, DC. Courtesy of the artist. Photo by Herbert Lotz.

Chapter Review

Recall List the four properties that you must learn about any type of clay you work with.

Understand Explain why potters generally use additives such as grog when building large ceramic pieces.

Apply Using a slab of clay and clay slip of a contrasting color, reproduce one of the design elements—reversal, repetition, outline, or maze—depicted on a piece of Mata Ortiz pottery.

Analyze Select one ceramic artwork from this chapter. Write a description of the work based on its sensory, formal, expressive, and technical qualities. Describe as many qualities as possible. Be prepared to discuss your analysis with the class.

Synthesize Compare paperclay to regular clay, based on the four basic properties of clay.

Evaluate Which technique of clay preparation—kneading or wedging—did you have most success with? Why?

Fig. 2–26. This paperclay sculpture features a powerful man-animal figure in a familiar pose. What do the tiger stripes and stance suggest?
Christopher Maxwell, *Untitled*, 2000.
Paperclay, paint, 8¼ x 6¼ x 8¼" (21 x 16 x 21 cm). Applecross Senior High School, Ardross, Perth, Western Australia. Photo by Graham Hay.

Fig. 2–27. Helen Kwok displays her paperclay mask. What technique would you use to finish this piece?
Helen Kwok, *The Face of Reflections*, 2001.
Paperclay, 7¾ x 7 x 2¾" (20 x 18 x 7 cm). Applecross Senior High School, Ardross, Perth, Western Australia. Photo by Graham Hay.

Writing about Art
Often when looking at a work of art we think about or discuss whether or not we like it. Select a clay piece from this book (or another source) that you dislike. Write a short, clear statement indicating why you do not like it. Then write a persuasive statement arguing why it is a good work of art.

For Your Portfolio
Photograph your paperclay structure. Document with title, date, and size. Write a statement about the construction of your work—tell what inspired you to build this piece. Explain who would use this building and what its function it might be.

Key Terms
pinch
coil
extruder
slab
mold

Fig. 3–1. The artist who created this vessel learned hand-building techniques that were passed down through generations of potters in Nigeria.
Magdalene Anyango N. Odundo, *Reduced Mixed-Color Symmetrical Piece*, 1990.
Ceramic, 13¾" (34.9 cm) high. Museum purchase, 91-4-2. Photograph by Frank Khoury. National Museum of African Art.

3 Hand-Built Forms

Hand-building techniques have remained unchanged for thousands of years. Today's clay artists often use the same methods as their predecessors. All one needs is an idea, some sketches, a few good tools, clay, and knowledge of how to join clay pieces together. The three methods of hand-building—pinch, coil, and slab—are the basis of most variations in clay construction.

You can use these methods, alone or in combination, to make simple tiles and elegant vessels. You can experiment with making musical instruments, masks, or lidded boxes. Or you might prefer to sculpt a fanciful horse, dragon, or bird. Clay hand-building offers a freedom that can lead you into sculptural expressions you may never have imagined you could explore.

coil

pinch

slab

Fig. 3–2. Pinching techniques offer the artist many expressive options. Surfaces may show finger marks or be scraped smooth. Shapes can be asymmetrical or balanced. How do you think these pinched cups were finished?
Japanese, *Sake cup and raku teacup*.
Glazed ceramic, 2" (5 cm) and 2½" (6.3 cm) diameter. Private collection.

Pinching

Using the **pinch** method, you hand-build forms by squeezing clay between thumb and fingers. Making a pinch pot may seem simple, but it is an art to hollow out a pot from a single piece of clay. Japanese ceramic art forms are ideal examples of this art, in which the form is perfected according to an acknowledged sense of beauty.

For example, each part of a tea bowl—its contours, rim, base, the feel and balance in the hand—amplifies its exquisite dignity. (For more about Japanese tea bowls, see page 51.)

To make a pinch pot, squeeze the clay between the thumb and fingers of one hand while your other hand holds and turns the clay. Thin and increase the height of a pot by repeating this rhythmic action. The product usually has a natural or *organic* quality marked by variations in balance and shape. The walls can feature the textural repetitions of finger marks as part of the design, have a surface textured by some other method such as paddling, or be scraped smooth with a metal *rib*.

Fig. 3–3. What qualities of this closed form suggest that it was pinched? How does the title redirect your attention?
Ryan Thomas, *No Peeking*.
Raku, pinch pot, closed form with wire base, 5" (12.7 cm) high x 3½" (8.9 cm) diameter. Stivers School for the Arts, Dayton, OH. Photo by Kim Megginson.

Note It Making a pinch pot is not just a beginner's method. Some of the world's most beautiful pottery has been created by pinching. The key to success lies in controlling the turning rhythm while keeping the amount of pressure even for each pinch.

Practice: Pinch Pot

To make a basic pinch pot, take a lump of clay about the size of a lemon. It should fit comfortably in your hand. Keep a damp sponge nearby to wet your hands.

• Press one thumb into the middle of the lump. The clay at the bottom will be the base of your pot, which should be roughly as thick as the walls. For this exercise, try to make the walls and the base about ¼" (.6 cm) thick. As you develop your tactile sense, you will be able to tell if the clay is too thick or too thin.

Press clay with one thumb.

• With your thumb inside at the center of the base, begin pinching the clay gently between the thumb and fingers of one hand while you support it and slowly turn it with the other hand.

Pinch while turning.

• Use a gentle, even pressure for each pinch to maintain an even thickness in the walls.

Fig. 3–4. The organic form and asymmetrical line of the lip on this pinched piece are typical elements found in traditional tea bowls.
Irene Casey, *Untitled*, 1997.
Stoneware, slip decorated with cone 10 glaze. Photo by Maureen Mackey.

• Make a complete rotation for each row of finger pinches.
• After you've gone around once, move your pinching thumb and fingers up a bit and start a new rotation.

Move up, pinch, and turn.

• Each succeeding row of pinches should slightly overlap the row below.
• Press your thumb and pinching fingers onto the dampened sponge when you feel the clay drying out. Smooth over any cracks with your moistened fingers. As the walls become thinner, the clay can become too flexible and lose its shape. If that happens, let the clay dry a bit before you finish the pot. Set the pot on the table upside down for a few minutes to let it firm up, or set the pot upright inside something (a jar, a paper tube, mug, or a frozen juice container) to help support the walls.

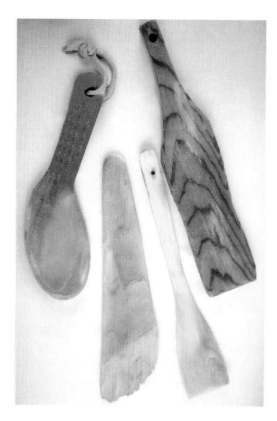

Fig. 3–5. Pinch and slab methods are combined to form these whistles.
Tim Ballingham, *Whistles*, 1998.
Burnished clay, colored slips, pit-fired in saggar, 9½ x 3" (24 x 7.6 cm). Courtesy of the artist.

Fig. 3–6. Paddle tools.

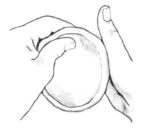

Smooth cracks with moistened fingers.

• After the clay has stiffened slightly, pinch the walls thinner and give the rim its final shape. You can either flare out the rim for a wider opening or gently ease the rim inward for a narrower opening.

Shape the rim.

You can change the appearance of your pinch pot after it has stiffened a bit:
• *Paddle* the walls to refine the form or change the shape.

• Add textures by impressing or carving.
• Add a *foot*, or base, to the pot to balance the form and help it to stand properly.
• Decide if you want the surface of the pot to be rough or smooth. You can leave finger marks on the surface for decoration or scrape the pot smooth with a metal rib when leather-hard.

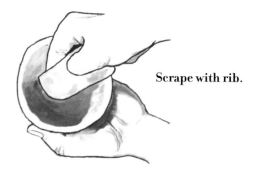

Scrape with rib.

Try It Make a few pinch pots with your eyes closed. You'll be surprised how easy it is to tell the thickness of the walls just by touching. Experience the process without visual distraction.

Join Two Pieces of Clay

Whether you're adding a foot to a pot, joining two pinch pots together, or assembling the pieces of a large clay sculpture, you need to know how to join pieces of clay securely before they dry out.

1 First, use an old fork or a rib with a serrated edge to score (scratch) the leather-hard clay surfaces you want to join.

3 Roll out a coil (a long, thin piece of clay) and wrap it around the place where the edges are joined.

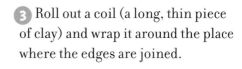

Slip scored edges.

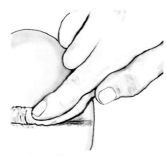

Apply coil to seam.

2 Use a paintbrush or wooden tool to coat the edges with slip (liquid clay). Then stick the two pieces together.

4 Using your fingers or a wooden tool, smooth the top of the coil over the top edge. Finish the join by smoothing the bottom of the coil over the bottom edge.

Join slipped pieces.

Smooth over edges.

Adding a Foot

Adding a "foot" to your pot not only balances the form but also gracefully lifts the entire pot. Be sure to add the foot before the pot dries out.

* Make sure your pot stands well by flattening the base slightly to keep it from rocking.
* Turn your pot upside down and mark the spot for the foot. (Try putting it just inside the edge of the base.)
* Draw a circle on the base of the pot and score its edges.

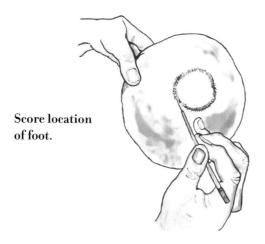

Score location of foot.

* Roll out a thin coil of clay and make a ring a little smaller than the base.
* Apply clay slip (liquid clay) to the base.
* Press the foot onto the pot and smooth the join with your finger or modeling tool.

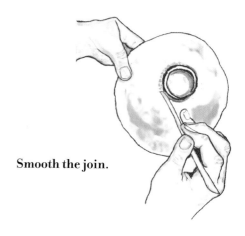

Smooth the join.

* When the pot is dry, scrape and smooth the surface.

Safety Note Sponge down the table after you finish working and rinse off your tools at the end of the class. Collect clay fragments and recycle them to prevent clay dust from entering the studio atmosphere.

Variations on the Basic Pinch Pot

Now that you've made a basic pinch pot, you can experiment with the form, using other techniques or playing with scale (making a very large pinch pot, for example).

Using a Dowel

This is a simple way to produce a tall, narrow pot or vase.

Fig. 3–7. What are the main elements of this composition? Which parts do you think were constructed first?

Shawnda Sneed, *Pea Pods*.

Stoneware, slab construction with pinched "peas," cone 6 oxidation, 4 x 15¾" (10.2 x 40 cm) each. Stivers School for the Arts, Dayton, OH. Photo by Kim Megginson.

- Begin with a ball of clay about the size of a small orange.
- Push a dowel (about 1" diameter) (2.5 cm) into the center of the ball.

Push a dowel through clay.

- Gently rotate the dowel and clay against a cloth-covered surface to produce a thin-walled cylinder.

Pound and rotate to thin walls.

- Slip the pot off the dowel occasionally to feel how thick and even the walls are.
- Create a base for your pot: Pat a small amount of clay into a disk shape and join it to the bottom of the cylinder in the same way that you joined the foot to your pinch pot (score the edges, apply slip, and smooth the edges).

A square pot can be formed by using a square or rectangular piece of wood instead of a dowel.

Large Shapes

You can use the pinch technique to form large shapes. This is a useful way to create sections for sculptural work.

- Pat a large piece of clay into a round shape.
- Set the clay on a turntable or banding wheel.

- Use your fist to punch a hollow center in the ball of clay.
- Brace one hand against the inner wall of the form. Place the other hand on the outside directly opposite the inside hand. Press your hands together to thin the wall and draw it upward as you rotate the form on the turntable or banding wheel.

Forming large shapes.

- Allow the clay to stiffen slightly as you shape the form.
- If you are forming a vessel, you might wish to attach coils to finish the *neck* and *lip*.

The Hollow Sphere

Learning to make a hollow sphere of clay can help you create a variety of shapes—sculptures of animals or humans, abstract pieces, and so on.

- Make two pinch pots of roughly the same size and allow them to stiffen.
- Join the pots together and allow the join to stiffen.

Fig. 3–8. **The rich luster of this raku form contrasts with the black matte surface of its coil-built stand.** Michelle Charles, *Untitled.* Raku pinch pot, closed form with coil stand, 3½" (8.9 cm) diameter x 8" (20.3 cm) high. Stivers School for the Arts, Dayton, OH. Photo by Kim Megginson.

- You can modify the shape of the hollow clay sphere by gently tapping it with a wooden paddle. The trapped air inside will support the walls of the pot.

Try It Make your hollow sphere the basis for a sculpture of an animal or imaginary creature. Add clay cutouts or coils for its head, limbs, and other appendages. Join each piece to the body by scoring and slipping the surfaces to be joined and pressing the pieces together.

When you're satisfied with your creation, use a needle tool to make a hole in the bottom of the hollow body. This will prevent the clay from exploding when it is fired.

Making a Rattle

You can use hollow pinch pots to make a clay rattle. The ancient Mayans made rattles out of hollow clay forms filled with tiny pieces of clay.

For fun, create a rattle that might be used as an instrument by a band you enjoy listening to.

- In your sketchbook, design some distinctive pieces that could symbolize the band's name, theme, or character. Select one or two ideas to illustrate in clay.

Fig. 3–9. This humorous Mayan rattle uses a man's legs as the handle and an exaggerated pot belly for the sound-maker.

100 BC–900 AD, Classical Mayan Period.

Drawing based on a rattle in the collection of the Museo Nacional de Antropologia e Historia, Mexico City.

Fig. 3–10. Do you think these were made for performing or for decoration? Nancy Baca makes rattles using both hand-built (pinch) and thrown techniques. What materials other than clay do you see in these two rattles? For other examples of mixed-media ceramic work see page 78.

Nancy Baca, *Rattles*, 1997.
Clay, mixed-media, 14" (35.5 cm) high, 4" (10.2 cm) diameter.
Courtesy of the artist.

- Roll out a series of small clay balls and let them dry. Wrap them loosely in a piece of newspaper.
- Make two pinched bowl shapes of the same diameter.
- Place the paper package holding the dried clay balls inside one of the spheres before joining it to the other (score, slip, and coil the join).
- Add shapes that will further distinguish the final piece.
- Pierce the hollow form before firing.
- The newspaper will burn during the firing, releasing the balls.

Tea and Its Influence on Ceramics

The tea plant is native to southern China, where tea drinking originated nearly 5,000 years ago. Spread by Buddhist monks and adopted by the aristocracy, tea drinking became a social custom throughout China and Japan. Later, it spread to the Near East, Europe, and the rest of the world and was adopted by people of all social classes. As the number of people drinking tea grew, so did demand for ceramic tea ware.

Many cultures have created rituals to govern tea drinking. But perhaps the most elaborate tea ritual arose in Japan. By the fifteenth century, the tea ceremony was widely practiced by Japanese aristocracy and had given rise to a style of ceramics used specifically for tea.

Japanese tea masters measured the beauty of an outstanding tea bowl against specific aesthetic standards:
• physical qualities—The bowl should offer a variety of textures, such as irregular, smooth, contoured, impressed, glossy, or unglazed surfaces that offer a range of subtle tactile sensations.
• visual appearance—The way the bowl looks should match its physical characteristics; for example, if a bowl looks heavy then it should be heavy to lift, or if it appears delicate, it should feel light.
• outside form—The bowl's shape should fit comfortably in the palm of one's hand, and the foot should soundly support and balance it. The seasons of the year govern the shape of the tea bowl. Winter bowls have higher walls that turn inward, while summer bowls are wide and shallow.
• rim—The rolling outline of a bowl's rim should suggest natural movement over stones, hills, or mountains.
• drinking point—Each bowl should have only one place on the lip to drink from. This should be opposite the "front" or decorated part of the bowl.
• interior form—A faint spiral relief that lets the tea flow gently into your mouth should be on the inside of the bowl. After you drink, the remaining tea should easily flow down the spiral to rest in a pool at the base.

Fig. 3–11. Pinching is the oldest method of shaping clay and an excellent technique for developing your sense of touch (tactile sense).
Otagaki Rengetsu (1791–1875), *Tea Bowl.* Glazed ceramic, 4¼" (10.8 cm) diameter. Museum of Art, Rhode Island School of Design. Edgar J. Lownes Fund. Photo by Eric Gould.

• thermal factors—An ideal bowl should keep tea warm on the inside, without causing your hands to be uncomfortably hot on the outside.
• glaze qualities—The glaze application should vary in thickness and coverage and harmonize with the bowl form. Areas left unglazed should add to the textural qualities of the surface.
• color—The colors of the bowl depend on the time of year it is used. Winter bowls should be dark with shadowy shades, while summer bowls should be bright with glowing colors.

- Select a decorative technique to finish the surface and complement the musical theme you wish to convey.
- Look carefully at your finished pinched forms. How can you tell they were made by the pinch method? Does the shape seem to lift up or does it appear low and squat? Is it lighter or heavier than you expected?
- Consider arranging a performance piece with your fellow students, using your rattles to accompany a favorite musical number.

Coiling

Like the pinch technique, coiling has existed since the beginning of ceramics. Coiling is a much more versatile technique than pinching. Contemporary arts and crafts potters as well as traditional African and Native American potters still use the technique.

Using the **coil** method, you hand-build forms by rolling clay into a long, thin piece like a snake or a rope. Potters usually use coils to build circular forms, adding the coils on top of one another. Coils can also be used to add straight lines or vertical elements to a pot.

Coiling's versatility makes it well-suited to building different types of pots. Coiling allows you to build a large pot fairly quickly—the only limit to the size of

Fig. 3–13. What do you think may have been the purpose of these pots? Although these hand-built vessels were made using the coil technique, forms such as these can also be constructed using the pinch technique shown on page 49.
Pima, *Human Effigy Jars*, 1926.
8" (20 cm) high. Courtesy of Arizona State Museum.

a ceramic coiled piece is the size of the kiln used to fire it. Large pieces can be engineered with a network of inside coil supports that reinforce the outside walls of the form.

Making a Coiled Pot

To create a coiled pot, you will need the following tools: bat or banding wheel, modeling tools, sponge or brush, rib tool, knife or flexible hacksaw blade for smoothing, and a smooth stone or metal spoon.

Think about how you want to shape your pot. The shape of your base affects the ultimate shape of your pot. A wide, flaring base will support a wider pot. A narrow, high base will suit a pot that's a bottle or bud-vase shape. Make a sketch and keep the silhouette nearby as **A banding wheel.** you proceed. Work on a *banding wheel* or bat (a round piece of wood) that can be easily turned.

Fig. 3–12. Although the coils used to make this vessel are clearly evident, some pots that are made using the coiled method have a perfectly smooth surface. Compare and contrast this artwork with the one shown in Fig. 3–14.
Ryan Thomas, *The Burp*.
Earthenware, coil construction, 11" (28 cm) high. Stivers School for the Arts, Dayton, OH. Photo by Kim Megginson.

Note It Potters usually start a coil pot by making a shallow bowl shape to support the base of the vessel. The size of the support doesn't limit the ultimate size of the pot—it keeps the weight of the coils from pressing down on the base and creating a squat shape.

To form the base of your pot:
• Take a piece of clay the size of a grapefruit and pinch it into a shallow bowl shape. Keep the walls fairly thick (about ⁵⁄₈") (1.6 cm).

Form the base.

• Smooth and compress the inside wall of the base with a rib tool while your other hand supports the wall from the outside.

Smooth the inside; support the outside.

• Score the edge of the base.
• Moisten it with a wet brush or damp sponge.

Moisten scored edge.

Now you're ready to add coils to build the walls.

Fig. 3–14. At first glance, does this pot appear to be made using the coil technique?
Courtney Teschner, *Untitled*.
Coil formed, sawdust fired in saggar, 14 x 12" (35.5 x 30.5 cm). Spruce Creek High School, Port Orange, FL.

How to Make Coils

Coils should be of uniform shape and long enough to fit around the edge of your pot. As a rule, the coil diameter should be twice as thick as the walls of the pinch pot you've created for the base. Later, you can thin the walls to the width you desire when you finish the piece by smoothing and scraping its surface.

Squeeze a thick lump of clay into a snake shape, roll the clay on a smooth surface with the palms of your hands, or use an extruder.

Fig. 3–15. Paul Roge's drum is coiled and glazed at cone 6 electric. The drum is strung with goatskin and laced with ¼" strips of goatskin.
Paul Roge, *Untitled*.
Coil-built, glazed at cone 6 electric. Bellarmine College Preparatory, San Jose, CA. Photo by Diane Levinson.

For Your Sketchbook
Sketching both silhouettes (outline shapes) and more detailed renderings that include surface treatment will help you decide what approach to take when planning a large or complex coil-built form. Draw several ideas and choose the best one before you begin working with clay.

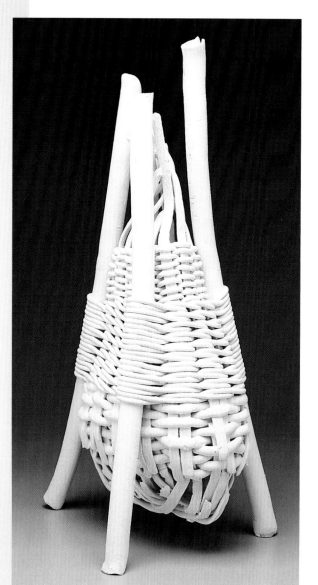

Fig. 3–16. Rina Peleg uses extruded coils to develop her basket forms.
Rina Peleg, *Nesting Structure*, 1983.
Clay, 31⅛ x 17¼ x 13⅛" (79 x 44 x 34 cm). Mint Museum of Craft & Design, Charlotte, NC. Allan Chassanoff Ceramics Collection.

Try It To make coils by hand, take a piece of clay and roll it into a snake shape, then lay it on a flat surface. Starting at the middle of the snake, roll the clay back and forth, keeping the palm and fingers flat while moving them lightly and gently to the outer edges of the coil.

Make a coil.

Fig. 3–17. Cynthia Villegas loads the extruder.

How to...

Extrude Clay

An **extruder** is a simple mechanical device that compresses clay and forces it into coils or hollow tubes of different sizes depending on the die you choose. You can make coiled or extruded forms that are symmetrical or asymmetrical, refined and smooth, or rough and primitive. Extruders are often used when many evenly-made coils are required, such as for a large sculptural work. (See Fig. 3–16.)

1 Prepare clay for extruding by wedging or kneading to the desired consistency.

2 Select and install a die for the shape you want, and load the extruder with clay.

3 Pull the handle down slowly and evenly.

4 Collect the clay and trim it to size.

Adding Coils to the Base

- Cut a coil the length of the base circumference and lay it in a ring onto the scored surface of the base.

Lay a coil on scored edge.

- To join the coil to the base, smooth the coil downward on the inside and smooth the base upward on the outside.

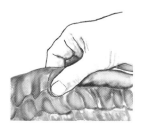

Join coil to base.

- Add a coil on top that matches the thickness of the one below it. The ends of the new coil should join to make a ring. If your coil is too long, cut off the excess; if it's too short, add in a shorter coil and join all the edges.

Join coil ends.

- Smooth the coils together. Join coils securely, so they won't crack or separate later.
- Continue to make new coils and increase the height of the walls.

If the coils are soft enough, they may be joined without scoring the edges. If you have to leave your pot and come back

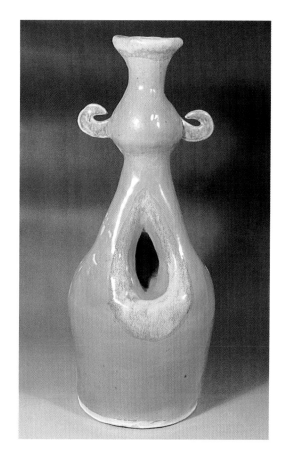

Fig. 3–18. Identify the base, body, shoulder, neck, and lip on this vessel. How did the artist maintain symmetry and balance?
Bryan Campbell, *Classic Elegance*.
Stoneware, coil-built, cone 6 oxidation, 19" (48.3 cm) high. Stivers School for the Arts, Dayton, OH. Photo by Kim Megginson.

later, the clay may have dried. In this case, score the edges of the pot and the new coil and moisten them with a brush dipped in water or a damp sponge before pressing together.

If your clay is damp, the weight of the coils may cause the walls to sag. If this happens, let the walls stiffen to support additional coils by leaving your piece (uncovered) for about twenty minutes. Keep the top ring moist by covering it with plastic or a damp cloth. When you resume coiling, if the surface ring has stiffened, score and slip it before joining the first new coil.

Fig. 3–19. **What areas of this sculpture do you consider to be dominant? How are they balanced?**

Pam Berard, *Untitled*.

Coil built, low-fire, 11 x 7" (27.9 x 17.8 cm). Spruce Creek High School, Port Orange, FL. Photo by Timothy Ludwig.

Note It Once formed, coils will dry out quickly because their large surface area comes into contact with air. Cover your coils with a piece of plastic or a moist cloth to keep them damp while you work.

As you continue, you can best control your pot's shape by following these hints:

- Start laying each new coil in a different place each time.
- Support the growing shape with both hands, one on the outside and the other inside, as you join and smooth each coil ring onto the one below.

Support pot and smooth coils inside.

- To change the wall's direction inward, attach the coil toward the inside of the rim. If you want the wall to flare out, place the coil toward the outer edge.
- Look at your pot from all angles, not just from above, as you construct it to see how the coiling is developing and adjust the shape.

Fig. 3–20. **How does repetition of the triangle shape in form and design create unity in this teapot?**

Jilian Davis, *Triangle Teapot*.

Earthenware, coil-built with underglazes, cone 04, 9" (22.8 cm) diameter, 10" (25.4 cm) high. Stivers School for the Arts, Dayton, OH. Photo by Kim Megginson.

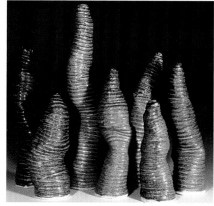

Fig. 3–21. **Consider the negative space as a design element. How does it contrast with the movement implied by the coil legs?**

Shawnda Sneed, *Mingling*.

Stoneware, coil built, cone 10 reduction, 9 to 17" (22.8 to 43.2 cm) high. Stivers School for the Arts, Dayton, OH. Photo by Kim Megginson.

Fig. 3–22. Observe how the profile of this cup and unusual "handle stand" imitate the shape of the teapot's body.
Linda Mruk, *Untitled*.
Coil built low-fire teapot with incised surface design, cone 04. Lancaster Central High School, Lancaster, NY. Photo by Anne Perry.

• Define the shape of your pot and compress the clay by gently tapping the surface with a wooden paddle when the walls are firm. Use light pressure when paddling.

Define shape and compress clay.

Fig. 3–23. The organic coil forms and the vertical direction of curving, shiny, circulating surfaces give this composition a special rhythmic quality. What does the color suggest?
Kanessa Herron, *Bronzed Buds*.
Stoneware, slab with coil construction, cone 6 oxidation, 15½" (39.4 cm) high. Stivers School for the Arts, Dayton, OH. Photo by Kim Megginson.

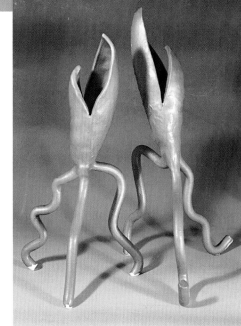

• Add the final coils to create the top edge of your pot.

Smooth top coils.

Safety Note Recycle clay so that it doesn't end up as dust and damage your lungs. Put a sheet of newspaper under your piece when you scrape or sand it to collect clay fragments and dust.

Scrape bottom of pot.

• Check the lip, or top edge, to make sure the angle and size balance and fit with your pot's character.
• Smooth the walls with a rib tool or scrape them with a flexible hacksaw blade when the pot is leather-hard.

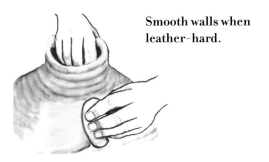

Smooth walls when leather-hard.

• Check to make sure that the weight is evenly distributed throughout the pot.
• Scrape the bottom with sandpaper or a rasp blade (a metal scraper) to even off the base if necessary.
• Allow your pot to dry slowly to avoid cracking.

Discovering Jomon Ware

Throughout history, potters have made beautiful storage containers out of clay. The ancient Egyptians made jars to hold the organs of the dead as part of their rituals relating to beliefs about an afterlife. The ancient Greeks made large vessels to hold their harvest grains. But the Jomon people, a preliterate Japanese culture (about 9000 to 300 BC), created storage pots beyond anything required in a simple object for practical use. Jomon vessels represent some of the most powerful and dynamic examples of coil work that exist.

The word *jomon* actually means "cord-impression pattern." The patterns that form the most elegant elements of decoration on these storage and cooking vessels are made from coiled clay. In addition to surface coils, the pots incorporate designs that are impressed or incised into the clay.

Jomon pottery is notable for another reason: its distinctive style came from a hunting and gathering (Paleolithic) society. Historically, storage vessels were not produced until people settled into the agrarian way of life and relied upon tilling the soil for planting and harvesting crops. Many Jomon designs incorporate animal imagery in a subtle way. The ornately embellished shapes drama-tize the artistic creativity of the potter, and the beauty of these utilitarian objects fills the viewer with curiosity about the Jomon people.

Little is known about the people who produced these fanciful earthen-ware vessels. We know they were the first people to settle on Japan's closely linked chain of islands. Surrounded by four great seas, warm currents influenced the climate on the south-ern and western shores resulting in luxuriant vegetation. The cold cur-rents of the northern and eastern waters nourished excellent fishing grounds for the coastal people. It is thought that because of the plentiful food supply on the land and in the sea, and the safety from invasion afforded by the surrounding waters, the Jomon people thrived and enjoyed a peaceful and bountiful life. Such relative peace and plenty relieved people of the simple struggle to survive, thus allow-ing them the luxury of making these artistic objects.

Fig. 3–24. Although they appear decorative, Jomon pots served an important function—they were used as storage vessels.
Flame-Style Storage Vessel. Japan, Middle Jomon period c. 2500–1500 BC.
Earthenware with carved and applied decoration, 22" (55.8 cm) diameter. © The Cleveland Museum of Art, John L. Severance Fund, 1984.68

Fig. 3–25. Would you agree that architectural clay forms lend themselves to slab-building techniques?
Duncan Warner, *Mosque*.
Saggar fired, cone 02, 12" (30.5 cm) wide. Spruce Creek High School, Port Orange, FL.

Slabs, Molds, and Tiles

A **slab** is nothing more than a flat piece of clay. Building with slabs offers new challenges and opportunities. With stiff clay slabs, you can fashion geometric shapes such as tiles or clay boxes. Using soft clay slabs, you can create everything from

Fig. 3–26. The playful composition and unlikely subject matter for this sculpture appeal to a viewer's sense of humor. What other expressive qualities does this artwork evoke?
Sarah Worman, *Frog on Wheels*.
Slab and sculpture. Whitmer High School, Toledo, OH. Photo by Corey Gray.

Fig. 3–27. This decorative slab is meant to hang on a wall. The artist used a black glossy glaze design in the center with sponge accents, and a matte crater glaze on the border.
Marcy Wrenn, *Untitled*.
Low fire with porcelain slip, 16" (40.6 cm) wide. Courtesy of the artist.

platters to wall pieces. Slabs are so versatile, you can use them to make a variety of sculptural pieces and expressive forms.

Note It When rolling slabs, and working with slabs in general, cover your work surface with a piece of canvas. The canvas absorbs moisture so the clay won't stick to the work area. The canvas also makes a sort of carrying sling for the slab—you can carry clay from one place to another, supporting part with one hand and draping part over your other arm without distorting the shape or thickness of the slab.

How to Make Slabs

You can make clay slabs using several different techniques and tools, including a mechanized roller. If a roller is unavailable, you can slam the clay down onto the floor or a table and repeat until you reach the desired thickness. Each time you lift the clay, turn and slam it on the alternate side. This forces the clay platelets closer together and strengthens the slab. The more compressed the clay becomes, the less likely it is to crack when fired.

A slab piece usually takes more clay that you would expect. Often, you will end up with a lot of unused clay from around the edges of cut pieces. You can wedge the excess clay and use it again before it dries out.

You can also form slabs by rolling clay by hand with a dowel or rolling pin. For the studio practice described in this book, you will roll out slabs.

Fig. 3–28. Slab rolling tools.

Fig. 3–29. Barbara Fransway uses a mechanical slab roller to quickly roll out a clay slab. She presses wedged clay evenly by hand to about 1" and places it on the roller atop a piece of canvas. Then she covers the clay with a second piece of canvas and turns the wheel.

Fig. 3–30. When the clay is flattened, she reverses the direction of the wheel and rolls it back over the clay until the roller clears the slab, then removes the top canvas. The bottom canvas functions as a sling for carrying the slab to a work table.

- Take a lump of wedged clay and level it first by pressing it to a flat, even thickness with the heel or palm of your hand.

- Turn the slab over and place it between two parallel guide sticks (wooden slats of equal thickness, about

Press clay flat.

⅜") (.7 cm). The slats help you to maintain the same thickness throughout the slab as you roll and flatten it. Using the dowel or rolling pin, roll slowly back and forth over the clay, and then roll diagonally to even out the corners.

Roll clay between guide sticks.

Fig. 3–31. The free-form edge of this geometric vase softens its shape and frames the garden painted on its walls. What other device does the artist use to frame the garden?
Lexy Durik, *Garden of Paradise.*
Slab vase with asymmetric lip. Whitmer High School, Toledo, OH. Photo by Corey Gray.

- Turn and reverse the flattened slab once or twice during the rolling process to help strengthen and compress it. Should some air bubbles appear in the slab while you are rolling, pierce them with a needle tool and press the hole smooth with your finger. You can easily create textured slabs by rolling out your clay over a patterned surface such as lace, burlap, straw matting, or any other textured material.

Fig. 3–32. Simplicity of surface and form is this piece's defining characteristic. Where does the artist use emphasis?
Corey Benscik, *Untitled*.
Soda fired, slab, 14 x 10" (35.5 x 25.4 cm). Spruce Creek High School, Port Orange, FL. Photo by Timothy Ludwig.

You can easily make small slabs by slicing them directly from a wedged lump of clay using a wire tool. Place several wooden slats of equal thickness on each side of the lump and use them as a horizontal guide for the cutting wire. Remove the slats gradually as you continue cutting slices from the lump. Small slabs can be pressed and joined together to make larger sheets if necessary.

Slicing slabs with wire.

Depending on your desired form, you can use slabs when they are soft and malleable, or you can let them stiffen to the leather-hard stage to make geometric creations such as boxes and tiles.

Safety Note Keep your fingers out of the way when you are cutting clay slabs.

Note It It's always better to use clay from the same source and roll out all your pieces simultaneously. This helps to maintain identical water content and minimizes distortion and cracking. Prepare as many slabs as you might need, and cover them with plastic to keep them moist.

Soft Slabs

Soft clay slabs are ideal for using with molds. While the clay is still flexible, it can be easily fashioned into a variety of shapes using simple molding techniques. Whether shaped in a sling, pressed into a mold, draped over a mold, or wrapped around a support, soft slabs are fun to work with.

Fig. 3–33. Lisette De Mars rolls a soft slab over a tube to make a cylindrical form.

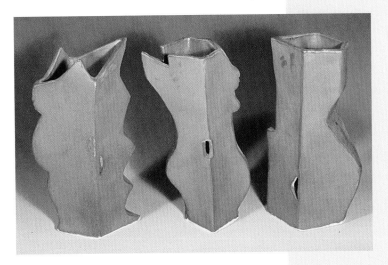

Fig. 3–34. What elements do the forms in this series have in common? See page 166 for more about artworks in a series.
William Penn, *Geometry*.
Stoneware, slab construction, cone 6, 9¾" (24.76 cm) high. Stivers School for the Arts, Dayton, OH. Photo by Kim Megginson.

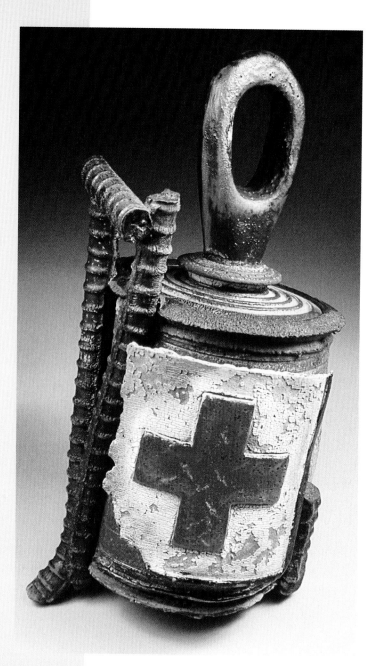

Fig. 3–35. Can you determine which parts of this sculpture were made using a mold?
Jim Koudelka, *First Aid Container,* 1998.
Multi-fired stoneware, 22 x 11 x 12" (56 x 28 x 30.5 cm).
Courtesy of the artist.

loons, smooth stones, tubes of various sizes, or even crumpled-up newspaper. When working with molds, it is easy to make multiples quickly. A molded piece can be changed by carving or by altering its shape. It can also be used as the basis for a composite work when combined with other molded shapes and forms.

Three different types of molds exist that are easy to use with clay slabs: the sling mold, the press mold, and the drape mold.

How to Use a Sling Mold

A sling mold is simply a suspended, secured piece of cloth that holds a slab until it stiffens. For a basic sling, you can use any box or container to hold the cloth. A slab that is allowed to dry in a sling mold acquires a graceful and subtle curve. The resulting pieces make beautiful platters or decorative plates. You can vary the shape of the mold depending on the size and shape of your slab. To make a long platter—one that could be used to serve fish, for example—you would secure your sling in a long rectangular box.

To make an oval-shaped platter, first cut out an oval shape from a piece of newspaper.

• Lay a cloth over the opening of a big trash pail. Take some string and tightly wrap it around the rim to secure the cloth. This is the sling mold.

• Roll out a slab of clay ⅜" (.7 cm) thick.

• Lay the oval paper pattern on top of the clay and trace around it with a needle tool or knife. Put the excess clay aside (you will need it to make feet for your platter).

Using Molds

Using the **mold** method, you hand-build forms by shaping clay inside, on top of, or around an object. People have used molds to shape clay objects for millennia. Some examples of molded clay objects are ancient Moche (50–800 AD) stirrup vessels from Peru and Chinese tomb figures (Qin Dynasty, 221–206 BC and Han Dynasty, 206–9 AD). Almost anything with a firm surface can act as a mold if its angles are not too sharp or pointed. Some commonly used molds are plaster forms, kitchen bowls, boxes, pans, balls, bal-

Cut clay around pattern.

• Lay the oval clay slab in the sling and allow it to stiffen. (This will take from a few hours to all day, depending upon humidity.) The clay should hang in a natural curve. Adjust the sling—tighten or loosen it—as necessary for the desired curvature.

• Roll out four short cone-shaped coils to use as feet. Put the feet in the sling alongside your slab so that all the pieces will dry at the same rate. Allow the clay to stiffen to leather-hard.

• Lift the slab out of the sling and invert it over a chunk of foam or other support while you attach the feet.

• Place the feet (with the wide ends touching your slab) at equidistant points on the base where the curve begins.

• Trace around the feet. Score and slip both areas to be joined and press the feet onto the base. Seal the join with a thin coil.

Adding feet.

• When the piece has stiffened, lift it from the foam chunk and set it onto a flat surface. If the feet are uneven, sand the bottoms to make them level.

The final shape.

• Round off and smooth the edge of the platter with a dry sponge or fine sandpaper. Carve, pierce, or paint a slip design on the top edge of the platter to finish the piece. (See Chapter 5, Surface Decoration.)

Fig. 3–36. Can you imagine making a platter such as this using a sling mold? What additional techniques did the artist use to shape this platter?
Corey Salah, *The Green Monster*.
Footed slab platter. Whitmer High School, Toledo, OH.

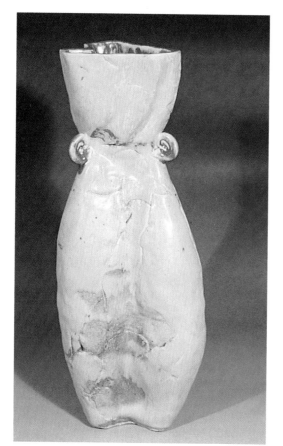

Fig. 3–37. This sculptural vessel was press molded.
Michelle Charles, *Antiquity*.
Stoneware, cone 10 reduction, 15" (38 cm) high. Stivers School for the Arts, Dayton, OH.

Find a form that appeals to you—a seashell, a plastic bowl, a cooking utensil. It could be an object from home, from nature, or from a secondhand store. This will be your press mold.

• Roll out a clay slab ⅜" (.7 cm) thick on a piece of canvas.

• Grasping the edges of the canvas, pick up the slab and invert the clay over the press mold.

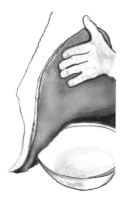

Lower clay over the mold.

• Using your fingers, gently press the clay into the mold.

How to Use a Press Mold

A press mold—also referred to as a slump mold—can be made from nearly any object. The potter presses a soft clay slab into something that has an interesting texture, shape, or design. Press molds can be used to make a single form, a series of the same form, or hollow forms when two or more pieces are joined together.

Note It Objects used for press molds should allow for easy removal.

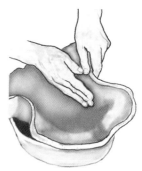

Press clay into mold.

Fig. 3–38. This creamer and sugar bowl are excellent examples of press-molded ceramic art. Original molds were handmade by the artist using plaster.
Alfred McCloud, *Compliment Your Joe*.
Stoneware, wood fired, 9 x 5 x 5½" (22.9 x 12.7 x 14 cm). Stivers School for the Arts, Dayton, OH.

- Smooth the surface carefully with a rib tool.

Smooth with rib.

- Let the clay stiffen until it is leather-hard.
- Turn the mold upside down and ease your clay out. If the clay sticks inside the mold, let it dry some more until you can remove it easily.
- Finish your piece with one of the design techniques described on pages 128-133.

Fig. 3–39. Do you think the artist applied texture before or after draping the slab in a mold?
Tiffany Carr, *Woodland Basin*.
Slab sculpture with textured bowl. Whitmer High School, Toledo, OH. Photo by Corey Gray.

How to Use a Drape Mold

Drape molds are useful when you will be working on the outside of your piece—for instance, when you make a mask, or part of a sculpture. Make a drape mold using any object that will support a slab of clay through the stiffening process. You might choose to drape a clay slab over a soft support, like crumpled paper or a piece of foam.

- Drape the slab over the mold and lightly press the clay over the shape.

Drape clay over the mold.

- Check the clay every ten or fifteen minutes as it dries. If it shrinks too tightly against the mold it will crack when removed, so remove it just as soon as the clay holds its shape.
- Set it carefully on a piece of foam to finish drying.

Try It You can drape a clay slab over an inflated balloon to make a round, closed form. When the clay is stiff enough to hold its own shape, pop the balloon with a needle tool. The hole will allow moisture to escape during the firing.

Fig. 3–40. One variation of a drape mold is to make a closed form by extending a slab around the entire circumference of a balloon. This artist used press mold additions to create a whimsical teapot.
Angela Jones, *Gourd Teapot*.
Stoneware, cone 10 reduction, 10½" (26.7 cm) high. Stivers School for the Arts, Dayton, OH.

Masks

The drape method of working with soft slabs is ideal for making masks. Masks have always been connected to the idea of transformation. For example, in many cultures they are associated with death and the idea of an afterlife. Like a chrysalis that protects the emerging butterfly from view, a mask shields an individual from recognition while this change takes place. The hidden one's behavior reflects the character or theme of their mask. Themes for masks come from nature (mammals, water creatures, birds, and reptiles); the theater, popular culture (such as Halloween masks), Mardi Gras celebrations, or other cultural rituals. Clay masks have been used as funerary objects. In mainstream American culture they are usually decorative—they would not likely be worn because of their fragility and weight.

Fig. 3–43. How has the artist used exaggeration to accent the features of this face?
Miranda Worthington, *Untitled.*
Slab-formed clay with acrylic paint, 8" (20.3 cm) high.
Courtesy of the artist. Photo by Maureen Mackey.

Try It Plan a mask you would like to make. Roll out a clay slab roughly 8 x 10" (20.3 x 25.4 cm) and cut out the desired shape (oval, circle, square) and drape it over a mold (such as a shallow plastic bowl) for support. Be sure to separate the clay from the mold with a sheet of plastic or thin cloth. Cut holes for eyes, nostrils, and mouth. Let the clay stiffen to almost leather-hard.

Embellish and decorate the mask. Use exaggeration to stress certain features—build them in relief, or add pinched pieces or slabs. Remove the mask from the mold when it has stiffened and holds

Fig. 3–41. Miranda Worthington makes clay masks by draping a slab on crumpled newspaper. While the clay stiffens, she models a face and adds decorative elements.
Photo by Maureen Mackey.

Fig. 3–42. What mood has the maker of this mask achieved? Can you tell how he formed the slabs for this piece?
Ben Swisher, *African Visage.*
Clay, mixed-media. Whitmer High School, Toledo, OH.

its shape. Decide how to hang the mask, perhaps by making holes in the clay to accommodate a wire or hook. Bisque fire, then finish with glaze or paint.

Fig. 3–44. The artist used stiff slabs to construct this piece. What shapes are dominant in the work, and how do they relate to each other?
Jenni McDonough, from *Pitcher Series*.
Slab formed pitcher with lid, sawdust fired, 16 x 12" (40.6 x 30.5 cm). Spruce Creek High School. Photo by Timothy Ludwig.

Stiff Slabs

Throughout history, potters have used stiff slabs of clay to make boxes and geometrically shaped containers, tiles, and sculptural pieces. Both ancient and modern clay sculptures are made from stiff slabs in combination with other clay techniques. Stiff slabs may be cut and assembled when leather-hard. Plan your piece carefully.

Note It When you work with stiff clay slabs, it helps to build a model. First sketch the idea and then put it together on a small scale. This process may reveal potential building or joining problems. You may decide to discard certain designs that prove unworkable. These preliminary clay sketches are called *maquettes*.

Follow this process when working with stiff clay slabs:

• Draw the form that you want to create.
• Construct a maquette to test the design.
• Cut out paper patterns for the shapes you want to use.
• Roll out your clay slab. Because clay shrinks as it dries, allow it to dry somewhat (until nearly leather-hard) before cutting it.
• Place patterns on top of slab and cut shapes from clay using a knife or needle tool.

Fig. 3–45. If you wanted to plan a series of clay dwellings, would you sketch them first? How could you make models, before cutting final, full-size slabs?
Michelle Charles, *The Village*.
Raku, tallest is 20" (50.8 cm) high. Stivers School for the Arts, Dayton, OH.

Safety Note Take care when you use sharp or pointed tools. Always cut away from yourself.

Merely joining four sides to the base as four walls creates a problem. Try it yourself and see what happens—the corners don't fit. The thickness of the clay wall is another dimension, which you must take into account. To make a successful clay box, prepare your wall pieces before joining them to the base and to each other.

- Place a ruler about ¼" (.6 cm) from the edge of a wall piece. Miter (cut at a 45° angle with a knife or needle tool) the two long (10") (25.4 cm) sides of each wall.

Miter side edges to 45°.

- Score and slip the mitered sides and the bottom edge of each wall.

Apply slip to scored edges.

Practice: Making a Clay Box

Because it takes time to attach the sides that form a box, be careful not to let the slabs dry out too much (stiff slabs will dry quickly). Keep unused pieces covered with plastic until you are ready to attach them.
- Cut out a 6 x 6" (15.2 cm) square of cardboard and a 6 x 10" (15.2 x 25.4 cm) rectangle of cardboard to use as templates.
- Place each cardboard cutout on a leather-hard clay slab and cut around it with a sharp knife or needle tool. Cut two 6 x 6" (15.2 cm) squares and four 6 x 10" (15.2 x 25.4 cm) rectangles. You now have four walls, a base, and a lid.

Cutting slab with template.

• Lay your square base flat on the work surface. Position the wall pieces flat on the work surface next to the base.

• Score the base's surface where the walls will join and apply slip.

The scored base ready for slip.

• Slip and join the walls and base together, one at a time. Press firmly into place.

Press walls down onto base.

• Roll out four coils the length of the box sides.

• Reinforce each join on the inside with a soft coil. Smooth the coils into the sides and base.

• Clean the inside edges and pinch the outside edges smooth with your thumb and forefinger or with a wooden tool.

Reinforce joins with coils.

• Slip and score the edges of the remaining square piece. Also, slip and score the top edges of your box.

• Attach the square to the top and press firmly to attach it.

• When the clay is leather-hard, use your knife or needle tool to cut—at a 45° angle—through the clay a couple of inches below the top. Cut all around the box. Include a notch (like a puzzle piece) on each side. This not only adds visual interest but helps to secure the lid.

Pinch outside edges smoothly together.

Box with lid.

Fig. 3–48. How does this simple cover complete the form beneath? How does the artist utilize patterns in the form? Marcy Wrenn, *Untitled*. Lidded and footed box, impressed design, saggar fired, 12 x 7 x 7" (30.5 x 17.8 x 17.8 cm). Courtesy of the artist.

Fig. 3–47. Notice the different areas where repetition is used on this box. Do you think this is a functional or non-functional piece? Kristie Martin, *Paisley Paradise*. Slab box with textured surface and hand-built additions. Whitmer High School, Toledo, OH. Photo by Corey Gray.

Adding a Knob

A knob is a solid piece of clay that makes it easier to lift a lid. Add a knob to your box:

* Remove the top from your box.
* Roll out a short coil or slab. Form it into whatever shape you want to create your knob.
* Score and slip the bottom edge of the knob as well as the area on the lid where you'll attach it.
* Press the knob onto the lid to attach firmly.
* Your box should be fired with the lid and knob in place.

Box with knob.

Making a Foot for Your Box

When the box has stiffened to leather-hard, you can add feet to your box. (See page 63 for foot-making instructions). Turn the box over and attach the feet in the corners.

Fig. 3–49. A box with a lid might be a house with a roof. What else might it be?
Jon DeVol, *The Fifth Wheeler.*
Lidded slab box with non-firing stain. Whitmer High School, Toledo, OH.

Alternatively, you can construct a rectangular foot. You'll essentially make another box on the bottom of the first box.

* Cut four strips of clay about 1 x 4" (2.5 x 10.2 cm).
* Gently turn your stiffened box upside down.
* Prepare and miter the four walls as you did above. Score and slip the surface of the base about 1" (2.5 cm) from the edge.
* Join the walls as before. Reinforce the joins with coils and allow them to stiffen.

You've just created an elegant box foot. If you like, you can decorate the walls of your box by carving into them or adding a slip design. See Chapter 5, Surface Decoration, for additional ideas.

Fig. 3–50. The relief on the front of this box conceals a drawer. Can you find the pull?
Lexy Durik, *Pandora's Box.*
Footed slab box. Whitmer High School, Toledo, OH. Photo by Corey Gray.

Fig. 3–51. The extensive use of tiles in architecture has endured for nearly 6,000 years.
Turkey, Ottoman. *4 Tiles from Isnik*, 16th–17th cent.
Glazed ceramic, 9½ x 9½" (24 x 24 cm) each. Private collection. Courtesy of Davis Art Slides.

Tile Making

It is difficult to consider the uses for flat slabs of clay without thinking of tiles. The tradition of tile making is quite old. The art form spread across Persia (Iran), Syria, and Turkey to Spain with the Moorish occupation in the eighth century. By the twelfth century, tiles were used in Portugal and Italy along the Mediterranean, and north to Holland and Germany. The Spanish brought the tradition with them to Mexico when they came to the New World in the 1500s.

Usually tiles embellished important buildings, such as castles, mosques, and cathedrals. Tiles are extremely versatile, able to withstand extremes in temperature, and always maintain their vibrant colors.

Due to these qualities, we still use tiles to beautify homes and public buildings.

Note It Handmade tiles tend to warp. To create successful tiles:
• Reduce shrinkage by using a clay body containing grog or sand.
• Cut grooves on the back ⅛" (.3 cm) deep and spaced about 1" (2.5 cm) apart for a good bonding surface.
• Dry tiles as slowly and evenly as possible. Place a flat board on top.
• Add relief at the leather-hard stage.
• Lay the dried tiles on flat kiln shelves sprinkled with a thin layer of sand to allow for movement as the tile shrinks.
• Increase kiln temperatures at a slow rate during early firing.

Fig. 3–52. Tell how the sensory qualities of this tile series are similar. How are they different?
Jane A. Archambeau, *Mona Series*.
Tiles with relief, stamps, and texture. Courtesy of the artist. Photo by Corey Gray.

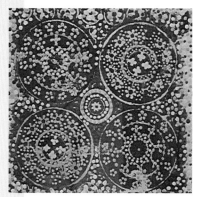

Fig. 3–53. Do you think the creator of this tile meant to include it in a larger composition? Raquel Durik, *Synergy*. Silkscreen on clay. Whitmer High School, Toledo, OH. Photo by Matt Squibb.

How to Make a Design with Clay Tiles

Sketch some square tile designs for individual and multiple arrangements. Select a design that you will produce on a clay tile.

Trace over the design with tracing paper, creating a paper stencil. Cut out the negative spaces around the dominant image. You may need to make more than one stencil depending on the design.

Thinking About Tile Design

A grouping of tiles can form any number of designs. Or, a single tile can be a complete composition. This illustration shows the dominant feature located in the center of the tile design.

A tile design.

When the original tile is placed in a grid pattern, design elements at the tile's corners now become part of a new design. The central design feature of an individual tile becomes less dominant as it becomes part of an overall design scheme.

Fig. 3–54. **Students from the Class of 2000 at Stivers School for the Arts designed and created a tile mural, which they installed and presented as a gift to the school.** Collaborative project, *Spirit of 2000*. Earthenware, cone 04 glazes, 7' (2.13 m) high. Photo by Kim Megginson.

Repeating tiles—notice new designs.

How the parts relate to the whole depends on which design element is dominant and how it affects the balance of the arrangement. Tiles are not always set in rows, adjacent to one another. In a composition that is similar to a painting, tile shapes can be used in a freely composed design without a grid arrangement.

- Roll out a clay slab (³/₈" thick) (.7 cm) on a piece of canvas.
- Place the canvas and slab on a board.
- To smooth the surface of the clay, draw a rubber rib or plastic squeegee across the top.
- Let the clay stiffen slightly before cutting out the tile square.
- Cut around a 6 x 6" (15.2 cm) pattern using a sharp knife and a square rule to get the edges clean and straight. Handle the tile as little as possible.

- Place a second piece of wood on top of the tile and reverse both boards with the tile in between. Take off the top board and remove the canvas.
- Cut horizontal grooves about 1" (2.5 cm) apart on the tile. The grooves can be ⅛" (.3 cm) deep. (The grooves not only help the clay to dry but also provide a bonding surface for the adhesive to stick to when installing the tile.)
- Turn the tile over, smooth side up.
- Arrange your stencils on the tile, and use your fingers to gently press them into the clay.

- Paint background color(s) on the tile using underglazes or slips. (See pages 126, 128.)
- Carefully remove paper stencils and clean smudges with a flat tool or knife.
- In areas where stencils were removed, you can now paint details using underglaze.
- Let the tile dry slowly on a flat surface for several days.
- When the tile no longer feels cold (damp) it is ready for the first firing (known as the bisque firing).
- You can add more color and details with underglazes after the bisque firing.
- Finish the bisqued piece by dipping the tile face lightly in transparent glaze, and fire a second time.

Fig. 3–55. Stephen Farley was awarded a commission to create and install a monumental tile mural (this view shows one of four walls) commemorating everyday people from the 1930s–50s in Tucson, Arizona. Individual tiles appear as singular pieces of abstract art. The blacks, whites, and gray glazes are separated by thin lines that allow some terracotta-toned tile to show through, providing warmth and depth. When viewed as a whole, the collected tiles form murals that are lustrous, clear, and deep.
Stephen Farley, *Windows to the Past, Gateway to the Future*, 1999.
15,000 hand-glazed 6 x 6" (15.2 x 15.2 cm) tiles. Courtesy of the artist.

For Your Sketchbook

Draw some animals, people, scenes, or symbols that you think might work as a clay relief. When you have a variety to choose from, imagine actually creating a relief based on one of your sketches. Which kind of relief will you use? Can you combine several of your ideas into an interesting, balanced composition?

Fig. 3–56. Which elements of this design remind you of the view through a kaleidoscope?
Cassie Johnson, *Kaleidoscopic Klowns*.
Clay formed with molds, stamps; underglazes brushed, sprayed, spattered. Whitmer High School, Toledo, OH.

Relief

Relief is an image that has been carved, modeled, or molded onto a fixed background. It may be:

- High—projects from the surface and appears nearly three-dimensional.
- Low—is elevated but remains part of the surface.
- Flat—has only a very slight elevation.
- Intaglio (sunken)—the image is incised or carved into the surface.

Practice: Relief Panels

Make a tile wall piece that includes relief in its composition. Use coils, slabs, and pinched pads of clay to build up the relief forms. Use your fingers and modeling tools to shape the forms, complete details, and add texture. Plan a ½–2" (1.3–5 cm) border to frame your creation.

Make some drawings in your sketchbook of people, animals, scenes from nature, a dream, or an abstract design. Select one and think about how you would

Principles of Design

Unity

When parts of a design combine to create a sense of harmony and oneness, they display the design principle of unity. A potter might achieve a harmonious design in many ways, including the use of color, texture, and repetition of shapes or lines. A successfully unified design also contains some variety, because too much repetition can be monotonous or boring. Look at the work shown in Fig. 3–57. How did the artist achieve unity?

Fig. 3–57. Notice how the four central tiles create movement within this piece. What areas provide harmony and unity?
Kristen Koka, *Fancy Floral*.
Press molded and stamped tiles. Underglazes brushed, sprayed, spattered. Whitmer High School, Toledo, OH. Photo by Corey Gray.

create it in relief (use at least two different types of relief) and adapt it to the size of a slab that is 2 x 1' (61 x 30.5 cm). Decide how the border will relate to the design.

You may decide to cut the tiles into organic shapes that follow the flow of your design. Think about how they will fit together and be attached to a wall or piece of wood.

• Gather the following materials: your drawing, a piece of cloth or canvas slightly larger than 2 x 1' (61 x 30.5 cm), a ³⁄₈" (.7 cm) thick slab of clay (2 x 1') (61 x 30.5 cm), a ruler, soft clay to use for making the relief additions, clay slip, a knife or needle tool, modeling tools, and a paper drawing that shows your design.

• Roll out a ³⁄₈" (.7 cm) thick clay slab on a canvas-covered board.

• Measure the slab and make sure the dimensions for your rectangle are even.

• Measure and mark the border.

• Place your drawing on the slab and trace the composition with a pencil.

• Remove the paper and begin to build up areas of relief within the outline of your composition. Model details and texture.

• Complete the design for the border in the same way.

• Cut the completed panel into shapes or squares.

• When clay is leather-hard, carefully cut horizontal grooves about 1" (2.5 cm) apart on the back of the tiles.

• Allow pieces to dry slowly.

• Finish your piece. You might paint your bisqued composition with an oxide wash, stain, or underglaze. Try gently wiping the surface with a damp sponge to add subtle contrast and surface interest for the final firing.

• Mount on plywood or directly on wall.

Fig. 3–59. Tiles are durable, so they make sense for use in public spaces. For more information about this artist, see page 82.
Barbara Grygutis, *Portal*, 1995 (detail).
Tile, cast concrete, 12' (3.6 m) high.

Fig. 3–58. A change in background color gives the same printed image two different looks.
Michael Borer, *Senior Snork Pic*.
Silkscreen on clay. Whitmer High School, Toledo, OH. Photo by Matt Squibb.

Sculpture

Many ceramic objects have a functional purpose such as storage, cooking, tableware, and tile floor or wall coverings. But clay is also well suited to creating sculpture.

Ceramic sculpture is often made using multiple techniques such as coil, slab, and pinch combined in one work. Its purpose may be representational (depicting a person, animal, or object) or nonrepresentational. A nonrepresentational or abstract work might seek to induce an emotion, mood, or intellectual state in a viewer through its sensory and formal qualities. Sculpture of this kind—for example, the work of Peter Voulkos (see page 169)—is an end in itself, formed as an expression of the artist's creativity.

Discuss It Search through ceramics magazines and books to find examples of ceramic sculptures that use a combination of forming methods (pinch, coil, or slab). Try to identify the methods used. How do you think the pieces were joined together? As the structure dried, would it need support? If you were the artist, what would you use to support it and where would you place supports? Read about the artist and share your thoughts about the idea he or she was trying to portray in the work. Do you think the piece is successful? Why or why not?

Using Supports and Braces

Sometimes your sculpture will need support while it dries. Moist clay may collapse or droop if left unsupported. Fortunately, you can use supports and braces to help create the form you want.

• Coiled clay braces may be constructed inside the form to add strength and support the basic shape.

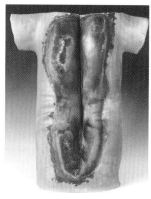

Fig. 3–61. Which slab-building methods do you think were used in the construction of this sculpture?
Rosemary Beitia, *Torso Series 1*, 2000.
Slab built, saggar fired, 24" (61 cm) high. Spruce Creek High School, Port Orange, FL.

Fig. 3–60. Nature deities were very important in Zapotec culture, and bat god images have been discovered in almost every major tomb. This representation of the bat god wears maize earrings and an elaborate headdress that resembles wings. Teeth protrude, vampire-like, from his lips.
Mexico, Zapotec, *"Bat God" Funerary Urn*, c. 400–800.
Ceramic, 17¾" (45 cm) high. © Art Resource, NY. Museum fuer Voelkerkunde, Staatliche Museen, Berlin, Germany.

- An *armature* (another type of support) can brace the clay while you construct the form around it. Armatures can be made from many different materials such as a cardboard cylinder, pieces of wire, rolled-up newspaper, or wooden dowels. They should be removed before firing.
- External supports can be added outside the piece. Rolled-up newspapers or foam chunks make excellent external supports.

Making a Solid Structure

If you sculpt a solid piece of clay, you'll need to hollow it out before firing so that it doesn't explode. Any piece of clay more than 1" (2.5 cm) thick will likely explode during firing.

- Cover the finished sculpture loosely with plastic to let it stiffen slowly. This could take a few days to a week depending on the thickness of your piece.
- Slice the solid-built piece into two or more sections with a wire tool when the final form has stiffened enough to hold its shape. Cut at a 45° angle to provide a wider surface for scoring and support when you rejoin the pieces.
- Remove the interior clay with a trimming tool. The remaining walls should be of uniform thickness.
- Reassemble the pieces by scoring the edges, applying slip, and pressing them together. Poke a small hole in the sculpture so that gases can escape during the firing process.
- Dry your sculpture slowly to avoid cracking at the joins.

Fig. 3–62. Where might the artist have used braces to support this work as she was preparing it to be fired?
Joan Tackett, *Bright Bird.*
Raku, pinch pot, closed form with additions, 11 x 12 x 10½" (28 x 30.5 x 26.7 cm). Stivers School for the Arts, Dayton, OH.

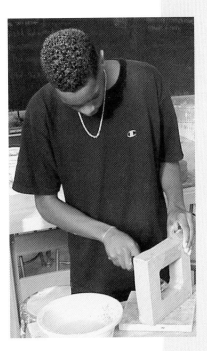

Fig. 3–63. Tony Watson creates a name sculpture using extruded clay; here he welds together hollow rectangular forms to make the letter "O".
Bellarmine College Preparatory, San Jose, CA. Photo by Diane Levinson.

Fig. 3–64. Consider the size of this sculpture. How much clay did the artist need to remove to keep it from exploding when fired?
Kirk Kirkland, *Chicken Little.*
Raku, 5 x 7 x 9½" (12.7 x 17.8 x 24 cm). Stivers School for the Arts, Dayton, OH.

Mixed-Media Sculpture

Mixed media is a term that describes an artwork that makes use of more than one technique or medium. American art movements featuring mixed media emerged in the late 1950–60s. Pop art, assemblage, and funk art are some names given to these expressions.

An incredible range of materials is used in mixed-media sculpture. A few examples include found objects like bolts, cans, computer parts, CDs, flowers, stones, glass, hardware, seashells, feathers, toys, sticks, copper tubing, paper products, leather, fur, and wire.

Fig. 3–65. Coil and pinch methods were used to shape this figurative piece. How does it express aspects of present-day society?
James A. Jones, *Food Chain Kingpin*, 1999.
Clay, acrylic paint, found objects, 29 x 16 x 14" (73.7 x 40.6 x 35.6 cm). Courtesy of the artist.

Elements of Design

Space

Space refers to the three-dimensionality of a pot or sculpture, the air around that object and the way they interact. Positive space is the structure itself, and negative space is the area surrounding the object. Space can be flowing—for example, in a clay form that is pierced with holes—or static. It can seem cramped or open. The effect of space might seem different when an artwork is viewed from different angles.

Fig. 3–66. Can you find the non-ceramic parts of this sculpture? The artist had recently moved from New York to California and "attempted to merge three things—the vessel, the figure, and the landscape." Did she succeed? Does her use of found objects add to the merging effect?
Diane Levinson, *I Dreamed I Was a Teapot*, 1993.
Clay, found objects, 21 x 15 x 15" (53.3 x 38 x 38 cm). Courtesy of the artist.

Fig. 3–67. In addition to using a variety of materials, the artist has dramatically varied the clay forms and surface treatments in this work. Made as a funerary urn to honor a friend, the sculpture incorporates a timer that symbolizes "Mr. C's time has run out."
Diane Levinson, *Flowers for Mr. C*, 1996.
Clay, marble, found objects, 32 x 21 x 22" (81.3 x 53.3 x 56 cm). Courtesy of the artist.

Fig. 3–68. At the time this sculpture was made, potters were experimenting with form and technique. Ceramics became a major art form.

China, Tang dynasty (618–906 AD).
Earthenware model of Tang original, 12" (30.9 cm) high. Courtesy Meitie Wilson. Photo by Maureen Mackey.

Clay Sculpture: Horses

The horse has held a special place in Asian cultures ever since it was domesticated in China around 3000 BC. Horses were believed to be powerful enough to carry their riders to immortality and provided inspiration for poems, songs, paintings, and sculptures in both stone and pottery.

This fascination with the horse was obvious during the Shang dynasty in China (about 1600–1100 BC), when real horses and their human charioteers were buried alive in royal tombs. This custom was later modified during the Qin dynasty (221–207 BC), when the dead emperor was entombed with hundreds of life-size terracotta horses and soldiers—clay stand-ins for his real army.

The horse achieved its highest status during the Tang dynasty (618–906 AD), a time of unparalleled political, artistic, and cultural greatness. It was used in battle, hunting, and sport. Thus, this popular animal became a favorite subject of Tang potters, who produced amazing numbers of sculptures, most of which were placed in their owners' tombs.

In Japan, at around the same time as the Tang dynasty, artisans were making large earthenware figures that encircled their burial mounds, preventing erosion. These sculptures of horses, soldiers, and other animals are called *haniwa*.

Fig. 3–69. Haniwa sculptures were made for burial mounds, and their subjects included animals and people. Because hundreds of figurines often were made for a single tomb, artisans developed a simple method of cylinder structure.

Japan, 200–552 AD.
Drawing based on a 26½" (67.3 cm) high sculpture in the collection of the Seattle Art Museum.

Studio Experience
Sculpting a Fantasy Animal

You will create an animal sculpture, combining at least two hand-building methods, (pinch, coil, and slab) to achieve the finished form.

Cultural groups throughout time and around the world have written about, painted, and sculpted animals that are important to them. Some animals are

unlike any creature that exists in real life. They can be mystical or symbolic—for example, see page 76. Artists may borrow characteristics from one animal and combine with those of a different animal or a person.

Before You Begin
• A bull's head sporting a human beard on a harp in ancient Mesopotamia, a terrifying sea creature on the prow of a Viking ship, and fierce winged animals guarding a Han Dynasty tomb in China are examples of the fantastic animals conceived by artists from various cultures through time. Research some of these artworks. What function did they serve? How did the artist change the original animal to make a unique creation? Find pictures of animals that interest you and imagine how you could invent a new creature from the original. You might decide to "animalize" a person by accentuating or exaggerating characteristics that parallel those of a particular animal.

• Sketch your ideas for an animal sculpture. Plan your design. How will you

Fig. 3–71. Tony Columbo and Zenon Zabinski create a dinosaur. Do you think this qualifies as a fantasy animal? Photo by Diane Levinson.

incorporate different hand-building methods? Will forms be organic or geometric? How will positive and negative space be utilized and balanced? What expressive properties will your sculpture portray? Will your creation have a purpose or function? What will it be?

• Consider your surface treatment. Will texture enhance the piece or should the surfaces be smooth?

You will need:
• sketches and plans for your sculpture
• clay, at least 5 pounds, with grog in it (Use groggy clay because it is less prone to shrinking and cracking than clay without additives.)
• hand-building tools, sponge, slip
• a ware board to hold your piece until it is ready for firing
• newspaper or foam for support

Create It
1 Depending on the complexity of your animal, you may want to build a quick model (maquette) first; otherwise, refer to the sketches you have made.
2 Combine at least two hand-building methods (pinch, coil, or slab) to achieve the finished form.
3 The walls or sections of the sculpture should be of even thickness. (Parts thicker than 1" (2.54 cm) may explode during firing.) Avoid the use of thin or especially delicate additions. Poke a hole in any section that is hollow or enclosed to allow gases to escape during the firing process.

4 Use supports for different segments, if needed, until the piece has sufficiently dried.

5 Remember, soft pieces of clay can be joined together by pushing and squeezing. Stiffer pieces must be scored on the surface and slipped before joining. See page 47.

6 Add surface decoration as desired, and sign your work.

7 Bisque fire, add further decoration, and glaze fire.

8 Be prepared to explain the techniques you used.

Check It What does this animal mean to you? Explain how you combined characteristics of different animals or created new ones. What expressive properties does your sculpture portray? Name and describe the hand-building techniques and surface treatments you used. Why did you choose them?

Sketchbook Connection

Illustrate ideas for parts of your composition. For example, sketch a series of ears or paws found on different animals. Try some variations to elicit a comical, majestic, or fierce characterization.

For Your Portfolio

Photograph your sculpture from various angles. Document the title, date, clay type, and dimensions as well as notes on glazing and firing. Write a short description of the methods you used to build your piece. Expand on the traits and symbolism expressed in your work.

Fig. 3–72. The head of this dragon was formed with pinch pot and slab techniques. What other methods do you think were used in its construction?
Richard Koong, *Dragon.* Hand-built, slipped and incised. Bellarmine College Preparatory, San Jose, CA. Photo by Diane Levinson.

Rubric: Studio Assessment

	4	3	2	1
Idea Communication • Fantastic animal figure • Expressive qualities • Optional purpose or function	Final figure is unusual and inventive combination of animals (may have human features). Expressive quality is fascinating and compelling. Alive, inventive, imaginative	Final figure is an interesting combination of animals (may have some human features). Expressive quality engages viewer interest. Expressive, interesting	Final figure is a somewhat interesting combination of animals (may have some human features). Expressive power somewhat bland or lacking. Moderate risk and expression	Final figure is lackluster OR depicts few animal features. Expressive power may be bland or lacking. Uninspired, stiff
Design Choices • Use of organic and/or geometric forms • Balanced positive and negative space • Surface treatment	Choice of form, interaction of positive/negative space, and surface treatment work smoothly together to add great vitality, interest, and unity to sculpture. Sophisticated, holistic	Choice of form, interaction of positive/negative space, and surface treatment add pleasing interest and unity to sculpture. Competent, unified	1 of these: Choice of form seems ineffective for intended purpose; little interaction or lack of balance between positive/negative space; surface treatment is neglected. Needs additions or edits	2–3 of the factors listed in level 2. Monotonous, unfinished
Media Use • Combines at least 2: pinch, coil, slab • Structural craftsmanship/stands up • Glaze application	No apparent mistakes in construction of clay form. Very successful glaze application. Sculpture freestanding. Polished finish	Few apparent mistakes in construction of clay form. Successful glaze application. Sculpture freestanding. Skillful finish	Some noticeable mistakes in media use. Glaze application may yield an uneven finish. Sculpture may not stand up. More care indicated	Many noticeable, significant mistakes in media use. Sculpture may not stand up. Rudimentary difficulties
Work Process • Research • Sketches • Optional maquette • Reflection/Evaluation	Thorough documentation; goes above and beyond assignment expectations. Thoughtful, thorough, independent	Complete documentation; meets assignment expectations. Meets expectations	Documentation is somewhat haphazard or incomplete. Incomplete, hit and miss	Documentation is minimal or very disorganized. Very incomplete

Career Profile:
Barbara Grygutis

Public art has been a part of society since the beginning of civilization. From the prehistoric cave murals in France and Spain to the sculptures and frescoes of Renaissance Europe, artists have created art for a public audience. Today murals and public sculpture appear on street corners and the sides of buildings, strengthening community feelings of presence and identity. Barbara Grygutis takes part in this ancient tradition by creating large-scale clay sculptures that enhance a specific outdoor site.

Fig. 3–73. Before beginning her work in clay, Grygutis makes small-scale models out of painted wood, which she presents along with tile samples so people can see the actual future surface of the sculpture. This piece is one in a series commissioned by the city of Albuquerque, New Mexico.
Barbara Grygutis, *Cruising San Mateo III*, 1991.
Tile, cast concrete, 3½ x 10 x 10' (1 x 3 x 3 m). Courtesy of the artist.

Why do you use clay to send your message?
Barbara: What's great about clay is its flexibility; it can be used not only to adorn or decorate architecture but also to express complex concepts and ideas.

Some of your works relate to history, others relate to the environment. How do you decide what the final work will look like?
Barbara: I'm very interested in bringing the idea of history and continuity into modern times, and my pieces are about the evolution and changes that have occurred in the human thought process. My work is very much about the site and community; they must be user-friendly. I study the site and think about what form of expression is most appropriate to convey the idea. Then I build wooden models and make samples of the ceramic tile to show the possibilities for the color or surface decoration.

What obstacles or challenges did you have to overcome to become a public artist?
Barbara: One of the greatest challenges in creating public art is to create a ceramic work that is durable and requires little maintenance. I create sculptures to last for a fifty- to one-hundred-year cycle to withstand the weather and not break apart. Developing the technical skills needed to build such large-scale clay pieces was a challenge.

How do you find your commissions?
Barbara: Public art has grown as a profession in this country, and all of the paid commissions and requests for proposals are advertised. Any ceramics person can access this advertising network. We're living in a very exciting time, a time when this kind of work is available and there's a lot of it.

Chapter Review

Recall What are three types of molds used with soft clay slabs?

Understand Study the pinch pots made by artists in this chapter. Describe their sensory qualities. What clues tell you that they were made by pinching?

Apply Create four tiles that show the four types of relief. Decide on a simple shape to repeat. Roll out a 3 x 12" clay slab, then divide it into four equal sections. Model your chosen shape in high, low, flat, and intaglio relief.

Analyze Study the Ottoman tiles shown in Fig. 3–51. First, describe the general features of the design that is repeated in each tile. Next, describe how the design on each tile creates a new composition when placed in a grid. Consider the original function of these tiles. Why is this design a good choice for such a use?

Fig. 3–74. Surface and shape balance these two vessels, while movement is implied in the contour of the forms. Notice how tension between the reflected light on the two surfaces is broken by negative space.
Courtney Teschner, *Untitled.*
Slab sculpture, Avery slip, soda fired, 14" (35.5 cm) high.
Spruce Creek High School, Port Orange, FL.

Synthesize Use the Internet or the library to find images of different English ceramic teacups from the same historical period. Examine their size, shape, texture, surface details, decorative elements, and so on. Based on these details, write a description of what you think are the aesthetic standards of English tea ware.

Evaluate In this chapter, find examples of pieces that can be used for storage. What are the requirements for a good storage container? Which forms seem better suited for this function? Why?

Writing about Art

Select a well-known contemporary clay artist. Be sure to consider global choices. Artists work with clay in every corner of the world. Investigate the artist's work in light of past clay traditions. Write a report indicating what clay traditions or artists of the past might have influenced the work of your selected artist. Conclude with your opinion about whether or not this artist might be an important influence on future clay artists. Be sure to support your opinion with well-considered reasons.

For Your Portfolio

Organize a sequence of images for an electronic portfolio. You can show your fantasy animal sculpture or another work of your choice. With a digital camera, photograph works in progress and final pieces. File photos electronically categorized by technique. Burn onto a CD or DVD to be used for a final critique. You can also use your electronic portfolio when you apply to college.

Key Terms
centering
coning
dome
collaring
trimming

Fig. 4–1. Throwing clay on a wheel is an ideal way to create round forms such as cups, vases, and bowls.
Ursula Mommens, *Untitled.*
Tenmoku glazed vessel, 10⅜" (26 cm) high. Photo by Graham Allan.

4 Thrown Forms

The practice of shaping clay on a fast-turning wheel is known as throwing. Throwing has an almost magical quality, whether you are watching the action or performing it yourself. In the potter's hands, a lump of clay is transformed into a cone shape, then opened and shaped into a vessel—almost like a flower unfolding.

The wheel exerts centrifugal force on the clay, so you can mold a pot with your hands fairly quickly. Ultimately you'll become comfortable with the steps as you center your clay on the wheel. Through practice and concentration, you will learn to master all the factors that affect throwing: placing the clay, positioning your body, applying the right amount of pressure, and controlling the speed of the wheel.

tableware

the wheel

lids, handles, spouts

Fig. 4–2. To begin throwing pots on the wheel, first pay attention to basic clay preparation. You will have a successful experience only when air bubbles are properly removed from the clay.
Mike Flinn, *Thrown bottle*.
Pit fired, 9" (22.8 cm) high. Blue Valley High School, Stilwell, KS. Photo by Janet Ryan.

The Wheel

Potters have historically used a round, spinning surface to throw pots. Early potters found it was much easier to build a pot if the piece was turned while being formed, rather than maneuvering around a stationary piece. The first turntables or pottery wheels were flat stones with curved bottoms that the potter slowly spun by hand. Often, potters used the neck and shoulders of a broken jar as a turning device.

Various types of wheels eventually developed from these simple turning systems. As the demand for pots grew, the use of wheels changed gradually to those powered by foot or by a turning stick. As potters continued using the wheel, they increased production of storage jars, dishes, bowls, mugs, and pitchers.

Fig. 4–3. The speed at which the wheel revolves and the moisture content of the clay are the most important variables in throwing.
Ryan Thomas, *Tin Men*.
Stoneware, wood fired, each 4½" (11.4 cm) diameter and 4" (10.2 cm) high. Stivers School for the Arts, Dayton, OH.

Studios typically are equipped with either electric wheels or kick wheels, both of which offer good speed control. Each step in the sequence of throwing a pot requires a different speed. First, you center the clay on the wheel, which is best done at a fairly high speed. Opening up the form and pulling up the walls can be done at a medium speed. The final shaping and trimming should be done at a low speed.

With an electric wheel, you control the speed by changing the amount of pressure on the foot pedal. Sit at the wheel and practice controlling the speed of the wheel head with the foot pedal. Get used to how much pressure your foot exerts for slow, medium, and fast speeds.

With a *kick wheel*, you "kick" the base to set the wheel turning and change the speed by kicking more or less often. Using a kick wheel requires rhythm and timing. Start with your foot near the inside of the wheel, near the shaft, and push diagonally outward toward the edge. Try to maintain an even pace and keep the intervals between kicks evenly spaced.

Be careful not to let the wheel slow down too much as you center and form your piece. When you kick, take your hands off the clay. The kicking motion

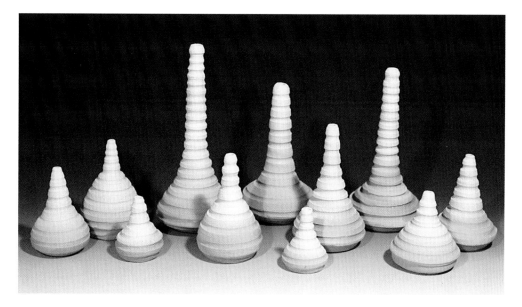

Fig. 4–4. What other type of forming technique do the lines circling the surface of these thrown objects bring to mind? What do you think the sculpture's title, *Shades of Evolution*, could be referring to?
Stuart Walker, *Shades of Evolution*.
Earthenware, wheel thrown, underglaze cone 04, to 11" (27.9 cm) high. Stivers School for the Arts, Dayon, OH. Photo by Kim Megginson.

produces vibrations within your whole body. If your arms quiver, the clay can move off-center. So as you get a sequence of movements going, concentrate on your rhythm.

Most wheels have a shelf for equipment. Keep the following tools within reach when throwing:

- small bucket of water
- sponges
- needle tool
- rib tool, preferably rubber
- pointed stick
- wire tool

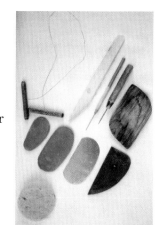

Fig. 4–5. Throwing tools.

Be sure to use clay that has been well prepared (see "Preparing the Clay" on page 28). Wedge or knead it to remove air bubbles.

Note It The clay's consistency is important. Clay that is overly stiff will be difficult to center, while the walls of too-soft clay can easily collapse as they are thinned out.

After you've prepared the clay, cut it, and form five or six balls, each about the size of a large grapefruit. Take four thumb-sized wads of clay and place them at equal distances apart on the surface of the wheel head near the edge. These wads will keep the bat fastened securely to the wheel. Seal the bat to the wheel head by pressing it down onto the clay wads. Next, dry your hands and place one ball of clay in the center of the dry bat, pressing firmly down without distorting its shape.

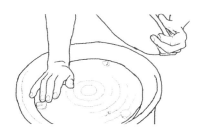

Placing bat on wheel.

Fig. 4–6. World-renowned
potter Bernard Leach
studied ceramic arts in
Japan and worked closely
with Shoja Hamada (page
130) to bring Japanese
design and firing methods
to England.
Bernard Leach, *Jar*,
c. 1920–48.
Glazed earthenware, 8¾ x 5"
(22.4 x 13 cm)
The Potteries Museum and Art
Gallery, Stoke-on-Trent, England.

Note It A *bat* is a disc or slab, made of plaster, plastic, plywood, or masonite, that supports the clay form and keeps it from sagging. It is usually attached to the wheel head. The bat and the completed pot are removed from the wheel together; once the pot has stiffened, it is cut from the bat.

Centering and Coning

Learning to center the clay on its surface is the first step in throwing pots. Centrifugal force is a good aid, but unless your clay is centered, you might not succeed. It's worth spending some time getting to know the wheel and regularly practicing **centering** your clay. Try out all the different speeds.

The following directions are for right-handed throwers. The wheel should turn counterclockwise. (Left-handed throwers may be more comfortable reversing hands and wheel direction.)

• Imagine the wheel head as a clock face. Train yourself to focus on the 3:00 position to help increase your concentration.

• Center yourself at the wheel. You will find that throwing can be physically demanding. Use your body weight, not

Fig. 4–7. To
center more
effectively, keep
your hands from
touching the bat
or wheel head.
Sarah Thomas
centering clay. Photo
by Ann Perry.

just your arm strength, as you work. Brace your arms firmly against your body. Lock your left elbow against your left hip and think of your left hip as the fulcrum, with your arm as a lever.

• Wet your hands before you begin centering. If you loosely place your hands on the clay, they will vibrate because of the clay's uneven surface. Instead, keep your left arm stiff and practice leaning forward and back again from the hips. The heel of the left hand exerts the necessary pressure to force the clay upward—a process known as **coning**. Leaning forward increases the pressure; moving back decreases it.

Press clay using your body weight.

Note It Coning facilitates the centering process by causing particles of clay to slide together and "line up" in the same direction.

• Don't let the clay push you around! If your arms are bouncing, slowly release your grip. Lock your arms against your hips again, and push the clay away from you with the heel of your left hand. Lean into the push with slow, steady pressure to gain control. Your right hand works opposite the left, guiding the clay into a cone.

Using heel of left hand to raise a cone.

• Think "slow motion." The wheel may be turning fast, but throwing movements

are slow. This is important for control, especially when you put your hands on the clay or remove them. Quick motions can knock the clay off-center. Practice touching and releasing the clay with your hands "in slow motion."

• Touch the clay only when the wheel is spinning. The wheel should be rotating relatively fast. Trying to center clay when the wheel is turning slowly or has stopped will only move it more off-center.

• Keep the clay lubricated. When you feel suction building between your hands and the surface of the clay, slowly release your grip and squeeze water over the clay with a sponge.

• Undercut at the base. Hold a sponge with your right hand and move it from the outside edge of the bat to the base of the cone. Clear away excess clay from the bat's surface.

Undercut with sponge to remove excess clay.

• Bring the cone down. With your left thumb resting on top of the cone (at 6:00), encircle the cone with your left hand. Press on top of the cone with the edge of your right fist at 4:00. Push the clay down with your right hand while using your left hand to control the expanding clay from the side. Your final product is called a **dome**.

Bring cone down.

• Is the dome centered? Place your right hand on the wheel splash pan and stretch out your right index finger until it touches the clay. Turn the wheel slowly. The clay is centered if your fingertip moves evenly on the surface. If your fingertip skips on the surface, the clay is not centered. Repeat the sequence until the clay is centered.

Is the dome centered?

Opening the Dome

When you feel comfortable with the centering process, create an opening in your clay. This is called *opening the dome*, and is part of making thrown vessels, pots, and plates. Your hands work in unison for these throwing movements. As you work, moisten the clay with your sponge when

you feel any suction, but be careful not to form a pool of water.

• Position your hands. Imagine them as a single implement. When you brace the thumbs or fingers of one hand against parts of the other, they work as one unit. Practice "hand-touching-hand" as you shape the clay.

Brace thumbs together.

• Hold your hands palms down and make a "**W**" by bracing your thumbs against each other. Drop your hands slowly onto the clay dome. Center your thumbs atop the clay while gently encircling the sides with your fingers. Focus on the center of the mound. With thumbs braced together, push

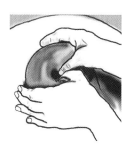

Press down and out from center.

straight downward and outward to open the dome.

• Test the thickness of the pot's base. A ³⁄₈" (.7 cm) thick base will provide enough clay to trim a foot when the pot is leatherhard. If the bottom is too thick (more than ³⁄₈"), push down again to open the base more. If the bottom is too thin, use your index and third finger to press clay from the edges of the opening and direct it toward the center.

• Finish the bottom. Press your left palm on top of your right hand between the wrist and knuckles. With the wheel spinning

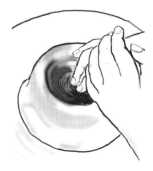

Make a smooth base.

Fig. 4–8. Throwing lines on this platter suggest energy radiating from the center of the abstract figure. Do you think the artist intended this result?
Maureen Mackey, *Platter*.
Stoneware, red shino glaze with brushed abstract figure design in black glaze. 14" dia. (35.5 cm), fired at cone 10. Courtesy of the artist.

moderately fast, use the fingers on your right hand to smooth and flatten the bottom. Your left hand provides balance and support.

Try It To finish the bottom, first place your right hand in the middle of the opening. Hold the fingers together as a unit. Beginning at the center, move your fingers across the base to the edge of the wall. Use slow, steady pressure to make a smooth base.

• True the rim. Even the lip of the pot by squeezing the rim gently between the thumb and index fingers of your left hand (thumb on the outside, index finger on the inside). Lay your right hand over the left between the knuckles and wrist, resting the edge of the right palm on top of the rim. Using your hands as a single unit, press down. The pressure from the edge of your hand compresses the top of your pot and helps it stay centered.

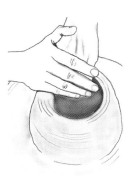

Squeeze and compress the rim.

Note It Practice the centering and opening actions until they happen automatically. Gradually, you will depend less on what your eyes tell you and more on what your hands tell you. If you close your eyes when throwing, you will notice that your concentration increases along with your sense of touch.

Fig. 4–9. AJ Santos applies pressure to even the rim of his cylinder.
Photo by Diane Levinson.

Safety Note Some production potters throw standing up. This position relieves pressure on their back muscles. Most wheels in classroom studios are set up to be used in a seated position. To lessen strain on your body as you throw:
• Fix the seat.
• Pat the clay into center before you start the wheel.
• Keep your back straight.
To minimize the amount of clay dust in the studio, after you finish your work at the wheel:
• Put all the clay slip from the splash pan into a recycling bucket.
• Clean the wheel and splash pan with a wet sponge and remove all traces of clay.

Fig. 4–10. This beautiful pot is basically a flared-out cylinder. Notice how the mouth and the foot are the same size.
Teressa Riney, *Untitled*.
Thrown pot, copper matte with luster glaze, raku, 6½ x 8" (16.5 x 20 cm). Courtesy of the artist. Photo by Maureen Mackey.

Fig. 4–11. **You can easily see how this work is based upon a cylindrical form. How can you tell that it is handmade rather than mass-produced?**
Janet Leach, *Untitled.*
14⅜" (36.3 cm) high. Photo by Graham Allen.

Throwing the Cylinder

The cylinder form is the foundation for a host of useful pieces—mugs, pitchers, jugs, vases, jars, and teapots, for example. By learning to throw cylinders, your potential repertoire of clay work increases tremendously.

* Wedge 3–4 pounds of clay and shape it into a ball.
* Center and open the clay.
* Undercut at the base.
* Raise the wall. Form a fist with your right hand, with the knuckle of your index finger slightly extended. Imagine the clay as a clock's face. Place the fingers of your left hand inside the pot at 4:00. Rest your fingers against the inside wall and hang your left thumb over the rim. Brace your left thumb on top of your right hand. Only the clay separates the fingers of your left hand from the knuckle of your right hand. Use your outside hand to press into the base while you squeeze the clay

Press clay from both sides.

evenly with inside fingers. Pull up slowly, toward your left shoulder, releasing pressure as you reach the top. (Pulling up at an angle helps to keep the top of your cylinder from flaring out.) Undercut the base and repeat the pulling movement a few times until your cylinder is the desired height.

Raise walls to final height.

* Collar the walls. If the walls of the cylinder tend to flare out between each pull, narrow the shape using a process called **collaring**. Form a ring with your thumbs and the tips of your index fingers encircling the pot. Gently push them together to narrow the cylinder. Repeat as needed.

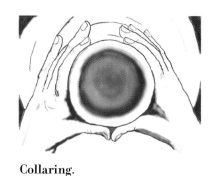

Collaring.

Fig. 4–12. **What features do the pieces in this series of altered cylinders have in common, other than shape and surface quality?**
Canaan Good, *Hip Hop Jesters*.
Stoneware, thrown and altered, cone 10 reduction, 5½" (13.9 cm) high. Stivers School for the Arts, Dayton, OH.

Fig. 4–13. **The cylinder is such an important form to master that some beginning potters throw only cylinders for many weeks.**
Teressa Riney, *Thrown vessel*.
Raku copper sand glaze, 13" (33 cm) high. Courtesy of the artist.

- Even the top edge. If the top rim is uneven, trim it with a needle tool. Use your fingers as a guide for making the cut. With the wheel turning slowly, gently grasp the wall just beneath the rim between your index finger on the inside and thumb on the outside. In your other hand, press a needle tool through the clay just above your thumb. Resting the tool on your thumb will steady it as you press the needle through the clay. As the wheel turns, the needle tool will slice through the pot. Lift the excess ribbon of clay cleanly with a single motion.

Cut rim to straighten.

- Finish the pot. The flexible rib tool can be used to further define a pot's shape and even out throwing marks. A small piece of wet plastic or *chamois* (leather) bent over the rim will compress the clay and create a smoothly finished edge.
- Cut the pot off the wheel. Let the wheel stop and hold the wire tool taut between your two hands, beginning at the far edge of the bat. Press the wire down against the bat and draw it steadily toward you, through the base of the pot. Let the pot firm up for about ten to fifteen minutes and lift it off the bat by grasping it at the base where the clay is thickest. Place it on a board to let it stiffen to the leather-hard stage for trimming. Cover it with plastic if you want to complete the trimming later.

Separate clay from bat with wire.

Fig. 4–14. When this casserole was leather-hard, a soft slab was draped over it and shaped with a moist sponge to form the lid. The leather-hard lid was trimmed to size and a strip of clay was added underneath for a flange.

Maureen Mackey, *Thrown casserole*, 1996. Stoneware, cone 10, 14" (35.5 cm) long x 4" (10.2 cm) high. Courtesy of the artist.

How to Make an Oval Casserole

A casserole is one of the many functional items that can be thrown on a wheel. To make an oval casserole:

• Throw a wide cylinder without a bottom, then wait for it to firm up (just enough to hold its shape) while preparing a slab for its base.

• Remove the cylinder from the bat and squeeze its sides together to achieve the desired oval shape.

• Brush slip onto the slab in a band approximately the shape of the oval. Lower the walls onto the slab, gently pressing into place.

• Seal the join on the inside with a coil and trim excess slab from the outside, smoothing edges with a metal rib.

Fig. 4–15. The handles on this casserole are clay loops.

Canaan Good, *Oval reduction*. Stoneware, wheel thrown and altered, cone 10 reduction, 15½ x 7 x 4½" (39 x 17.8 x 11.4 cm). Stivers School for the Arts, Dayton, OH.

Balance

In a sense, throwing on the wheel is all about balance. The physical balance achieved when you create a tall cylinder is akin to the balance you feel when standing, walking, or skateboarding. Artists consider the design principle of visual balance when composing a painting, photograph, or other two-dimensional art as well as when forming a three-dimensional sculpture or functional ware. Balance may be symmetrical (two sides mirror each other, like butterfly wings) asymmetrical, or show approximate symmetry. Art that is symmetrically balanced tends to appear stable, dignified, and calm. Look at Fig. 4–15. How did the artist achieve balance? Is the work symmetrically balanced? Why or why not?

Rookwood Pottery

The Industrial Revolution of the late eighteenth and nineteenth centuries greatly impacted crafts and design. Prior to this time, an individual skilled craftsman or artisan worked on a single object from beginning to end. With the advent of machines, however, assembly lines replaced the artisan and the creation of an object was divided into separate tasks. This division of labor saved time and money, but many saw it as a loss of craftsmanship and quality.

In particular, English poet and architect William Morris (1834–96) set out to renew handcrafted designs. Morris advocated for the Arts and Crafts movement, which proposed that an object's aesthetic qualities have greater value than its function. These ideas soon reached America, where the craze to collect the porcelains of such countries as China and Japan fueled a growing interest in ceramics. It was within this context that the American Art Pottery movement began to take shape.

The Rookwood Pottery Company of Cincinnati, Ohio, became the most successful American Art Pottery manufacturer. The pottery was founded in 1880 by Maria Longworth Nichols (1849–1932), who assembled many of the country's best art potters, including A. R. Valentien, Matthew Daly, and Kataro Shirayamadani. Women played an important role in the Art Pottery movement—for example, painters Sarah Sax and Laura Fry were among Rookwood's top decorators.

The Rookwood Pottery became known for its fine craftsmanship and attention to detail as well as for its highly decorative surfaces and experimental use of glazes. Rookwood artists were inspired by such ethnically diverse influences as Japanese porcelain and Greek vase-painting motifs. They created unique works of art through the use of innovative painting techniques, namely an airbrushlike method of applying glaze with a mouth-blown atomizer. This early glaze became known as the Standard glaze, a deep yellow, orange, or red decoration over a dark brown background, finished with a high gloss. Other glazes included Vellum, which produced a soft, fuzzy finish; Sea Green, often used with fish or floral scenes; and Ombroso, a matte glaze used on incised pieces. Rookwood wares feature both highly realistic and simplified, abstracted decorations that range from landscape, flower, and animal scenes to those portraying portraits or human figures.

Over the course of its long history, Rookwood produced all kinds of utilitarian wares, including vases, tea services, pitchers, jugs, plaques, bookends, and bowls and dishes. But in later years, the company focused increasingly on commercial success rather than artistic expression. The quality of its wares declined, and the pottery closed in 1967.

Fig. 4–16. The Rookwood Pottery Company survived two world wars, spanned the Arts and Crafts movement, and continually exhibited fresh lines, glaze techniques, and artistic excellence.
E.T. Hurley, *Vase*, 1915.
Vellum glaze, 16½" (41.9 cm) high. Courtesy of Cincinnati Art Galleries. Photo by Riley Humler.

Lindsay Reckson, *Tumblers.*
Soda fired, cone 10. Spruce Creek High School, Port Orange, FL. Photo by Timothy Ludwig.

Trimming

After you cut the pot off the wheel, your cylinder may still have a few rough spots where the clay is of uneven thickness. Refine the appearance of your pot by **trimming**. While trimming, you can also add a foot to your pot by cutting away extra clay. This raises your pot, gives it a more well-crafted look, and helps to keep extra glaze from sticking to the pot's base.

Wait until your pot is leather-hard before trimming. If the pot is too wet, it can easily become distorted. Stand your pot upside down and allow the base to dry to leather-hard. If your pot is too dry, you can rehydrate it by immersing it in a bucket of water for a few seconds. Wrap it in plastic for several hours or more to allow the water to absorb evenly before attempting to trim it again.

Note It Your pot is too dry if the walls are hard. The friction on a dry pot dulls your trimming tool and produces clay dust rather than smooth, damp shavings.

• Examine the pot. Feel the walls of your pot with one hand inside and one hand outside. Do you feel a place where the wall begins to thicken? Mark it with your thumbnail on the outside.

Mark thickest area of wall with thumbnail.

• Mark the base. The width of the base will determine how much you can trim as you shape the foot. Measure the inside

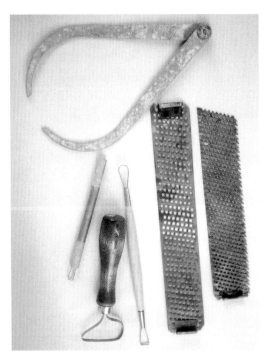

Fig. 4–18. Trimming tools.

Chapter 4

diameter by placing one fingertip at the edge of the base *inside* the pot. Now place a finger *outside* on the pot base that matches up to where your inside finger is, and make a mark. This is where the foot will begin.

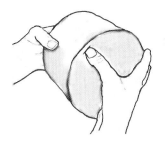

Mark base for foot.

• Center the pot on the wheel. Place the pot upside down on the wheelhead as close to center as possible. Anchor your hand on the wheel splash pan and extend your right finger out to the pot. Turn the wheel slowly to test for center. Stop the wheel and move the pot as necessary. Keep adjusting until the pot touches your finger evenly as it revolves.

Fig. 4–19. The decorative feet on this thrown vessel were made from slabs embellished with coils.
Maureen Mackey, *Raku-fired vessel with copper luster glaze*, 2001.
Raku fired, 9" (22.9 cm) diameter, 11" (27.9 cm) high. Courtesy of the artist.

Check for center.

Note It Remember, the sense of touch increases when you close your eyes and concentrate. Close your eyes and focus on feeling.

• Anchor your pot. Secure it in place by pressing some clay coils around your pot's rim. Press coils down onto the wheelhead so that your pot won't travel off center when you start turning the wheel.

Stabilize the centered pot.

• Trim your pot. Spin the wheel at medium speed. Using a trimming tool, trim away the excess clay between the two marks on the outside of the pot. Trim starting at the mark on the outside wall and work toward the mark on the base.

Remove clay between mark on wall and mark on base.

For Your Sketchbook

Consider the many functions served by bowls. When are bowls nonfunctional? In your sketchbook, sketch designs for both functional and nonfunctional bowls.

Try It When you first start trimming, use this trick to keep from removing too much clay: Before you turn your pot over on the wheelhead, press a thumbtack into the middle of your pot's base. You will know you've trimmed far enough when your tool scrapes the tack point. When finished, remove the tack and smooth over the tack hole. After a few tries you'll sense the depth and thickness without needing a tack.

• Create the foot. The thickness of your pot's base will determine the height of the foot. (If you trim too deeply, you can make a hole in your pot!) Outline the foot by trimming around the mark you made to indicate the diameter of the base. With your trimming tool, trim the side walls inward to where you want the foot ring to begin.

Create the foot (outside).

• Clean the inside of the foot. Decide upon a width for the foot and begin trimming away clay in the middle. Trim downward, moving toward the center as you go. Make several passes. Your finished foot should look like a flat donut on the base of your pot.

Clean the foot (inside).

• Burnish the foot. Use a wooden tool, dry sponge, or leather to smooth the foot's surface.

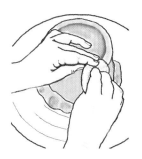

Burnish the foot.

Fig. 4–20. Cups, tumblers, and mugs are tableware forms based on the cylinder.
Gabe Apraiz, *Untitled*.
Thrown tumblers, soda fired, 3" (7.6 cm) diameter, 3" (7.6 cm) high. Spruce Creek High School, Port Orange, FL. Photo by Timothy Ludwig.

Thrown Tableware

Using the same basic technique you learned in throwing a cylinder with a few variations, you can create a bowl and a plate.

Throwing the Bowl

Throwing the bowl is only slightly different from throwing a cylinder. A cylinder's walls are pulled straight up, while the bowl's walls are eased outward as you raise them. The bowl also requires a wider base to support its walls.

A bowl can be functional or nonfunctional (decorative). Think of some different bowl forms. How does the bowl's function influence its shape? How can a bowl be used in a nonfunctional way? Sketch some different bowl shapes in your sketchbook and name their functions.

Fig. 4–21. By glazing only the insides of these bowls, how has the artist affected our sense of how they might be used?
John Silva, *Bowls.*
Bellarmine College Preparatory, San Jose, CA. Photo by Diane Levinson.

Imagine your inside hand determining the bowl's shape. Your outside hand will support the wall and follow the force of the inside hand. You will save making the rim for last, after you are satisfied with the bowl's basic shape. Think about the rim treatment. Does it relate to the bowl's function? Where is the bowl's focal

Fig. 4–22. Would you say this bowl is strictly decorative, or does it seem functional as well?
Jessica Schell, *Thrown and altered bowl.*
Raku fired, 11½" (29.2 cm) diameter. Blue Valley High School, Stillwater, KS. Photo by Janet Ryan.

point—inside or outside? Think about how the interior of a bowl should contrast with its exterior.

* Center 3–5 pounds of clay on a bat attached to the wheel head.
* Widen the centered clay. Press the clay down and outward to expand the diameter of the base.
* Slow the wheel and open the dome. Keep the opening wide on top and leave a ³⁄₈" (.7 cm) base. Push the clay outward from the center of the hole, forming a curve at the base.

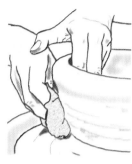

Shaping the bowl.

* Strengthen the bottom by compressing it. Brace your arms against your sides and use your inside fingers to press against the bottom from the edge to the center. Repeat until the curve is even and the bottom is compressed. You can use a rib tool for this operation as well. Undercut slightly at the base.

Compress the base.

* Raise and flare the wall. Keep the wheel turning at a slow speed for more control. The walls of the bowl should be slightly thicker than those of the cylinder. Give more attention to the inside of the bowl than the outside as you move the clay. Try two or three gentle pulls with your fingers or a rib tool to finish the bowl. Take care not to expand the walls too far over the base.

Fig. 4–23. Although this wheel-thrown plate is a functional piece, the artist has given much attention to visual effects and decoration.

John Parker Glick, *Plate*, 2001.
Stoneware with multiple glazes and glaze painting techniques, 22½" (57 cm) diameter, 4½" (11.4 cm) deep. Courtesy of the artist.

• Finish the rim using the method described on page 93. Even it with a needle tool if necessary, then finish with a chamois. Cut through the bottom with a wire tool. Remove the bat from the wheel and

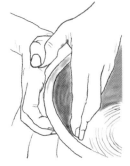

Raise and flare the wall.

allow the bowl to stiffen to leather-hard before trimming the foot.

• Trim a foot. Examine the contour of the inside walls and bottom of your bowl. Follow the curve as you trim and add the foot rim. The foot's diameter should match the bottom of the bowl and is usually smaller than the curve where the walls begin to flare out. Try to achieve a flowing unbroken line from the foot to the body of your bowl.

Trim a foot.

Throwing the Plate

The plate—a flat, low functional form—has provided unique surfaces for decorative treatments throughout history. The process of throwing this wide-open form is similar to that used for the bowl—in fact, the plate really is a low bowl. Plates can be functional as well as nonfunctional.

Discuss It What are some specific occasions when plates serve a prominent functional purpose? Name some ways plates perform a nonfunctional purpose.

• Center a 6-pound ball of clay on the bat.
• Slow the wheel speed and widen the clay. Place the heel of your left hand at 9:00 on the outside base of the clay dome. Pressure at the heel will help keep the clay centered while your right hand presses the clay down to expand the diameter for the base.

Keep clay centered while pressing down to expand.

Fig. 4–24. This artist uses the elements of line and shape to decorate her platter's surface. How would you describe its formal qualities—unity, rhythm, balance, proportion, and emphasis?

Ann Perry, *Untitled*.
Carved platter, midrange clay body with cone 6 glaze. Courtesy of the artist.

• Open the plate. Keeping the hole wide on top and leaving a thicker base than for the cylinder, use the inside hand to push the clay horizontally outward from the center. Gradually curve it toward the edges to form a shallow bowl shape.

Open from center into shallow bowl shape.

Check the thickness of the center with a needle tool.

• Compress the bottom. Press outward from the center to the far edge and back several times with your fingers or the flat edge of a rib tool. This will strengthen the bottom, and the pressure helps to mini-

Compress the base.

mize warping and cracking when the plates dries.

• Undercut at the base. Clear away excess clay from the edge of the bat to the outside base of the plate.

Fig. 4–25. What words describe the tension created by the flowing glaze color's hue and intensity on the surface of this piece?

Laura Kennicutt, *Untitled*.
Thrown bowl, poured glazes, cone 10 reduction, 9½" (24.1 cm) diameter. Courtesy of the artist. Photo by Maureen Mackey.

• Raise the wall. Complete all hand movements in slow motion, avoiding any uneven pressure. The wheel should be turning at slow speed. Release pressure slowly as your pull nears the rim area. Pay more attention to the inside than the outside as you move the clay. Apply pressure with the inside fingers and compress the rim after the final pull, to help keep a rounded shape.

• Finish the bottom. Use the fingers to smooth the inside of the bottom and shape a curved transition from the bottom to the wall.

• Finish the rim. With the wheel turning very slowly, hold the wall between the thumb and fingers of one hand (fingers inside, thumb on outside). Use your other hand to support the wall and absorb pressure from the inside hand. Keep the hands connected. Gently

Shape the rim.

and slowly push the rim downward with your index finger. (The thumb supports the rim underneath while your opposite-hand index finger compresses the edge and controls the flare.) You can also flare the rim by using a smooth stick or rib tool instead of fingers to press downward on the clay. (The outside hand is only supporting the walls, not pressing.)

• Cut through the bottom. First, use the needle tool to cut between the bat and the base of your plate, making just enough of a groove to get the wire tool under the edge of the plate. Then insert the wire and pull downward on the grippers, taking care to keep the wire taut. Remove the bat from the wheel and allow the plate to stiffen before removing it from the bat.

• Trim the plate. Feel the thickness of the bottom and edges to determine how much to trim. Feel where the edge of the

Fig. 4–26. **When do you think the appliqué design was added to this plate? How does the glaze application add an extra dimension of interest?**
Mike Flinn, *Untitled*.
Stoneware, cone 6 electric, thrown and altered plate, 16" (40.6 cm) diameter. Blue Valley High School, Stilwell, KS. Photo by Janet Ryan.

bottom curves into the wall and mark that place on the base. This is where the foot should be located. Turn the plate over. Attach it to the wheel head with clay anchors, and trim the outline of the foot. Trim the outside curve from the foot to the walls. Wide flat pieces sometimes have a second foot ring about 2" (5 cm) in diameter in the center the base. This adds support and prevents sagging. Finish trimming by removing excess clay from the base between the foot rings.

Fig. 4–27. **Michelle Fransway pulls a wire through the base of her plate to release it from the bat.**
Photo by Maureen Mackey.

• Flatten the bulge. The pressure from trimming such a wide surface can make the inside of the plate bulge slightly. After trimming, set the plate upright on a board or table and gently push down on the inside surface with the palm of your hand to flatten it again.

Fig. 4–28. A lid is simple to make, but fitting it to its pot takes some practice. How would the character of this jar be different without its lid?
Lindsay Reckson, *Lidded Jar.*
Soda fired–Barium matte, cone 10, 8" (20.3 cm) high. Spruce Creek High School, Port Orange, FL.

Lids and Spouts

Whether intended for a jar, pot, or dish, the lid's function is to shield the opening and protect the contents of its "partner" pot. Making a lid requires thinking ahead—you'll want to make the lid from the same type of clay and at the same time as its pot. This ensures that both pieces will shrink at the same rate and create an even fit.

Top, left to right: **Flat lid with raised lip, flat lid with flange, simple lid on jar flange.**
Bottom, left to right: **teapot lid with deep flange, cover lid, dome lid.**

Note It The lid should not only fit the opening securely but it should also complete the shape of the pot. Consider it an extension of the main body of the pot as you choose a type and design.

Think about the focus area of your lid. For a pot with a strong form, perhaps your lid should be recessed and nonintrusive.

However, you could also create a strong, visible lid that complements the pot to strengthen and unify the form. By contrast, if you wish to draw attention away from the pot form, your lid could be the main focal point, especially if supplied with a distinctive knob.

Another important feature of a lid—the *flange*—is a little ridge that is either part of the pot's rim or part of the lid. When it is part of the rim, it acts as a shelf or seat where the lid rests. When it is part of the lid, the flange fits inside the rim of the pot to provide balance and stability. A lid for a pouring vessel, such as a teapot, should be designed with a deep flange that will anchor the lid when the pot is tipped for pouring.

Lids can be thrown right-side up (flat lid) or upside down (domed lid). Their purpose can be functional or non-functional.

Throwing a Flat Lid with a Knob

A knob can be thrown by itself and attached to the lid with slip, thrown on a trimmed lid, or hand fashioned and attached with slip. Follow these steps for throwing a flat lid that sits inside the neck of a pot:

Flat lid resting on angled rim.

- Wedge, cone, center, and throw a simple pot.
- Flare the rim at a 45° angle. The angled rim will act as a subtle flange where the lid rests.

Measure with calipers.

- Use *calipers* to measure the diameter of the rim. The inside diameter of the rim equals the outside diameter of the lid. Place the calipers against a ruler to record the diameter.
- Center the clay for the lid. About 1 lb. of clay is sufficient for an average-sized lid. Throw the lid and pot at the same sitting in order to maintain similar moisture content.
- Flatten the centered mound until it is at least 1" (2.5 cm) thick, and 1" less than the diameter of the rim in width.
- Beginning about an inch from the center of the mound, use the fingers of your right hand, braced by your left hand, to push the clay down.

Shape the lid.

- Spread the clay out from the center to the desired width, taking care not to let the outside edges of the clay get too thin. You're going to use a wire tool to cut it from the bat, so make the lid thicker than it will be when finished—at least ¼" to ⅜" (.7 to .6 cm) extra is good.
- Smooth the edge with a damp sponge or leather.

Smooth with a sponge or leather.

- While the lid is still on the wheel, drop a hole in the clay that remains in the center of the mound. Leave a fairly thick bottom and pull up a small cylinder.
- Raise the cylinder by squeezing it near the base. Slightly flare and shape the top into a knob that will be easy to grasp.

Shaping a knob.

- Trim the top edge with a needle tool and smooth it with a sponge. No further trimming is necessary.
- Hold a wooden tool against the outside edge of the lid and trim at a 45° angle. The lid will match the angle of the rim for a secure fit. Check the

Angle the edge of the lid.

final measurements against the inside diameter of the pot.
- Use a wire to cut the lid from the bat.
- Dry the pot and lid together. When they are bone dry you may want to do a final fitting, or fine-tuning, to make sure the pieces are right.

Fig. 4–29. How would you describe the lids of these pots? Discuss the sensory, formal, technical, and expressive qualities of the series.
Emily Collins, *Blue Black Series*. Stoneware, cone 10 reduction, each 5¼" (13.3 cm) dia. x 8" (22.9 cm) high. Stivers School for the Arts, Dayton, OH.

Note It Achieve a good fit. Tip your leather-hard work sideways and hold it with the lid in place. Gently rotate the lid back and forth against the pot several times as though unscrewing the lid from a jar. Remove the lid, make a quarter turn, position it in the seat and rotate it gently again. Repeat, making a quarter turn each time. The friction helps to adjust both pieces and completes the fit.

Throwing a Flat Lid with a Flange

To make a flat lid with a flange, you need a pot with a shoulder for the lid to sit on.

Flat lid with flange resting on pot shoulder.

* Wedge, cone, center, and throw a simple pot with a substantial shoulder.
* Measure the diameter of the rim with calipers (see page 104).
* Center a dome of clay for the lid (1–1½ lbs). The diameter of the lid should be slightly less than the diameter of the inside edge of the pot.
* Measure the base of the lid with calipers. This stem will fit inside the opening of the pot.
* Midway between the center and the edge of the dome, press down and spread the clay outward leaving the clay in the center for the knob.

* Make a horizontal shelf to complete the rim.
* Finish the edges of the lid with a soft sponge or leather.

Shape the lid.

* Fashion a knob from the remaining clay in the center, as for the flat lid (described on page 104).

Smooth flange with a sponge or leather.

Throwing a Dome Lid

A dome lid does not have a flange, so the pot must be designed with a special rim for the lid to sit on. The dome lid is thrown upside down in the shape of a bowl. You can leave a thick bottom (about 1½–2", or 3.8–5 cm) for trimming a knob, or you can attach a knob later when the piece is leather-hard.

Dome lid resting on flanged rim.

- Throw a pot, keeping the top edge thick to allow enough clay for a flange—about ³⁄₈" (.7 cm).

Make a pot with a wide rim.

- Make a seat for the lid by holding the top wall of the pot base steady with one hand. Split the top edge. Use a flat-bottomed rib tool or wooden stick to position it in the middle of the rim. Press straight down about ³⁄₈" (.7 cm) on the inside.

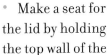

"Split" the rim.

- Measure its inside rim with calipers.
- Throw a smaller bowl (the lid). The diameter of the outside wall should match the diameter of the inside edge of the pot just above the flange (seat). Flatten the lid's top edge to make a lip that will rest on the shelflike edge of the pot's flange.
- Cut the lid off the bat with a wire tool.

- When the lid has stiffened, turn it over. Center it on the wheel and trim a knob on the top.

Remember to dry the pot and lid together. When the pieces have stiffened, they should be fitted (see page 104) and dried as one piece.

Fig. 4–30. What type of lid completes the opening for this teapot? Explain how it could have been made.
Gabe Apraiz, *Untitled*.
Thrown teapot, soda fired, 8 x 6" (20.3 x 15.2 cm). Spruce Creek High School, Port Orange, FL. Photo by Timothy Ludwig.

Pouring Lips and Spouts

A pouring lip is at the top of the vessel, and is made seamlessly from the clay that is thrown. Pouring lips are typically found on pitchers. A spout is an attached piece, made separately. Spouts are found on teapots, for example.

Fig. 4–31. Can you name some vessels that have spouts but are not teapots?
Emily Collins, *Cruets*.
Stoneware, cone 10 reduction, each 7½ x 3 x 5" (19 x 7.5 x 12.7 cm). Stivers School for the Arts, Dayton, OH.

Fig. 4–32. Notice how the shapes of the handles on the tray, cup, and teapot balance each other and contribute to the rhythm of the grouping. What other shapes are repeated in this composition?
Erin Fitzsimmons, *Untitled (Strawberry tea service)*.
Midrange clay body with cone 04 glaze. Lancaster High School, Cheektowaga, NY. Photo by Anne Perry.

Making a Pouring Lip

Pouring lips are formed while the pot is still plastic and attached to the wheel. The rim of the pot is stretched and pulled outward by one finger while supported by the thumb and second finger of the opposite hand. If you make a mistake, just stretch another lip. Set the wheel in motion, collar the neck and rim, and try again.

• Throw a cylinder, collar the neck, and finish the rim with a sponge or leather. Stop the wheel.

• Place one hand inside the pot and pull a groove upward and slightly outward with your middle finger. Support the outside wall with the thumb and index finger of your other hand.

• Pinch the edges of the rim and create a smooth channel for the liquid by drawing it forward. Keep your fingers well lubricated.

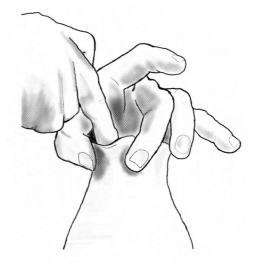

Shape a pouring lip; smooth the channel.

• Attach a handle on the opposite side of the pot after trimming. (See section on handles, page 109.)

Make a Spout

You can create spouts for flasks, teapots, or coffeepots. It is wise to throw a few extra spouts because some spouts fit better than others.

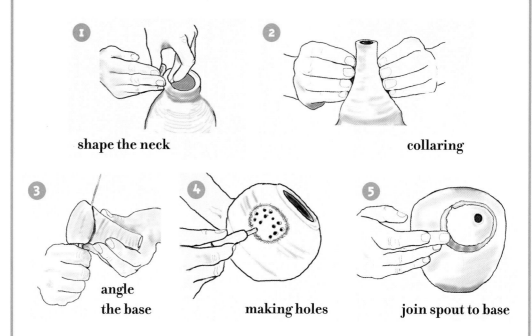

① shape the neck

② collaring

③ angle the base

④ making holes

⑤ join spout to base

① Throw a small, wide-based cylinder (about 1–1½ lbs.) with a narrow neck, using one finger on the inside to pull the wall upward. You can use a damp sponge on the outside to help smooth the pull.

② Alternate pulling with collaring. Finish the lip with a slight outward curve. Smooth the edge with a chamois or fine sponge. Allow the spout to stiffen. Mark the spout location on the pot. Place it high enough so that the top of the spout will be higher than the liquid inside when the pot is filled.

③ When the spout dries to leather-hard, position the spout on the mark you made. You may need to angle the spout's base so it will conform to the shape of the pot.

④ Rest the spout on the pot and trace around it with a needle tool or dull pencil. Remove the spout. Score the outline and the base of the spout. Within the traced outline, make small holes in the wall (for the liquid to pour through).

⑤ Slip the scored edges of both pot and spout, and press them firmly together. You can reinforce the join with a thin coil and smooth it with your finger or the edge of a wooden tool.

Fig. 4–33. This teapot's elegant stance is created by the height of its foot and the fanciful knob on its lid, balanced by the flowing movement of its handle and spout. What mood is created by the color treatment?
Emily Collins, *Tea for 200*.
Earthenware, cone 04, 26" (66 cm) high. Stivers School for the Arts, Dayton, OH. Photo by Don Clark.

Fig. 4–34. How would it feel to drink from one of these cups? Would you use the handle? Why might a clay artist want to place handles in this unusual position?
Lindsay Reckson, *Cups*.
Soda fired, cone 10. Spruce Creek High School, Port Orange, FL.

Handles

Handles can be functional or decorative. For example, in the twelfth century, Cistercian monks in England made vessels with multiple pulled handles that surrounded the neck and shoulders of the pot. The handles were purely utilitarian; if one handle broke, another was available—as long as one handle remained, the vessel was still useful.

Handles may be pulled, coiled, or thrown. Consider the following when planning to make a handle:

• Will the handle function as a handle or will it be merely a decorative attachment?

• If it is functional, how will it work? Will you grasp it with the whole hand or just a few fingers?

• If it is decorative, will you place it on the side, shoulder, or neck? How many handles do you want to create?

• Think about the negative space inside the handle's curve. Does it complement the shape of the pot?

Making a Pulled Handle

Each handle is unique, so you may want to pull many handles in order to have a wide selection. Keep a few extras on hand in case the first one doesn't fit.

• Wedge about 2–3 pounds of clay and shape it into a short, fat coil.

• Grasp the coil in one hand and hold it so that the coil hangs down.

• Encircle the top of the coil with your hand, your thumb facing you. This hand will remain stationary while your other hand pulls.

Hand position for beginning pull.

• Under the holding hand, make a ring around the coil with the thumb and forefinger of your other hand (this will be your pulling hand).

• With your pulling hand, pull down very gently. It helps to have your pulling hand slightly wet but not dripping for each pull.

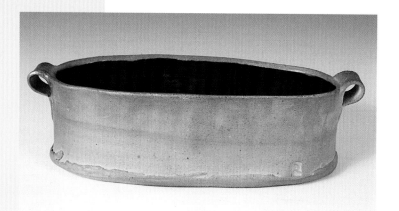

Pulling clay down.

- After each pull, rotate the coil a quarter turn with your holding hand.
- Repeat until the handle is pulled to the desired thickness.
- With your pulling hand, close the thumb and forefinger to form an oval shape.
- Flatten the ring of clay into an oval shape with one more pull.
- For the final pull, place the thumb of your pulling hand smack against the coil.
- Pull all the way down to make a groove.
  - Pinch off excess clay at the bottom.
  - Anchor the top of the clay by pressing it onto a board. The tug of gravity forms a natural curve on the handle. Allow the handle to stiffen to almost leather-hard before attaching to the pot.

Final pull with thumb making groove.

Note It When you're pulling a handle, you want your pulling hand to be moist but not dripping wet. Keep a small bucket of water nearby. Touch the water with your pulling hand and shake off the excess prior to each pull.

Making Lug Handles

Lug handles are attached horizontally to the sides of a pot. These handles are good for casseroles, large bowls, baking dishes, and jars. Lugs can be made from pulled handles, coils, or thrown sections.

Try It Throw a pair of lug handles.
- Throw a bottomless cylinder about 1" (2.5 cm) tall and 3" (7.6 cm) in diameter. Smooth the top edge with a sponge or piece of leather.
- Allow the cylinder to stiffen—about 20 minutes or until it holds its shape.
- Run a wire tool under the pot to release it from the

A lug handle.

wheel head or bat. Cut the cylinder in half vertically to form the two handles.
- Score and slip the bottom edge of each handle. Attach handles opposite each other on the pot's shoulder, taking care to balance their placement.
- Add a coil under each handle and against the pot for added strength. Press and seal the joins.

Making Thrown Handles

You can form several handles from one cylinder using this technique.

• Throw a cylinder with walls at least ⅜" (.7 cm) thick. Finish the rim. Support the inside walls near the top with the fingers of your stabilizing hand while the tip of your other thumb presses against the outside wall to form a slight groove. The wheel should be turning at a slow speed.

• Position the needle tool below the bottom of the groove, and trim through the clay. Lift the ring from the cylinder and put it on a board.

• Cut the ring in one place, open it to form the handle's curve, and allow it to stiffen until it is firm enough to keep its shape.

• Smooth the cut edge with a damp sponge. Score and slip the edges of the handle and the area where you'll join the handle to the pot.

Attaching the Handle

• Examine the profile of the curve on your pot's wall where you will attach the handle.

• Cut the top of the handle to match the contour of the wall's curve.

Determine angle for cut.

• Test the size and shape of your handle against the pot.

• If necessary, cut the bottom of the handle to fit the pot.

• View the join from above to make sure the handle is straight, not slanted. Adjust as needed.

• Trace around areas where the handle will join the wall.

• Score and slip the handle ends and wall

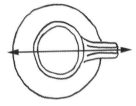

View from above to check position.

joins, and use gentle pressure to attach the handle to the pot.

• Seal the joins with your thumb or a

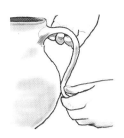

Attach with slip, and seal joins.

wooden tool, gently pulling the clay from the handle to the walls.

• Smooth the surface of the joined sections with a slightly damp sponge or leather.

Teapots

Making a teapot combines everything you've learned so far about using the wheel to throw clay. It's a challenging exercise, and it may require several tries to get it right. Don't give up! If you end up making a few nonfunctional teapots, you can always turn them into pieces of sculpture.

Planning Your Teapot

Before you begin, decide on your desired teapot shape. It can be squat, tall, narrow, or cone-shaped. Make a simple drawing of the shape and outline the profile. Then

Fig. 4–37. The shape of the cup and its handle mirrors that of its companion teapot. What two functions does the cup serve?
Bethany Krull, *Untitled (Stacking Tea Set)*.
Low fire clay and cone 04 glaze. Lancaster Central High School, Lancaster, NY. Photo by Ann Perry.

Fig. 4–38. Thrown forms are often altered. Some are barely recognizable as thrown work when they are complete. How do you think this teapot was constructed?
Susan Beiner, *Vegetable Medley*, 1998.
Porcelain, 8 x 11 x 6" (20.3 x 28 x 15.2 cm). Courtesy of Ferrin Gallery.

sketch a lid. As you consider your ideas about a teapot, ask yourself:
· Will the lid be flat or domed?
· Will it rise out of the pot or sink into the opening?
· What type of knob will it have—thrown or hand-built?
· Does the lid shape complement the form?

Handle over lid.

· Do you want to place the handle over the lid, on top of the shoulders of the pot—or on the side, opposite the spout?
· What size spout complements the shape?

Handle on side.

Line

When you think of line and the way it can be used in ceramic art, what comes to mind? In general, lines connect two points and are longer than they are wide. But more importantly, lines have a personality—they can be straight or curved, thick or thin, continuous or interrupted. A bold line with sharp edges that abruptly changes direction produces a different feeling than a thin, flowing line. While line's most obvious use might be that of surface decoration (drawing, incising, or carving), you might want to consider other ways to incorporate this powerful element into your work.

Fig. 4–39. Using line thoughtfully in your design can make the difference between a dull artwork and an exciting one.
Ann Perry, *Ginko Green Tea*.
Sculptural tea set cone 6 fired with cone 6 and 04 glaze. Courtesy of the artist.

Making a Teapot

Use the same clay for every part of your teapot: body, lid, spout, and handle. Be sure to throw or form these pieces at the same time. Then, all the components will shrink at the same rate, they'll fit better together, and the measurements will be more accurate. You can assemble the pieces at another time, but remember to cover them in plastic to keep them workable.

- Throw the body of the teapot.
- Measure the diameter of the opening and create a flanged lid.
- Pull or throw the handle. Shape it and allow it to stiffen.
- Throw the spout (and a few extras).
- Let all pieces stiffen to leather-hard.
- Trim a foot ring on your pot before you attach the spout and handle.
- Hold the spout against the side wall and adjust its fit.

Fig. 4–40. A teapot is one of the more complex objects that can be developed from wheel-thrown forms.
Robert Putnam, *Untitled*.
Thrown and altered teapot. Stoneware, cone 9 reduction with multiple glazes, 8 x 12½ x 6" (20.3 x 31.7 x 15.2 cm). Courtesy of the artist.

Note It Make sure the top of the spout is as high as or higher than the top of the pot. If the spout is too low, tea will spill out when the pot is filled.

- Trace around the spout on the pot wall.
- Supporting the wall, cut a series of holes within the outline.
- Smooth rough edges with a damp sponge.
- Score and slip the base of the spout and the traced outline on the pot.
- Press the two pieces firmly together and smooth around the join. You can reinforce the join with a thin coil and smooth it with your finger or the edge of a wooden tool.
- Balance the placement of the handle.
- Score, slip, and join the handle to the pot.
- Let your teapot dry slowly with the lid in place.
- Bisque fire, decorate, and glaze fire.

Fig. 4–41. The circulating and flowing applied decoration on this diminutive teapot unifies and balances its shape. How does the exaggerated handle further your perception of space and volume?
Jessica Schell, *Untitled*.
Stoneware, cone 6 electric, 8½ x 10" (21.6 x 25.4 cm). Blue Valley High School, Stilwell, KS. Photo by Janet Ryan.

Studio Experience:
Mixed-Media Sculpture

You will study the works of a well-known artist (painter, sculptor, or clay artist) and create a sculpture that reflects his or her style. Plan to stack at least three sections, or levels, to make a totem-like form. Distinct parts should be thrown and hand-built, and relate thematically and stylistically to your artist's body of work. Include found objects or other mixed media in your sculpture.

For inspiration, you might want to consider artists in the last half of the twentieth century. After World War II, painters and sculptors began boldly experimenting with new styles and themes. Their departure from tradition inspired clay artists to work in new ways too. As innovative styles merged with form and design, ceramics became an art form that could stand apart from its historical ties to function.

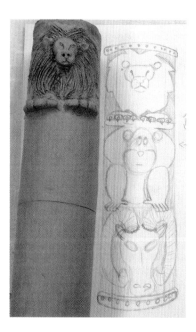

Fig. 4–42. Patrick made a drawing to help visualize his clay sculpture. Do you think he might have been inspired by the work of Henri Rousseau? How would you use found objects to add to this design?

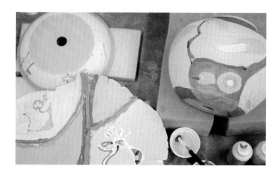

Fig. 4–43. Before bisque firing, Cassie Gonzales painted underglaze on her greenware pieces. Note the center holes.

Before You Begin

• Research a painter, sculptor, or clay artist whose work interests you. What stylistic qualities help you to identify this artist's work? Consider how you can integrate them into your sculpture. Will you emphasize form, color, or surface decoration? Make some drawings to help you visualize your composition.

• Plan how you will make each section relate to the theme. What imagery will you use? Will your sculpture have a separate base? Where will you use hand-building? Will you make molded pieces? How will you incorporate thrown pieces?

• Gather mixed-media materials for your piece. Think about how you will use them. Will you attach them after the firing?

You will need:
• hand-building and throwing tools
• molds, if desired
• decorating and glazing tools and brushes
• materials for bonding and attaching pieces

Create It

1 Make the individual pieces for each level, hand-building and wheel throwing as appropriate. Keep the clay to a uniform thickness, about ³⁄₈". Consider poking holes if you will attach pieces using wire,

or cutting a center hole if you will connect pieces with a dowel or threaded metal rod.

2 Bisque fire the pieces when they have dried sufficiently.

3 Add further decoration and glaze fire.

4 Erect your sculpture, combining pieces securely with a dowel or rod and hardware, wire, or adhesives. Attach mixed-media materials and found objects.

5 Be prepared to share information about the artist you researched, and to explain the techniques you used.

Check It Does your piece have a theme that reflects the style of the artist you selected? Does each section echo that theme? How? How many different forming techniques did you incorporate in your piece? Were you able to attach found objects successfully? Were you able to assemble the sculpture securely? What did you learn from this project? What would you do differently if you had to do it again?

Sketchbook Connection

As you plan your design, refine your ideas by drawing not only the front of your sculpture but also the back and sides. Draw each section from different angles. After your work is complete, sketch ideas for some ways you might utilize mixed media in other clay sculptures.

Fig. 4–44. Placing "earrings" on the figurative sculpture. The center pole was made from an overturned broom. What other found objects were used? Cassie Gonzales, *A Whole Lot of Miro*, 2002. Slab and thrown clay, mixed media, cone 04, 50" (127 cm) high. Photo by Maureen Mackey.

Rubric: Studio Assessment

4	3	2	1
Style and Theme • Style and theme used relates to that of a specific artist • Consistent style/theme between sections			
Final sculpture is a perceptive, inventive transfer of important aspects of researched artist's ideas. Style and theme very consistent among sections. Inventive, knowledgeable	Final sculpture is an accurate transfer of important aspects of researched artist's ideas. Style and theme consistent among sections. Related, consistent	Final sculpture exhibits a somewhat rough or superficial relationship to researched artist's ideas OR style and theme inconsistent. Some understanding	Final sculpture exhibits a limited relationship to researched artist's ideas OR style and theme highly inconsistent. Uninspired or insufficient
Design Elements • Interaction of forms with surrounding space • Use of found objects or mixed media • Surface treatment			
Interaction of forms and space, found objects (or mixed media additions) and surface treatment work smoothly together to add great interest and unity to sculpture. Sophisticated, holistic	Interaction of forms and space, found objects (or mixed media additions) and surface treatment add pleasing interest and unity to sculpture. Pleasing, unified	1 of these: little interaction of forms and space; little attention given or haphazard incorporation of mixed media/found objects; surface treatment is neglected. Needs additions or edits	2–3 of the factors listed in level 2. Monotonous, unfinished
Media Use • Thrown and handbuilt techniques • Other media included • Structural craftsmanship • Glaze application			
No apparent mistakes in techniques used and construction of sculpture. Very successful glaze application. Polished finish	Few apparent mistakes in techniques used and construction of sculpture. Successful glaze application. Skillful finish	Some noticeable mistakes in media use. Glaze application may yield an uneven finish. More care indicated	Many noticeable, significant mistakes in media use. Rudimentary difficulties
Work Process • Research • Sketches • Reflection/Evaluation			
Thorough documentation; goes above and beyond assignment expectations. Thoughtful, thorough, independent	Complete documentation; meets assignment expectations. Meets expectations	Documentation is somewhat haphazard or incomplete. Incomplete, hit and miss	Documentation is minimal or very disorganized. Very incomplete

Web Links

The American Ceramic Society home page offers a variety of information for the professional potter.
www.acers.org

Photographs and descriptions of pottery made by artists from Finland to Nigeria, over 4,000 pages of pictures and information.
www.studiopottery.com

Career Profile:
Charles Smith

Photo: Edmond Dean.

Charles Smith creates raku and stoneware pottery that is influenced and inspired by nature and the art of pre-Columbian, African, and Native American cultures. After junior college, Smith applied to Jackson State University in Mississippi but did not receive a scholarship. He stubbornly requested an interview to show his "portfolio"—boxes filled with pots—and was offered a scholarship that same day. He graduated with a degree in art education and taught for awhile, but found that he needed to be able to work on his craft twenty-four hours a day. Today Smith works in his own studio, where he is in control of his time and is always ready when the creative spirit arrives.

How do you decorate your pottery?
Charles: I love carving—I could carve all day long. People should be able to recognize a pot by the design, and the carving is my "signature." My designs are simple but look complex. I have also worked out a special tripod process that merges into a single element with the bottom of the pot.

Fig. 4–46. Smith uses line to balance out his work and capture the eye of the viewer. The carved surface design on this ceremonial jar is made of flowing lines that subtly turn into serpents as they move around the piece.
Photo: Edmond Dean.

Fig. 4–45. Smith often carves shapes with the pot upside down. He says, "Nature has been my biggest teacher."
Photo: Edmond Dean.

What is most rewarding about being a studio artist?
Charles: The studio is my own space, and it's where I work through problems and challenges. In your own studio you can leave things in a mess and clean up later because studio work is an ongoing process. I listen to music when I'm working. I like jazz when I'm doing big pots and blues for the smaller ones.

What is your advice to a young person interested in a career as a studio artist?
Charles: Listen to positive criticism of your work, even if you don't act on it immediately. It's also important to find a space—in a shed, on a table, under a tree—to make truly your own. And practice, practice, practice! Remember that you're never in total control. Pots blow up. Glazes fail. When this happens, don't throw away the mistakes. Learn from them as you work to master the challenges of the material.

Chapter Review

Recall List the steps for throwing a cylinder.

Understand Explain why centering is important when throwing pottery on a wheel.

Apply Throw a small cylinder. Then change its appearance by adding handles or a spout. Have you made it more functional or less functional?

Analyze Examine Ursula Mommens's vase shown on page 84. Describe the form, paying particular attention to its foot, body, shoulders, neck, and lip.

Synthesize Can an abstract claywork be functional? Give an example from the chapter to support your argument.

Evaluate Work with your classmates to test the pouring abilities of the clay pieces you've made that have spouts. Are there any that pour especially well? Identify and explain the qualities of a good pouring spout.

Fig. 4–48. **Attach handles when leather-hard. Carefully seal all the joined areas with your fingers and smooth the connection. Check negative space inside the handle and make final adjustments to the curve.**
Photo by Randy O'Brien.

Writing about Art
Review the clay pieces you have created so far for this course. Write a critique of your work. Include comments on your intent versus the actual result. List the strengths and weaknesses of your creations. Follow up by writing a plan of action for improving your skills and furthering your artistic development.

Fig. 4–47. **How do surface, color, and form reflect the title of this piece?**
Tim Ballingham,
Lotus Lantern.
Mishima technique.
Courtesy of the artist.

For Your Portfolio
Photograph your mixed-media sculpture and document with title, date, and size. Write a brief description of the methods you used to build, assemble, glaze, and fire your piece. Note your sources of inspiration.

Key Terms

sprigging
oxides
carbonates
flux
bisque ware
greenware

Fig. 5–1. Kurt Weiser uses china paint to decorate porcelain that is bisque fired and glazed white. Most of Weiser's complex pieces are fired about five times, due to the different temperatures at which the overglaze colors mature.

Kurt Weiser, *Blue Horizon*, 1992.

Porcelain with china paint, 11⅞ x 12½ x 4¾" (30.4 x 31.7 x 12 cm). © Mint Museum of Craft and Design, museum purchase: Delhom Service League Fund.

5 Surface Decoration

What makes a ceramic object beautiful or striking? Sometimes it is difficult to distinguish the effect of the object's shape or function from its surface appearance. Is it the deep and full body of a mug that we find so appealing, or is it the mug's warm and welcoming color? Would a sacred object made of clay appear so powerful and mysterious without ornamentation?

Since ancient times, potters have used a variety of techniques to decorate the surface of their clay pieces—from carving or incising grooves in moist clay to burnishing the surface of leather-hard clay, from painting with liquid slip of a different-colored clay to glazing or underglazing. Ideally, decisions made about surface decoration relate to a work's shape and form, and the whole piece is enhanced as a result.

color

texture

glaze

Now that you know how to make several forms in clay, you are about to discover the vast range of treatments and techniques available for surface decoration. At times, the many options may feel overwhelming. Slow down and thoroughly acquaint yourself with a few tools, colorants, and glazes. Learn how to use tools to create different textures. Discover how *colorants*, such as slips or oxides, affect textures and glazes and how glazes respond to thick or thin applications. Keep an organized record of what you learn.

The techniques you choose for your work are likely to involve two significant categories of surface decoration: texture and color. As you study the works of other clay artists, consider how these two elements of design affect each ceramic piece.

Fig. 5–2. What story does this artwork tell?
Nichole Suchy, *Mystic Morning*.
Slab-built platter with extensions, non-fired finish. Whitmer High School, Toledo, OH. Photo by Corey Gray.

Texture

Clay works inevitably include a textural aspect. Soft clay responds to a single touch that is recorded on its surface. Clay surfaces have historically served as a means for artists to tell a story, display symbols of religious significance, or beautify a form with a realistic or abstract design. When working with clay, it is fulfilling to know that even one fingertip can leave a mark that is eternally unique—just as fingerprints on prehistoric ceramic pots are connected to a single person.

Fig. 5–3. How does this work use texture combinations to achieve a particular mood?
Michael Zigler, *Temple Container*.
Slab-built vessel with coil design. Whitmer High School, Toledo, OH. Photo by Corey Gray.

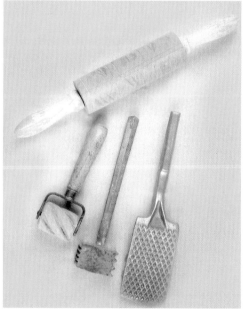

Fig. 5–4. Impressing and texture tools.

You can add texture anytime before your piece is fired, when the clay is at the various stages in between soft and leather-hard. Impressing is best done when clay is soft. Incising and appliqué can be done at any time. Piercing, inlaying, and burnishing should be done when the clay is leather-hard.

Impressing

Press with a tool into a clay surface, and the texture, design, or mark left on the clay becomes a low relief of your tool. Tool possibilities include almost anything: a fingernail, button, stamping tool, textured wooden beater, string, rope, burlap, lace, and whatever your imagination leads you to.

Fig. 5–5. Bisque fired clay stamps made by Doris Walenta. Stamps may also be carved from rubber or plaster, or cut into a sponge.

You can make your own stamps out of clay by carving a design or image on a clay disc that you've fitted with a ridge or handle on the back. After they're fired, these stamps can be used to impress patterns on your other clay works.

Note It You can achieve interesting effects when you press crumbled, dried, colored clays into surfaces of contrasting color. Or, press organic materials such as seeds, leaves, or sawdust into soft clay. They will burn away in the firing, leaving a recessed textural surface.

Fig. 5–6. Stamps add texture to a pot, demonstrated here by Jan Bell.
Photo by Maureen Mackey.

Experiment with different tools to make impressions on a clay slab. Oxide washes and colored slips (see page 124) can further accentuate the pattern after the clay has stiffened to leather-hard.

Incising

Cutting into the surface of the clay is called incising. You can carve designs or even remove whole parts of the surface. Any device that cuts into the clay, from a wooden tool to a cheese cutter, is good for incising. Both hand-built and thrown forms lend themselves to this form of decoration.

Experiment by seeing how your incised marks change

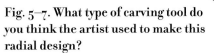

Fig. 5–7. What type of carving tool do you think the artist used to make this radial design?
Chris Hlavaty, *Mandala Indian Bottle*.
Slab-built vessel with incised design, cone 04 glaze, 11 x 9 x 2" (27.9 x 23 x 5 cm). Lancaster High School, Lancaster, NY. Photo by Ann Perry.

when you stretch or manipulate the clay. For instance, try throwing a thick cylinder. Incise a series of vertical marks around the walls, then press from the inside to make the form bulge out. How do the incised marks change?

You can make a carving tool by inserting a bent staple into an eraser.

Appliqué

The technique of appliqué involves applying one piece of clay onto another. Appliqué pieces can be coils, cut-out pieces of clay, pads, or clay designs that are pressed on the soft walls or rim of a form. Add these to the surface of your piece by applying some pressure, smoothing the appliqué on, or beating it on with a paddle. Make sure to support the inside wall of any hollow form while you add the appliqué. If surfaces have dried somewhat, score and slip the pieces

for better adhesion. (See page 47, "How to Join Two Pieces of Clay.")

When the appliqué itself is a molded piece with a lot of detail, add it gently so that the delicate details remain intact. To do so, attach the appliqué with slip. This technique is known as **sprigging.**

Fig. 5–9. This thrown pitcher features a sprigged lizard design.
Wynn Conover, *Untitled*.
Stoneware, cone 6 electric, 4½ x 6½ x 5" (11.4 x 16.5 x 12.7 cm). Blue Valley High School, Stilwell, KS. Photo by Janet Ryan.

Piercing

Piercing holes in clay is a decorative technique used to create dramatic effects by playing with light and the contrast between inside and outside surfaces. You can use knives, hollow cutting tubes of various shapes and sizes, needle tools, or anything that punctures the clay with a clean edge. The clay should be leather-hard. Be sure to support it carefully to prevent cracking.

Fig. 5–8. Appliqué is a method of creating texture by adding pieces of clay to the surface. How would this plate be different without the added texture? Would it appear to be more functional?
Erin Adriance, *Untitled*.
Thrown plate with appliqué and thick slip; stoneware, cone 6 electric, 11½" (29.2 cm) diameter. Blue Valley High School, Stilwell, KS. Photo by Janet Ryan.

Fig. 5–10. Where did the artist use piercing? What effect is achieved with this technique? What do you think inspired this work?
Jesse Ives, *Chaos*, 2002.
Glazed ceramic, 13 x 8 x 4" (33 x 20 x 10 cm). Omaha North High School, Omaha, NE.

Once you've completed the pierced design, smooth any projecting bits of clay on the inside surface with a fine piece of sandpaper or a dry sponge. You can also use the side of a needle tool to clean the corners of the "windows."

Note It When you glaze a pierced form, run a needle tool around each of the holes to clear out any glaze that may have collected there. This will prevent the glaze from pooling in the hole or running on the surface.

Fig. 5–11. The walls of this pot were burnished with a smooth stone and oiled.
Photo by M. Mackey.

Burnishing

This ancient method of finishing an unglazed leather-hard pot involves rubbing its surface smooth with a stone or the back of a spoon. Burnishing has a practical use: the pressure of rubbing packs the clay particles together (making the pot more watertight) and produces a shiny finish. The burnishing operation takes time, but a light application of cooking or furniture oil on the surface of the pot speeds up the process. You can also burnish certain sections of a piece. Burnishing works best with clays that are fired at low temperatures in pit firings (see page 172) or other primitive firing environments. Otherwise the burnished/polished effect is lost due to vitrification or clay shrinkage.

Elements of Design

Value

Value refers to how light or dark a color is. Each color, or hue, has a range of intensity between white and black with an unlimited number of values in between. Values may be gray (the absence of color), or tints and shades—a light or pale color is called a tint, and a dark color is a shade. The way we perceive value depends upon the amount of light absorbed or reflected by an object's surface. In ceramics, an unglazed or matte-glazed surface will absorb light so its value tends to remain stable. Burnished and gloss-glazed surfaces reflect light, so they appear to have multiple or changing values.

Fig. 5–12. Although this pot is all black, light reflects differently from its burnished and unburnished areas to create a contrast in value.
Maria Martinez, *Maria Bowl*.
Courtesy of Gilbert and Jean Davis.

Fig. 5–13. **Can you name some sensory qualities, technical qualities, expressive qualities, and formal qualities of this work?**
Bennett Bean, *Untitled (Triple Series)*, 1998.
White earthenware, pit fired, acrylic, gold leaf interior, $17\frac{1}{2}$ x $30\frac{1}{2}$ x 14" (44.5 x 77.5 x 35.6 cm). Private collection, NY.

Color

Adding color to your ceramic work opens up enormous creative possibilities. Color can complete your original vision of a piece. Or you can add it even when the clay is dry and about to be fired for the first time. Experimenting with different ways to add color can produce unexpected effects that reveal an entirely new perspective. Keep in mind that the temperature and kiln atmosphere will also affect the outcome of different colorants.

Clays of different types have their own individual colors; you might decide to mix clays to create variations in color. Use **oxides** (natural earth minerals such as iron, cobalt, and copper) to produce varying hues of reds, blues, and greens, and earth tones like browns and yellows. Or paint your clay with underglazes. (See page 128.)

Colored Clay

Create beautiful marbled or other dramatic effects by using clays of different colors in the same piece. The color of any ceramic piece depends on the clay it was made from and the temperature at which it was fired. For example, a piece made from a red clay body can become pink or reddish brown depending on the firing temperature. You can create an interesting contrast in colors by incorporating a layer of a white clay body.

Fig. 5–14. **A ceramic work with colorful glazes can brighten a room. How did the artist apply color to this piece?**
Barb Worman, *Floral Clock*.
Slab-built. Whitmer High School, Toledo, OH. Photo by Corey Gray.

Fig. 5–15. You can combine different colored clays by wedging them together, such as this artist did to create her hand-built neriage vase. To achieve success, use clay bodies that fire at the same temperature and shrink at the same rate.
Alissa Gigliotti, *Untitled*.
Brown and white stoneware, cone 6 electric, 7 x 5 x 5" (17.8 x 12.7 x 12.7 cm). Blue Valley High School, Stilwell, KS.

Try It The Japanese technique known as neriage incorporates clays of different colors in hand-built or thrown pieces. Try combining two different colored clays by wedging, twisting, or stretching to achieve a marbled effect. Use slices for a hand-building project, or form the clay into a ball for throwing a neriage form. For a thrown form, lightly sand or scrape the surface after the piece has dried to reveal and sharpen the colors.

Inlaying

You can fill impressed or incised marks with soft clay of a contrasting color or with a colored slip (see Mishima on page 132). This technique is called *inlaying*. The inlay is the clay filling.

Fig. 5–16. Slips or colorants can be wedged into soft clay to get different colors. **Would you use colored slab pieces or coils for the inlay decoration on this plate? Why? What do you think the artist used?**
Diana Lott, *Celebration*.
Plate with inlaid clay designs. Whitmer High School, Toledo, OH. Photo by Corey Gray.

Because the clay you use in the inlay will be moister than the surface clay, it will shrink more dramatically as it dries. For this reason, overfill the inlay areas and then scrape off any excess once the inlay has dried completely. To scrape the surface down to the design pattern, use a metal rib tool or old hacksaw blade. Take care not to apply too much pressure as you remove the excess. Go over the surface several times lightly rather than risk pulling the inlay out.

Oxides and Carbonates

Anyone who explores color in ceramic art will also learn a bit about chemistry, for what gives clays, glazes, and underglazes their colors are minerals and metals. When these substances are subjected to high temperatures, they change color. Oxides and **carbonates** are basic metals combined with oxygen (oxide) or carbon (carbonate). Some common combinations are iron (black and red), cobalt (blue), chrome (green), rutile (yellow), manganese (black), and copper (green). These metals produce a variety of glaze colors when used alone or in combination with other colorants. They are also basic materials for underglazes and slips. (See page 126.) Manufactured stains, made from a blend of oxides and opacifiers, are also available.

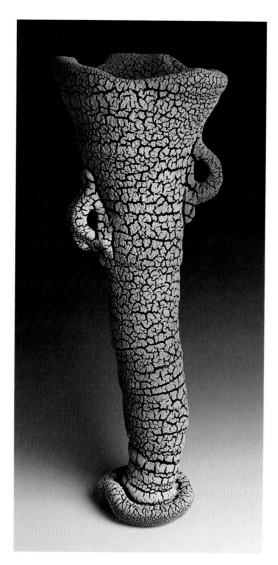

Fig. 5–17. One advantage of using a commercially-made stain is that you can achieve color consistency from batch to batch. Why might this be important?
Randy O'Brien, *What Flowers?*
Thrown and altered low fire clay, volcanic ash crawl glaze with Mason stains, sprayed in multiple layers, 22" (55.9 cm) high. Courtesy of the artist.

Try It If your clay piece has any surface texture, try creating color contrasts that enhance the textural details. Simply apply a wash of an oxide or carbonate to the piece, then wipe the surface. The color will remain more concentrated in the recessed areas. Glaze the piece with transparent glaze and refire. Remember that colors are more intense when they are used with white or transparent glazes. (The darker the glaze, the more subtle the color contrast.)

Safety Note Wear latex or rubber gloves when you sponge or rub an oxide or stain onto the surface of your piece. Always wash your hands thoroughly after glazing.

Colored Slips

A slip is a mix of extremely fine clay with water. Available in commercial preparations, a slip can be colored with oxides or other stains that can change your pot's color or add decorative interest. You can

Note It While oxides and carbonates are ingredients that give glazes their color, they can also be applied directly to the clay.

Oxides and carbonates can be diluted with water and sponged or painted on bisqued surfaces. They can be applied under a glaze for muted color or over a glaze for more intense color.

Experiment by using oxides and carbonates alone or with other colorants. Sometimes, you can achieve more dramatic effects with a limited color palette. For instance, the simple glaze and oxide combination that constitutes the popular blue-and-white ware (see page 127) has endured in many cultures through the ages.

Fig. 5–18. Where are points and dots repeated on this work? How do they create unity as well as add interest to this traditional shape?
Rosa Díaz, *Vejigantes*, 2001.
Redware, low fire, commercial underglazes and slips. Courtesy of the artist.

Blue-and-White Ware

Blue-and-white pottery has been much loved worldwide for centuries. The story of this ware involves the exchange of ideas and material among cultures over time.

The striking blue in blue-and-white ware is the result of cobalt, a ground-up mineral which is an ideal component for glazes. Potters used cobalt decoration as early as the eighth century AD in the Middle East and China. Middle Eastern cobalt was of higher quality than that found in China, and by the fourteenth century, the Chinese were importing pure cobalt from the Middle East. The resulting blue-and-white decorated porcelain, known as "Mohammedan Blue," was considered to be as precious as gold.

By the fifteenth and sixteenth centuries, Chinese blue-and-white ware was in great demand throughout the Near and Middle East. Camels carried the pottery via the Silk Route through central Asia. Ships transported it to ports worldwide.

Popular in Europe, blue-and-white ware had its admirers in Asia, too. During the late sixteenth century, Korean potters who were brought to Japan began to experiment with the blue-and-white combination and the industry expanded quickly. In the early seventeenth century, the Dutch East India Company requested that Japan produce blue-and-white ware for the European market. Japanese potters imported cobalt blue, copied Chinese designs, and made vast quantities of porcelain ware.

In southern Europe, faience and majolica (low-temperature glazes) evolved from techniques based on Islamic attempts to imitate Chinese wares. The Arabs had carried these methods to Spain during the Moorish occupation from the ninth through thirteenth centuries. In turn, Spanish colonists brought the blue-and-white techniques to Mexico in the sixteenth century.

The superbly painted translucent porcelain ware from China was never equaled. European potters continued their efforts for a couple of centuries until their products satisfied local demand. Only then did blue-and-white imports from China taper off.

When the English began to make porcelain, they invented a design-transfer method that eliminated costly hand painting. In the late 1780s, a potter in Staffordshire (believed to be either Thomas Turner or Thomas Minton) created a pattern known as "Blue Willow" based on traditional Chinese design elements. It featured a willow tree, two birds, a fence, tea house, boat, and a bridge.

By the early 1800s, willow ware was transported on steamboats and carried in covered wagons. In the 1900s it was manufactured in America, Japan, France, Germany, Holland, Poland, Spain, Finland, and Mexico. Although blue-and-white combinations inspired by Chinese imagery gradually faded in the latter part of the twentieth century, contemporary cobalt blue designs on a white background continue to dazzle the viewer.

Fig. 5–19. During the Great Depression in the early 1930s, Blue Willow plates were found in so many restaurants that a meal was often advertised as a "blue plate special." *Bowl*, c. 1910. Blue-and-white glazes, 8¾" (22.2 cm) diameter. Courtesy of Myra Byrnes-O'Leary. Photo by Tom Fiorelli.

apply a slip with a brush, a dropper, or
whatever tool your imagination conjures
up. Apply slips to clay after it has dried, or
when it is leather-hard. Some clay artists
even apply slip to **bisque ware** (pieces
that have already been fired once). You
can make your own slip. See the Appendix
page 187 for a sample formula.

Note It The slip must fit the clay body.
Before using slip, check to be sure it is the
right kind of slip for the clay you are
using.

Underglaze

Underglazing involves painting on the
surface of **greenware** (pottery that has
never been fired) or bisque ware. Some
commercial underglazes are specifically
made for bisque ware. The advantage of
using underglazes is that they don't
change substantially during firing,
whereas glazes might—so, they are suited
to all kinds of painterly effects, including
fine-line or detail work. Try using them
under a transparent glaze to bring out the
colors' brilliance.

Commercial underglazes come premixed and are simple to use. They come
in jars or sets that look like watercolor
pans. Some are available as pencils. To
make your own underglaze color, put a
small amount of oxide or stain—about the
size of a dime—on a plastic container lid.
Add the same amount of **flux** (transparent glaze) and a few drops of the vehicle
(equal parts glycerine and water). Mix it
all with a spatula until your underglaze is
smooth and creamy. The vehicle makes it
easier to brush the mixture on the ware,
while the flux helps the underglaze to
fuse, or combine, with the ware when it is
fired. When you decorate and fire your
piece, the color will be sealed to the ware.

Techniques for Using Color

You can add color to your work using a
number of techniques. If you are applying
underglaze as your color, use the following techniques on bisque ware for easy
water cleanup of errors. Stains or oxides
tend to be absorbed by bisque ware, so
you may wish to apply them to slightly

Fig. 5–21. In this contemporary reference to blue-and-white porcelain, what area dominates or stands out? Is your aesthetic experience enhanced by knowing the history of blue-and-white ware? Explain why or why not.

Babs Haenen, *Piece de Millieu: L'Eternal Reteur*, 1994.

Colored porcelain, stain, barium glaze, 9½ x 14¼ x 12" (24 x 36.2 x 30.5 cm) © Mint Museum of Craft and Design. From the Allan Chasanoff Ceramics Collection.

damp greenware instead. If you want to make a change, the stain or oxide can be removed with a damp sponge. When applying oxides, slips, or underglazes to bisque ware, work quickly—the materials dry faster than if applied to greenware.

Sponging

Sponges vary from rough to smooth grain and give different textures and depth of color when daubed onto clay surfaces. Try making your own sponge designs.

• Cut several small pieces of foam, or use cosmetic sponges.

• Draw a simple design on each sponge. Cut around its shape with sharp scissors.

• Dip your sponges in colored slip, then press the designs lightly on leather-hard clay.

Fig. 5–22. Brushes for decorating and glazing.

• Repeat, overlapping shapes and colors as desired.

This technique may also be used to sponge color over a base glaze.

Spattering

A toothbrush or a common household bristle brush can be used to generate a spattered background. Dip the brush in the underglaze, slip, or oxide, hold it above the clay surface, and use your (gloved) fingers to flick the bristles.

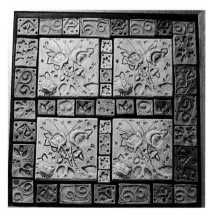

Fig. 5–23. Underglazes were brushed, sprayed, and spattered by this artist for a rich effect.

Kresta Opperman, *Floral Tiles*.

Clay tile with molded and stamped forms. Whitmer High School, Toledo, OH.

Fig. 5–24. Hamada believed in the timeless beauty that exists in simple handmade objects. The richness of his ideas can be seen in this bottle. How does the trailed white slip decoration balance the natural dignity of the form?

Shoji Hamada, *Square Vase*.
Stoneware, glazed, 7¾ x 4¾ x 2¾" (19.7 x 11 x 7 cm). Gift of David and Ann Shaner, Schein-Joseph International Museum of Ceramic Art, 1997.134. Photo by Brian Oglesbee.

Fig. 5–25. This artist applied multiple resists with multiple glazes on the surface of her plate. Look closely at the different colors. Can you determine how many layers were used to achieve the end result?

Katy Vicory, *Untitled*.
Stoneware, cone 6 electric, 9½" diameter (24 cm). Blue Valley High School, Stilwell, KS. Photo by Janet Ryan.

Brushing

A paintbrush is good for blocking in areas of color or painting fine, delicate lines or strong gestures. Brushes can be used to finish details on top of a background, outline a design, or emphasize a certain aspect of the form. Artists usually choose among watercolor brushes, oriental brushes, or brushes with stiff bristles. See page 146 for a description of airbrush technique. You can even use the end of a brush handle to add dots of color.

Try It Practice working with different brush types and sizes. Begin with strong strokes and move on to delicate markings. Observe what happens when you change the speed of your strokes. Get to know the characteristic marks that each brush produces.

Masking

Stencils can enclose or outline background shapes or foreground designs. Cut out a design from a piece of paper, lay the paper on the clay surface, and apply color through the opening using one of the methods you've learned (sponge, spatter, brush). Duplicate or overlap the design as many times as you wish, to create an interesting pattern. Masking tape cut into lines or shapes also makes an effective stencil.

Paper Resist

Paper resist is similar to masking. Cut shapes or patterns from damp paper and lay these shapes on the clay surface. Brush, spray, or sponge some color over and around the paper. After the slip has dried, peel the paper off to show the uncolored portion of the clay surface. Repeat this process to get various color tones and to complete a design.

Fig. 5–26. What mood
or feeling do you get
from the surface
design of this raku-
fired work?

Kimberly Hardiman,
Untitled.
Slab-built vase, sgraffito and
wax resist, 5 x 8 x 7" (12.7 x
20.3 x 17.8 cm). Blue Valley
High School, Stilwell, KS.
Photo by Janet Ryan.

Wax Resist

Wax resist is a versatile masking technique used on both leather-hard clay and
bisque ware. You can use melted wax,
commercial resist emulsions, or even
white glue thinned with water. A few
drops of food coloring added to the resist
make it more visible after application.

Here are some wax resist methods:

• Paint a design with liquid wax (or other
resist material) on leather-hard clay.
When the wax is dry, wipe the piece with a
wet sponge. The top layers of the unwaxed
clay will melt away, leaving the waxed area
intact as a raised design.

• Paint over a wax design with an oxide
or underglaze. The waxed area will remain
clear while the unwaxed area will hold
color.

• Apply wax directly on bisque ware.
When this is done, the wax application
will resist any glaze that is applied. The
wax melts away during firing, leaving raw
fired clay as a contrast to the glazed area.

• Apply wax details over a glaze. Brush or
dip another glaze over it, or carve away
parts of the waxed area and apply glaze to
the exposed surfaces.

Slip Trailing

This method of surface decoration
involves squeezing a line of slip onto
damp clay to produce a raised line. Slip
trailing was common in the seventeenth
and eighteenth centuries in Britain. Slip
trailers can be made from pastry bags,
mustard dispensers, rubber syringes, or
anything that produces a steady flow of

Fig. 5–27. Dipping
this jar in black
glaze was one step
of the creative
process. What
additional steps
do you think the
artist followed?
Stuart Goldberg,
Untitled.
Stoneware, wax resist on
base glaze, 8" (20.3 cm)
high. Courtesy of the
artist.

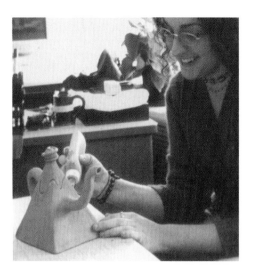

Fig. 5–28. Jolene Zanghi slip trails a design onto her teapot. Slip that is used for decorating is a fine-grained slip, different than the clay-and-water mixture that is used for attaching two pieces of clay by the "score and slip" method.
Photo by Ann Perry.

slip. The slip must be well mixed and free of lumps.

You can make various sizes of lines and dots by using different-sized nozzles. Practice trailing slip designs on a clay slab before attempting to decorate a vessel or plate. If you make a mistake, a slip-trailed design is usually fairly easy to scrape off. Lines of slip applied to a wet surface can be feathered (by drawing a fine point across them) or combed to produce interesting effects.

Sgraffito

The **sgraffito** (*sgrah FEE toe*) technique involves scratching designs in a colored slip to reveal the color of the clay body beneath. The quality of the line varies depending on whether the clay is damp or dry. Almost anything you can scratch with is a good tool for sgraffito—old pens, wooden modeling tools, manicuring tools, or trimming tools.

Mishima

In this method, a pattern or design is incised or carved into the surface of leather-hard ware. Slip is brushed onto the surface, filling the incised lines with contrasting color. When dry, the extra slip is scraped off so that only the incised lines show the added color. Mishima is similar to inlay (page 125), but requires that slip rather than clay be used for filling.

Fig. 5–29. The artist combined two surface decorating techniques: mishima on the border and sgraffito on the base. See page 148 for a Studio Experience using these techniques.
Teri Bingham, *Untitled*, 2001.
Unglazed bisque ware, 8" (20.3 cm) diameter. Courtesy of the artist.

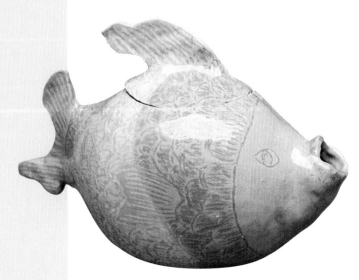

Fig. 5–30. Sometimes whimsy masks a functional purpose, as in this imaginative teapot. How do the glaze and color treatments suggest an underwater theme? How did the artist use line and shape to imply movement?
Marybeth Harry, *Fish Teapot*.
Coil-built, layered with colored slips and carved to show layers, clear glaze fired to cone 04. Lancaster High School, Cheektowaga, NY. Photo by Ann Perry.

Terra Sigillata

Terra sigillata means "sealed earth." In ancient Greece and Rome, this material was used before the invention of glaze. Terra sigillata is an exceptionally fine-grained clay suspension in water, similar to colored slip, that is best applied to greenware of low-firing clay. It can be sprayed, brushed, poured, or dipped. It can be colored with oxides or stains and has a natural sheen when fired cone 08 to cone 03.

Burnishing or polishing a work that incorporates terra sigillata can produce dramatic results, especially when contrasting colors are used. Some artists burnish the surface with a stone or other object prior to firing; others polish it with beeswax or tung oil after firing. Many variations of the technique are possible. Try a final sawdust or pit firing (after bisque firing) to achieve interesting effects.

Printing Techniques

There are many ways you can print on clay. You might work with a photograph or scanned image, or a design you draw on paper and then duplicate on a plate or mug. You can print just one ceramic piece, or create multiple pieces with the same design. Along with the methods described below, other printing methods such as silkscreening can be adapted for use on clay (see the tile image on page 75). New techniques also continue to be developed.

Transfer Printing

This print method was the basis for the proliferation of English blue-and-white ware during the 1800s (see page 127). It is suited to mass production and requires specialized tools and equipment. A pattern or design is etched onto a copper plate, inked with a mixture of oil and color (underglaze, oxide, or stain) and

Fig. 5–31. This artist burnishes his terra sigillata-coated forms with the palms of his hands and fine plastic. He then applies colored slip with a fine brush and fires once. Can you see evidence of his Apache/Yaqui Indian heritage in the design?
Ricky Maldonado, *Tri Becca*, 2002.
Coil-built, with terra sigillata/oxide slips, 16 x 15 x 16" (40.6 x 38 x 40.6 cm). Courtesy of the artist.

Fig. 5–32. Can you see where this piece is printed? How does the rest of the piece work to emphasize the printed area?
Mark Burleson, *Frontier*, 2001.
Ceramic with photographic imaging, 22 x 22" (55.9 x 55.9 cm). Courtesy of the artist. Photo by Steve Mann.

transferred to a pottery tissue—a special type of paper—that is pressed against the plate's surface. The paper is then placed onto bisque ware and soaked with water, which transfers the design to the piece. It becomes permanent when fired.

You may want to try a less complicated version of transfer printing. Press very thin damp paperclay sheets directly onto an inked plate. The printed sheets can be used in wall pieces, shaped over simple molds, or used in sculpture.

Monoprints

A monoprint (single print) can be made in a variety of ways. Here are two options:

• Paint a design with underglaze, stains, or colored slips onto a damp canvas. Place a slab of damp white clay over the colored canvas and roll it lightly with a dowel or rolling pin to press it evenly onto the surface. When you pull the slab away, the clay will be printed with a mirror image of the design. A second slab can be printed from the same canvas; however, the colors will be more subtle.

• Use a photocopy to monoprint an image on a clay surface. This process can be fun because a print can be hidden from view only to mysteriously appear after the bisque firing. Copy an image but turn off the photocopy machine and remove the paper before it passes through heated rollers (otherwise the heat will permanently fix the toner to the

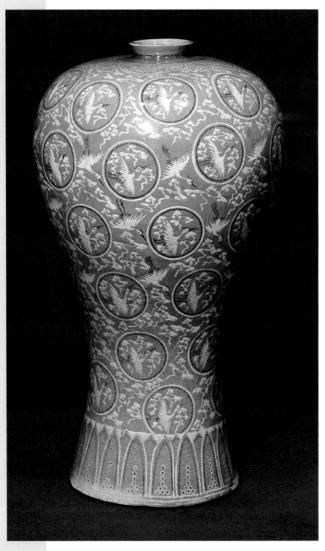

Fig. 5–33. A maebyong is a form that features a small mouth, expanding shoulders, and a body tapering to a cylindrical base. How does the quality of the inlay decoration and glaze balance the powerful form of this vase?
Korean, Koryu, *Vase*, c. 1150.
Porcelain. Courtesy of Davis Art Slides.

Pattern

What patterns do you see in Fig. 5–33? A visual pattern occurs when shapes, colors, and other elements are repeated at regular intervals. Patterns seen in nature include ocean waves, fish scales, flower petals, and tiger stripes. Artists plan patterns to organize and unify, and also to provide interest. The repeated unit in a planned pattern is called a motif. You can organize motifs into rows or grids, or use them to create a border. The motifs in nature's patterns are a rich resource for designers and clay artists. How did nature inspire the artist who developed the pattern shown here?

Fig. 5–34. **Cricket Appel forms her clay using molds she makes herself, fires her work with a clear glaze and then adds silk-screen printed decals of her own design. Each piece is fired ten to twelve times.**
Cricket Appel, *Crazy Comfort*, 1998.
Porcelain, china paint with decals and burnished Roman gold, 13 x 9 x 5½" (33 x 22.9 x 14 cm). Courtesy of the artist.

surface of the paper). Place the paper, print-side down, on a damp slab of clay and carefully roll over it with a rolling pin. The image may or may not show up on the clay. After the piece has been bisqued apply an underglaze color to the surface, wipe it with a clean sponge and the print will appear! Finish the piece with a glaze and final firing.

Photo Emulsions

In this darkroom procedure, the artist applies a photo emulsion to the surface of glazed and fired clay. When the emulsion is dry, a negative is placed over it and the piece is exposed to light. The "print" is developed according to photographic processing techniques using a developer and stop bath. This technique results in a delicate, fragile surface, so it is used mainly on nonfunctional pieces and sculpture.

Safety Note Use gloves and tongs to protect skin from contact with photo processing chemicals and follow proper darkroom ventilation procedures.

Computer-generated Decal Transfers

- Produce an image on a computer using paint or draw software, or scan your own artwork. Contour drawings with ink work well.
- Using a laser printer, print the image on decal paper. (Use manual feed.)
- Spray clear acrylic protective coating on the printed decal paper.
- Paint a covercoat over the entire image with a foam brush.
- Leave to dry for twenty-four hours.
- Soak the printed decal in water for one minute. The image will adhere to the cover coat and will separate from the paper.
- Lift the image and place it on a glazed tile.
- With your fingers, gently push out any air bubbles trapped under the image.
- Allow tile to dry for thirty minutes.
- Fire to cone 012–08.

Safety Note Acrylic spray and covercoat materials can irritate eyes and skin. Wear goggles and gloves for protection and work in a well-ventilated area.

Fig. 5–35. **This tile with a scanned image of a Botticelli artwork was made as a demonstration of the computer-generated decal transfer process.**
Courtesy of Ellen Kong. Photo by Tom Fiorelli.

Glazes

A glaze has the same characteristics as glass when it melts and fuses onto a clay surface. It waterproofs the clay, gives it a hard, smooth coating, and adds color and textural effects. Glazes are composed of powdered minerals that interact when mixed together and melted under ideal temperatures specific to each glaze.

All glazes are made from three basic ingredients:

1. **Silica**—the glass former. Silica is found naturally in sand and flint. Quartz, a form of pure silica, is what sparkles in sand grains. When silica is heated to 3119°F (1700°C) it melts, forming glass as it cools. Most clays cannot withstand such high temperatures, so a flux (an ingredient to lower the melting point of silica) is added to the mix.

2. **Flux**—the temperature reducer. A flux is a mineral component that helps the glaze to melt. Many fluxes exist, each with its own particular quality; they can produce matte or shiny finishes depending on the percentages added to a glaze. Low-temperature glazes require stronger fluxes, such as lead or calcium-borate frits. Stoneware or high-temperature glazes use less powerful fluxes like whiting, dolomite, and magnesium carbonate.

Fig. 5–36. How do you think the artist's choice of design may have been inspired by the natural environment? What glaze techniques lend themselves to this type of design?
Canaan Good, *Asymmetry*.
Wheel thrown, cone 04 majolica. Stivers School for the Arts, Dayton, OH. Photo by Kim Megginson.

3. **Alumina**—the stabilizer. *Alumina* is added to the mix to keep a glaze from running off the pot when it reaches its melting temperature. Alumina gives the glaze stability and sticking power and is found in feldspars, lithium compounds, and powdered clay.

Fig. 5–37. **Can you determine how the artist applied the glaze to this sculpture? He has stated: "Earth and fire, light, time, space—my work is a meditation on the relationship between human mind and material existence." What might his work say that goes beyond a simple presention of landscape?** Wayne Higby, *Dove Creek*, 2000.
Tile sculpture, earthenware, raku, 10 x 11 x 3" (25.4 x 27.9 x 7.6 cm). Photo by Brian Oglesbee. Private collection.

Note It A glaze adds strength to a pot and is a necessary hygienic finish for functional ware. If left unglazed, the walls of low-fired ware absorb liquids and bits of food, creating a perfect environment for bacterial growth. Glazing seals the pores, makes the pot safe for eating, and facilitates cleaning.

Fig. 5–38. **Early alkaline glazes were stabilized by adding a thick paste of slip, in order to prevent the glaze from running and smudging when fired. Kashan, in present-day Iran, was a commercial center for some of the most advanced pottery of medieval times.** Persian, *Jar.* 13th cent.
12¾" (22.3 cm) high, 6¼" (16 cm) diameter. Brooklyn Museum of Art, Gift of Horace Havemeyer, 42.212.41.

Types of Glazes

Potters choose glazes that are suited to the type of clay used and the temperature needed to fire it. A clay that is best fired at relatively low temperatures should be matched with a glaze that fires in the same temperature range. Most schools and studios have prepared glaze formulations that are well matched for the clay you use. When working with any glaze, be sure to note the temperature it needs to be fired at. This information is available in the Appendix, page 188, and on glaze packaging.

Keep a section in your sketchbook for glaze formulas and recording the results of glazes you make yourself. For general use, refer to the PV Glaze Base on page 187. You can also find glaze recipes in books, magazines, and on the Internet.

Wear a mask and rubber gloves when handling glaze ingredients. Weigh ingredients carefully. Holding a sieve and rubber scraper over a piece of non-absorbent paper, combine ingredients. Mix with colorant in a small bucket with enough water to achieve the consistency of light cream. Pour through a sieve again before using. Glaze and fire your work; document the procedures and results.

Fig. 5–39. **This piece is full of rhythm and movement. When you look at it, what area first captures your eye? What devices does the artist use to draw your attention into and out of the center?** Steve Marx, *Spanish Sunburst*, 2000. Low-fire underglazes, cone 06. Whitmer High School, Toledo, OH. Photo by Matt Squibb.

Low-Fire: The First Glazes

The original glazes were low-fire—that is, they melt at relatively low temperatures. Some of these ancient glaze types are still used, but because of their toxic ingredients, only experienced potters should use them.

Alkaline glazes were the first types of glazes. Developed by the ancient Egyptians, these glazes employ soda, borax, and potassium—common minerals in Egypt and the Near East—as fluxes. When oxides are added, alkaline glazes produce brilliant colors; but they are difficult to fit to the clay body. They are used mainly on nonfunctional decorative ware because of their tendency to develop cracks or surface scratches.

Safety Note When a glaze has not matured properly, it can release metallic compounds into acidic foods. This action, referred to as leaching, can be toxic when glazes contain lead, barium, chrome, manganese, or copper. Eating tomato sauce out of a lead-glazed dish, for example, may cause a person to develop lead poisoning.

Other ingredients used in early glazes were lead and tin. These low-fire glazes tend to flow well, have a wide range of colors, and are usually glossy. A lead base produces a transparent glaze that can be colored with various oxides and carbonates. Adding tin oxide changes the glaze from clear to opaque and from transpar-

Fig. 5–40. **Raku glazes can have flashy and dazzling effects due to the reduction of metallic oxides in the glaze surface. How does raku complement this piece? Would it be as dramatic with a different type of glaze?**
Angela Jones, *Waves*.
Raku fired, 3½" (8.9 cm) diameter. Stivers School for the Arts, Dayton, OH.

ent to white. Adding colorants to the lead/tin mix produces opaque colored glazes. When it was discovered that lead is poisonous, however, glazes using safer fluxing agents, such as zinc oxide and colemanite, were developed.

Raku glazes are applied to bisqued pieces that are raku-fired: quickly brought up to temperature, then removed from the kiln as soon as the glaze has melted and placed in an oxygen-reducing atmosphere with organic material. See page 176 for more about raku firing. These low-temperature glazes produce unusual and interesting surfaces under reduction. Some beautiful effects produced by raku glazes include crackle, metallic, shiny, and matte surfaces.

Note It The raku work shown in this book and used widely in North America was established and popularized in the 1960s by Paul Soldner and others. Soldner developed a unique method of raku firing based on techniques that originated in sixteenth-century Japan.

High-Fire: Later Discoveries

High-fire glazes (glazes that must be fired at high temperatures) are used on stoneware and porcelain clay bodies. They fuse or join with the clay to create a strong, impervious surface. The first high-fire glazes were developed in China around 2000 BC.

Ash glazes originated in China and Japan. These early stoneware glazes were

discovered accidentally when wood ash landed on the ware during firing. Ashes contain a variety of glaze-forming materials and colorants. Organic sources such as wood, grasses, and seeds have different chemical components, and their ashes produce unique qualities in a glaze. An ash glaze can be used alone or in combination with other high-fire glazes. Ashes should be soaked in water and sieved before being added to the glaze mixture.

Safety Note Wear protective gloves when handling or disposing of the ash/water combination, because the water the ashes soak in picks up lye from the ashes. This can burn your skin.

Fig. 5–41. **The surface of this wood-fired pot shows warm flashings caused by the interaction of iron in the clay with wood ash from the firing.**
Gelindo Ferrin, *Untitled*.
Thrown, wood fired, ash glaze. Courtesy of the artist.

Salt glazes were developed in Germany during the Middle Ages. This type of glaze was used to produce large quantities of functional ware that was exported throughout Europe. When salt is thrown or sprayed into the kiln chamber at a particular temperature, the salt instantly turns to a vapor that settles on the ware. The sodium vapor combines with silica in the clay to form sodium silicate, a glassy coat that glazes the clay surface. The results of salt glazing are unpredictable, but typically result in an "orange peel" pitted type of surface with interesting color variation. Salt, unfortunately, is corrosive to kilns and can produce harmful fumes containing hydrochloric acid.

Soda glazes are more environmentally friendly than salt glazes. Subtle color variation is one of the effects that put soda-glazed work in a category similar to that of salt-fired work. As in a salt firing, a substance is added to the kiln resulting in a vapor that coats the ware. For those who enjoy experimenting, soda firings offer the excitement of the unknown.

Slip glazes are simply clay slips that can produce a glaze. Some highly plastic clays contain enough flux to form a glaze alone or with few additives. The presence of powdered clay in a glaze helps suspend the materials in the mix and strengthens the raw glaze on the pot. Slip glazes give a smooth matte surface and are typically applied to high-fire ware.

Fig. 5–42. This salt-glazed pitcher with a hinged pewter lid is typical of utilitarian stoneware produced in Germany during the 18th century. A wash of cobalt oxide provides background color for the deeply incised design. Unknown artist. 14" (35.5 cm) high. Private collection. Photo by Maureen Mackey.

Fig. 5–43. These subtle colors were caused by spraying a solution of soda ash (sodium carbonate) mixed with water into a hot kiln near the end of the firing. Intense heat causes the chemicals to vaporize and combine with the clay's silica content to form a smooth finish. Lindsay Reckson, *Rice Bowls*. Soda fired, cone 10. Spruce Creek High School, Port Orange, FL.

Fig. 5–44. The design of this baluster jar was based on Chinese porcelain ware. A popular style, it was widely exported to the West and later copied by English, Dutch, and German potters.
Japanese, *Jar*, Edo period, late 17th century. Porcelain, 16" (40.4 cm) high, 12¼" (31 cm) diameter. Freer Gallery of Art, Smithsonian Institution, Washington, D.C.: Purchase, F1956.13.

Crystalline glazes are most often used with porcelain or low-fire white earthenware, and contain materials such as zinc, titanium, and lithium that form crystals under certain heating and cooling conditions. White porcelain best shows off the crystalline glaze's stunning effects. While high temperatures facilitate crystal growth in a glaze, lithium has the capacity to stimulate crystal growth in a low-temperature glaze.

Note It The degree of glossiness is an important quality to consider in the final design of an object. Some glazes are shiny, others have surfaces that range from satiny to a dry smooth surface. To achieve a matte (nonshiny) surface, add clay to the glaze mix or underfire a glossy glaze. The surface quality of a pot can determine whether a glossy or matte glaze will enhance work already established in the clay—for instance, detailed and intricate work may be lost in a glossy surface.

Overglazes and Paints

Once a ceramic piece has been glazed and fired you can decorate it more by applying an overglaze. The overglaze colors are bright and include reds, golds, lusters, enamels, and china paints. These are low-temperature glazes, but the low-temperature firing does not change the original glaze, which has already been fired to maturity. Low-temperature overglaze firings can be repeated as often as needed.

The glaze colors are usually applied and fired, then additional layers of colors are applied to enrich surface decorations.

When layering overglazes, apply the highest-firing glaze first and fire it. Then apply the glaze with the next-highest firing temperature, and so on.

Types of overglaze include:

China paints and enamels are versatile and have a wide color spectrum. They have a matte or glossy finish and are either transparent or opaque. (See Fig. 5–1 and 5–44.)

Lusters are usually translucent, allowing the color of the glaze they cover to shine through and adding a distinctive sheen to the surface of a piece.

Metallic lusters (in shades of gold, platinum, and copper) are opaque and are used to embellish or complement the glazed surface. These fire around cone 018 (1323°F).

Safety Note Kilns should be properly vented when firing china paints and lusters. Fumes are toxic.

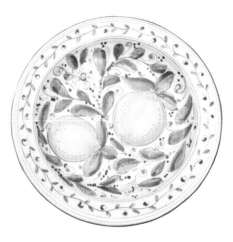

Fig. 5–45. **A careful, steady hand is evident in the painted images that embellish this plate. Broad brushstrokes are used to define shapes. How did the artist use line to achieve a feeling of lightness and rhythm?**
Unknown artist.
10" (25.4 cm) diameter. Private collection. Photo by Maureen Mackey.

Majolica *(mye-OH-li-ca)* is a method of overglaze decoration that involves painting a colored glaze on top of a base coat before the piece has been fired. Majolica features an opaque tin-based glaze that is usually white or cream-colored. Majolica ware can be fired from low to mid-range levels depending upon the clay body and glazes used.

Paint has been part of the ceramic tradition since ancient times. Oils, acrylics, enamels, wood stains, and fabric paints can be used on bisque ware and sealed with a sealer, such as a clear shellac. They function well as a surface treatment that can be totally controlled and they supply a dramatic and colorful covering to the form.

Safety Note Paints are toxic if ingested and should *never* be used on pottery that will come in contact with food or drink.

Try It To apply an overglaze, make sure the surface of the piece is smooth and clean. Let the base glaze dry thoroughly. Spray the base glaze with any type of hairspray or a solution of CMC gum mixed with water, then paint over it with the colored overglaze.

Applying Glazes

Before glazing a bisqued pot, remove any dust particles or other impurities from the surface. Wipe it with a damp sponge or rinse it quickly under the tap. Paint wax on the areas that you want to remain glaze-free, such as the foot, and let the wax dry before applying a glaze.

Fig. 5–47. **Laura Kennicut and Cynthia Villegas paint liquid wax on areas that will remain unglazed.**

Fig. 5–46. **The surface decoration of this piece embodies both control and happenstance. The painted images and gilded embellishments were created by the artist, who considers the smoke effects from the sawdust to be a gift of the fire. Whom do you think has the "last word" in the process of creation, the artist or the fire?**
Ellen Kong, *Garden of Mirth*, 2001.
Sawdust fired clay, terra sigillata, acrylic paint, gold leaf, 13½ x 13½ x 3" (39.3 x 39.3 x 7.6 cm). Courtesy of the artist.

A bisqued pot is porous and quickly absorbs moisture from the glaze. Test the glaze thickness by scratching through it with your thumbnail or a pin. If the glaze is too thin (less substantial than a card), apply another layer; if it is too thick (more substantial than a card), wash it off and reapply when your piece is no longer damp. Glaze that is too thick in some areas can be tapered and thinned by rubbing it lightly with your (gloved) fingers or a paper towel.

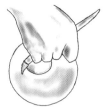

Painting wax on foot.

Note It Before every application, make sure that the glaze is thoroughly mixed and free of lumps.

Dipping

Dipping is the easiest way to glaze a bisqued pot and is the best method for bowl shapes and cylindrical forms. To glaze by dipping:

Hand dipping.

• Stir the glaze and put it in a large container. It should be the consistency of tomato juice or cream, not as thin as water or as thick as gravy.

• Grasp your piece with two gloved fingers, or glazing tongs, and dip it in and out of the glaze with a single motion.

• Twist and shake it to help spread the glaze, and drain off any excess.

• Use a brush to touch up the finger or tong marks and wipe the bottom (foot), clean with a damp sponge.

• Test for the correct thickness and adjust if necessary.

• Taper or thin the glaze near the foot by wiping some off with a sponge.

Fig. 5–49. Describe the parts of this vessel— the mouth, lip, neck, shoulder, body, and foot. How do the contrasting areas on the surface tie the parts together?
Katy Vicory, *Untitled*.
Thrown and slab-built stoneware, cone 6 electric, 7 x 4 x 4" (17.8 x 10.2 x 10.2 cm). Blue Valley High School, Stilwell, KS.

Fig. 5–48. A good coat of glaze on the pot's surface should be about as thick as a postcard.

Wear a mask or respirator when you:

- measure and blend dry chemicals.
- apply glazes with an airbrush.
- clean up spilled chemicals.

Wear latex or rubber gloves when you:

- mix glazes.
- dip a piece in glaze solution.
- sponge or rub an oxide or stain onto your piece.

Always wash your hands thoroughly with soap and water after glazing. Do not eat in the studio.

Fig. 5–50. When using the poured method, always glaze the inside of the piece first.
Laura Kennicut, *Untitled*.
Stoneware vase, poured glazes, cone 10 reduction. Courtesy of the artist.

Pouring

Pouring works best on larger pieces, forms with narrow necks, and plates.

- Pour the glaze inside and tip with a swirling motion to cover the work's interior surface.

Pouring glaze.

- Pour out any leftover glaze while rotating the piece, and shake any drops from the rim.

To glaze the outside surface:

- Invert the piece on a grate inside a bowl or container large enough to catch the poured glaze.
- Place the bowl on a turntable or wheel and rotate it slowly while pouring glaze on the pot.
- Shake the drops of glaze from the rim and remove any glaze drips with your gloved finger or a dry paper towel when the glaze is dry. Touch up any damaged areas using a brush filled with the same glaze.
- Clean the base with a damp sponge. Thin out the glaze around the base to prevent it from sticking to the shelf when fired.

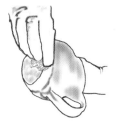

Cleaning glaze from base.

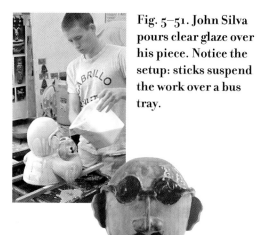

Fig. 5–51. John Silva pours clear glaze over his piece. Notice the setup: sticks suspend the work over a bus tray.

Fig. 5–52. John constructed his sculpture by throwing the body part forms and then connecting them when leather-hard.
John Silva, *Untitled*.
Slip decorated, clear glazed, cone 6, 10" (25.4 cm) high. Bellarmine College Preparatory, San Jose, CA.

Fig. 5–53. Why is the spray method of applying glaze effective for this artist's design?
Don Jones, *Full Moon and Clouds*.
White earthenware, underglaze decorated, 16" (40.6 cm) high.
Courtesy of the artist.

Brushing

In this method, you use a soft paintbrush to apply glaze. Brush at least three layers of glaze onto the surface in different directions. Don't let the coat of glaze dry out before you brush on the next layer. Because you can't allow the glaze to dry between layers, brushing is only practical for small pieces. Brushing works best on low-fire ware and raku.

Fig. 5–54. This pot was thrown in sections and altered. How would you describe its sensory qualities?
Jackson Medford, *Untitled*, 1985.
Airbrushed Mason stains and porcelain slips, 24" (61 cm) high. Courtesy of the artist.

Spraying

Sprayed glazes result in a look that is different from all other glazing techniques. Use a spray gun or airbrush to apply a base glaze, layer a contrasting color, or spray within, or over, masked areas for decorative effects. Spray guns are best for covering large areas or applying a base coat. Airbrushes are the tool of choice for more detailed work.

Prepare your piece for glazing (clean it; wax the foot) and stand it on a turntable inside the booth. To apply glaze, turn the piece as you move the spray gun back and forth in a sweeping motion. Spraying at an angle can heighten the visual effects of textured surfaces. Different colors can also be layered or sprayed from opposite directions to obtain gradations of contrasting colors. Spray two or three light coats of color on your piece rather than one heavy layer.

Safety Note Wear a mask or respirator over your nose and mouth to prevent inhalation of glaze vapors. Spray only in a booth with a vented exhaust system. Do not spray oxides. Wear a mask and rubber gloves when spraying glazes and cleaning spray booth.

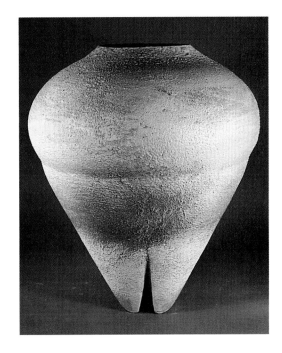

Spray Glazes

To obtain the most even glaze coat, work in a studio equipped with a spray booth, an exhaust fan, and vent to accompany a spray gun and compressor. Note, however, that spraying wastes glaze.

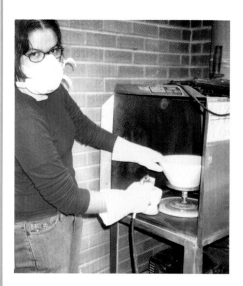

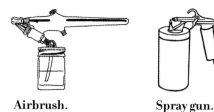

Airbrush.   **Spray gun.**

Fig. 5–55. Placing your work on a turntable helps you to achieve an even glaze coat as you rotate and spray the piece.
Cassie Gonzales. Photo by Maureen Mackey.

1 Practice spraying water on paper to get a feel for how the spray gun or airbrush works. Tape a piece of absorbent colored paper (construction paper works well) to the inside back of the spray booth and test a series of sprays with each tool. Begin spraying at the top of the paper and move slowly down across the surface while holding the gun about 12" (30.5 cm) away. Move in closer and continue spraying. The object is to visibly wet the surface. You are too close when the spray begins to run down. Experiment with pressure settings to discover which works best.

2 If using an airbrush, alter the width of the nozzle to achieve a spatter effect. Practice spraying freehand dots and lines. Cut shapes from a piece of paper, flexible cardboard, thin plastic, or acetate to make a template. Become familiar with airbrushing over templates and masks to discover the qualities of each.

3 Load the spray gun or airbrush reservoir about half full of glaze and dilute it with water by adding water until it is full and mixing together with the glaze to get an even application. Masking and surface designs in contrasting colors can be applied either under or over the base glaze. Work on the inside surface of your piece first. Turn it over to finish the outside. Test for correct thickness. (See page 142 "Applying Glazes.") If the glaze spatters or clogs, cover the nozzle with your finger to force air into the reservoir, or adjust the regulator to a higher pressure.

4 When you finish spraying, detach the reservoir and return leftover glaze to its container. Point the tip of the airbrush or gun into a sponge and spray until there is no color left in the spray. Submerge the nozzle of the brush or gun into a container of water and spray underwater until no color enters the water. Finally, spray out any water left in the tool. (Check the airbrush cleaning directions for additional steps.) Wipe the spray booth clean.

Glazing Problems and Solutions

Glazes do not always turn out as you might wish. They can be disappointing, spectacular, or somewhere in between. Record glazing details about each of your pieces in your notebook. The information will be invaluable as you attempt to determine why some glazes fail and some work well. You can also prepare and fire test tiles, a useful way to experiment with glaze effects. Document carefully by marking the back of each tile and keeping a written log or setting up a database.

Some glaze defects you might encounter are:

Crawling

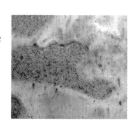

This occurs when the glaze coat has separated to expose the clay body beneath. The bare spots can be the result of several problems:

1. dirt on the pot's surface, under the glaze
2. glaze that is too thickly applied
3. an underfired piece, or
4. a glaze formula that needs adjusting.

It is possible to reglaze and refire a piece with a crawling glaze defect.

Crazing

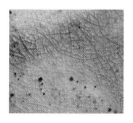

When the shrinkage rates of the clay body and glaze differ, tiny cracks, or crazing, appear on the surface—sometimes as soon as the piece is removed from the kiln, other times weeks later. Some potters appreciate the crackle pattern and work with it. Others track down the cause, which may be in the glaze or clay body, and work to eliminate it. Chinese crackle glazes were developed to intensify the characteristics of crazing.

Blistering

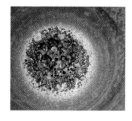

Blisters and craters are the result of escaping gases that occur when the glaze firing is too fast or the coat of glaze is too thick. Sometimes refiring the piece will smooth out the blistering.

Pinholes

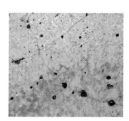

These usually result from air holes in the clay. For example, the bisque ware may be too porous and vapor trapped in the pores breaks through the surface of the glaze during the firing. Sometimes pinholes are caused by rapid firing or rapid cooling. Firing the bisque to a higher temperature and lengthening the glaze firing could remedy this defect.

Running

When a glaze runs and pools on the kiln shelf, the glaze was probably over-fired or there was too much flux in the glaze. Reducing the flux and increasing the alumina in the glaze should eliminate running. When glaze runs, pieces often fuse to the shelf. Break the piece off and chip or sand away any remaining fragments.

Rough Surface

A rough surface will occur if the glaze was applied too thinly.

For information about repairing cracks and breaks, see the Appendix on page 185.

Studio Experience:

Incised Design: Mishima and Sgraffito

You will use colored slip with two incising techniques—mishima and sgraffito—to decorate a plate. Mishima involves incising or carving lines into the surface of leather-hard clay and painting with colored slip to fill in the design. Sgraffito is the reverse, where slip is painted on the surface first and incising or carving reveals the color of the clay body beneath. Your design should feature one technique on the inside and the other on the rim as a contrast.

Mishima and sgraffito are proven techniques. Mishima is a Japanese word that describes a distinctive method of incision and inlay that originated in Korea during the twelfth century (see page 134 for an example). Sgraffito describes a method of incision that is used on a slipped surface. Ancient Greeks used this technique on their classic red-and-black ware in the fifth century BC.

Before You Begin

• Decide on the shape of your plate—for example, consider making a flared rim. You can either throw or hand-build your plate. When it is leather-hard, trim a foot and cover with plastic to keep it leather-hard.

• Observe patterns around you. Notice how lines accentuate the patterns. Make drawings in your sketchbook to develop a simple design for your piece. Use narrow and wide lines to add variety and intensity. Frame with a border that repeats parts of your design. The design can be abstract or realistic, tight or loose.

• Think about how you will transfer lines to the plate. Will you place your design on

Fig. 5–56. Plate made with sgraffito and mishima techniques.
Holly Weston, *Untitled*, 2002.
Clay, slip, and glaze, 8" (20.3 cm) diameter. Shorewood High School, Shoreline, WA. Photo by Nancy Skullerud.

the clay and trace it? Will you draw it on freehand?

• Determine how you want to balance your design. Do you want to emphasize the center of your plate or the border? What mood are you trying to create? What colors fit best with your design?

You will need:
• pencil and paper
• leather-hard plate
• tools for incising or carving
• soft dry brush
• paintbrush to apply slip
• metal rib
• paper towels, sponge
• colored slip

Create It

1 Select the area for your mishima design and draw or trace it onto the clay.
2 Use pointed tools to incise the lines. With a dry brush, clear away dust and clay particles.
3 Paint over the mishima area with colored slip.
4 After the slip has dried, use a metal rib to lightly scrape away the excess.
5 Dust the plate with the soft dry brush.
6 Paint the area for the second part of

Fig. 5–57. Incising center of plate with sgraffito design.
Photo by Nancy Skullerud.

your design (sgraffito) with three coats of colored slip.

7 When the slip has dried enough to handle, either trace or draw the outline of your design on the surface.

8 Use different tools to carve or scratch through the slip to the clay body beneath.

9 Clean your sgraffito design with a soft dry brush.

Fig. 5–58. Scraping slip off greenware.
Photo by Nancy Skullerud.

10 Bisque fire your piece. Apply a transparent glaze, and complete with a final glaze firing.

Check It Have you successfully used two different incising techniques? How did you balance your composition? Of the two techniques, which had the subtler outcome? Which had the stronger impact? Describe what you learned from this exercise. Can you think of other ways in which you would use these techniques again?

Sketchbook Connection

Set aside a section of your sketchbook for designs that lend themselves to sgraffito or mishima applications. Think of shapes and forms that could be used for this type of surface decoration, and sketch various ways the design could be arranged on the piece. Consider using these ideas for works in a series.

Rubric: Studio Assessment

4	3	2	1
Design Elements • Line, pattern, color, contrast, balance • Shape of plate • Unity of overall design • Choice of style			
Use of incised line, pattern, and color work very well with shape of plate. Balance and/or emphasis, contrast and/or similarity are all used to great effect resulting in a dynamic, unified overall design. Sophisticated, holistic	Use of incised line, pattern, and color work nicely with shape of plate. Balance and/or emphasis, contrast and/or similarity are integrated into a pleasing, unified overall design. Pleasing, unified	Use of incised line, pattern, and color is somewhat unrelated to shape of plate OR overall design shows limited use of elements and principles OR not unified. Needs additions or edits	Few marks or designs on plate surface or too many designs/marks appear thoughtlessly applied. Monotonous, unfinished, underdeveloped
Media Use • Mishima AND sgraffito techniques, contrasted on rim/interior • Craftsmanship • Glaze application			
No apparent mistakes in both techniques and plate construction. Very successful glaze application. Ample evidence of experimentation with techniques. Polished finish, experimental	Few apparent mistakes in both techniques and plate construction; successful glaze application. Some evidence of experimentation with techniques. Skillful finish	Some noticeable mistakes in one or both techniques, or in plate construction. Glaze application may yield an uneven finish. More care indicated	Glaring and significant mistakes in use of media and/or techniques. Rudimentary difficulties
Work Process • Research • Sketches • Reflection/Evaluation			
Thorough documentation; goes above and beyond assignment expectations. Thoughtful, thorough, independent	Complete documentation; meets assignment expectations. Meets expectations	Documentation is somewhat haphazard or incomplete. Incomplete, hit and miss	Documentation is minimal or very disorganized. Very incomplete

Web Link

Visit The Clay Studio, an educational arts organization dedicated to the promotion and development of the ceramic arts and the work of new clay artists.

www.theclaystudio.org

Career Profile:
Heeseung Lee

Studio artist Heeseung Lee was drawn to art from an early age. She confesses that

she devoted most of her homework time to her art classes. In college, Lee majored in ceramics and minored in art history, receiving her Bachelor of Fine Arts degree from the Maryland Institute College of Art. She has been an artist-in-residence at The Clay Studio in Philadelphia, a program that offers artists free living and studio space so that they can concentrate on their work. After leaving her position as director of admissions at Moore College of Art and Design, Lee spends nearly all her time in the studio while also teaching community-outreach classes.

Describe your influences and inspirations.
Heeseung: Influences are ever changing. In high school, my influences were mostly the painters that I learned about in art history classes. I was most compelled by the Fauvists and the German Expressionists. They are no longer direct influ-

ences, but I am still impacted by their color palette and bold, expressive strokes. At the moment, I am inspired by works that draw from nature, such as stylized Korean screen paintings, 1950s kimono and textile patterns, and Japanese lacquerware.

What advice do you have for a young person interested in a career in clay?
Heeseung: Ask a lot of questions to discover what kind of artist you want to be. Do you want to teach or be a production potter, ceramics historian, or fine artist? Once you have narrowed your interest, get the proper training. Also take advantage of the experience of your art teacher or contact your local art center, community college, or art school. Most art colleges offer preparatory classes for high school students. It is also wise to do an internship to gain experience and contacts. Networking is very important to an artist.

What are the advantages of being an artist-in-residence?
Heeseung: My residency at The Clay Studio has been a wonderful experience. It has given me the opportunity to show in their gallery, teach in their school, and make contacts with other artists. I highly recommend getting involved in residency programs.

Fig. 5–59. Heeseung Lee believes that "artists can glean influence by whatever surrounds them such as the natural world, the evolution of technology, history, or anything that interests them."
Heeseung Lee, *Lucky Vase*, 2002.
14 x 8 x 4" (35.6 x 20.3 x 10.2 cm). Courtesy of the artist.

Chapter Review

Recall List three methods of creating texture on the surface of a ceramic object.

Understand Explain why it is important to know the correct firing temperature of a glaze.

Apply Create a display that shows the surface design techniques discussed in this chapter. Cut 4 x 4" square tiles from a clay slab. Pierce holes for hanging. Use a different technique to decorate each tile.

Analyze Study the Blue Willow bowl shown in Fig. 5–19. How many borders does the bowl have? Describe how the artist used them to frame the central design. Explain how and where lines, patterns, and repetition are used to create balance and rhythm.

Synthesize Formulate at least three guidelines, or rules of thumb, for creating a successful match between a ceramic work and its surface decoration. Consider aesthetics as well as process.

Evaluate Which decorative techniques featured in this chapter appeal to you? Explain your choices.

Fig. 5–60. **This covered jar's main form is made from two thrown elements unified by surface color and glaze. Notice how the foot and body are part of the jar, while the shoulders and neck are shaped by the lid.**
Maureen Mackey, *Untitled*, 1998.
Stoneware, cone 10, 7" (17.8 cm) high, 3½" (8.9 cm) diameter.

Writing about Art

Review the careers that are explored in each chapter's Career Profile. Select one of these careers (or another clay-related career that interests you) to research further and evaluate. Using the library and Internet, gather as much information about the career as possible. Prepare a basic data table about the career (e.g., education, salary range, skill or experience required, best geographical location) and then write a concise description of the job itself. Add an analysis of whether or not you might be well suited to the demands of the career. Conclude with an objective evaluation of the pros and cons of this as a career choice.

For Your Portfolio

Photograph your finished sgraffito and mishima piece. Remember to document with title, date, and size. Write a short paragraph explaining why you chose your particular design to work with and how the two different techniques altered the outcome. Include information on glazing and firing.

Key Words

atmosphere
pyrometer
pyrometric cone
saggar
raku

Fig. 6–1. Jun Kaneko is a prolific clay artist who produces both small- and grand-scale sculptures. His oval-shaped "dango" pieces astonish the viewer with their incredible size. This eleven-foot-tall dango was fired in one piece.

Jun Kaneko, *Untitled (Fremont Dango)*, 1996.

11' x 6' x 2' 6" (3.3 x 1.8 x .8 m). Photo by Dirk Bakker.

6 The Firing Process

The kiln is the potter's most important piece of equipment. Although you can make a clay pot or sculpture with only your hands, to create a durable ceramic form you must fire your work.

Whether simple or elaborate, the kiln should reasonably fit the needs of the studio or classroom. As a student, you may not be firing kilns initially; but you should have a basic understanding of the firing process, types of kilns, firing sequences, and the expected outcomes.

Kilns evolved from simple open-fire constructions that used grasses, wood, or dung for fuel to ones powered by oil, coal, wood, natural gas, propane, or electricity. Firing devices can be as primitive as a hole in the ground or as sophisticated as a computer-programmed structure.

variables

kilns

techniques

Common Kiln Types

When you start out, you will likely use the kiln in your school's clay studio. These powerful kilns can produce very high temperatures suitable for firing a wide range of clays and glazes. Most studio kilns are powered either by gas or electricity. Due to the high energy demand of kilns, it has not been easy to power them using solar or other alternative fuel sources—hopefully, this will change.

Safety Note Make sure indoor kilns and kiln areas are properly vented. Know where fire extinguishers are located and how to use them.

Electric Kilns

The electric kiln is simple to run and easy to manage. It is fitted with evenly spaced heating elements that encircle the firing chamber. Some electric kilns have built-in safety features like a timer and an automatic turn-off switch that activates when the desired temperature is reached.

Fig. 6–2. Guardian kings ("lokapala"), commonly about three feet high and made from painted and glazed earthenware, were placed in the tombs of Chinese emperors and noblemen for protection in the afterlife. What kind of kilns do you think early Chinese artists used?
Chinese, Tang dynasty, *Lokapala*, 8th–9th cent.
Seattle Art Museum, Eugene Fuller Memorial Collection. Photo by Paul Macapia.

Fig. 6–4. When stacking or loading an electric kiln, leave space between the walls and the ware. Nothing should touch the electrical elements (wires) in the kiln walls.
Richard Bersamina, teaching assistant.
Photo by Diane Levinson.

Fig. 6–3. Inspired by a William Carlos Williams poem, this work was thrown and hand-built, then glazed and fired in an electric kiln.
Dan daSilva, *Poem Piece*.
Slips, underglazes, cone o6 oxidation. Bellarmine College Preparatory, San Jose, CA. Photo by Diane Levinson.

Electricity is much safer and cleaner to use than other power sources, but for indoor firing it is important to have good ventilation regardless of the power source. Gases such as sulfur and carbon monoxide are released during firings and must be removed from the indoor air.

Note It An electric kiln can be used for bisque as well as glaze firings. See page 161 to learn about the stages of firing.

Gas Kilns

Gas kilns are fueled by natural gas that is delivered either via hookup to municipal utilities or from tanks similar to those used for liquid propane. These kilns are fairly easy to build and are usually made of soft brick or a special insulating fiber within a metal casing. Insulation makes the firing more economical and efficient: the kiln is heated and cooled more rapidly because it absorbs so little heat. Adequate ventilation is essential not only to disperse the exhaust gases, but also to avoid any dangerous buildup of fumes around the kiln.

When loading the kiln, leave space between the ware and the chamber's walls to allow unrestricted circulation of heat and to prevent the burner flame from touching the pottery. With gas kilns, you can control the temperature by increasing or decreasing the amount of fuel during a firing. You can also restrict or increase the amount of oxygen (air) that flows through the chamber by closing or opening dampers (vents). See page 157, Atmosphere, for further information.

Safety Note Always leave the door ajar when lighting a gas kiln. If gasses build up in a closed area they can ignite and explode.

Fig. 6–5. **This car kiln can accommodate a large volume of work in a short amount of time. The housing sits on a track and can be wheeled back and forth over two beds. While one bed's load is cooling, the other can be stacked.**
Photo by Maureen Mackey.

Fig. 6–6. **Compare this work and the one by Jun Kaneko on page 152. How are they alike? Make a guess as to what kind of kilns Kaneko and Takaezu most likely use.**
Toshiko Takaezu, *Untitled (Porcelain Form)*, 1989.
Gas-fired, cone 10, 14¼" (36.2 cm) high, 7¼" (18.4 cm) diameter. Courtesy of the artist and Charles Cowles Gallery, NY.

1

2

3

4

5

6

7

8

Fig. 6–7. You can build your own kiln. This series of photographs shows students at Spruce Creek High School making a kiln that has now been in use for several years.
Photos by Timothy Ludwig.

1. A pattern attached to the wall where the kiln will be installed.

2. The brick floor, atop a cement block foundation.

3. Cutting notches in a plywood support panel.

4. Tim Ludwig (teacher) helps assemble the support.

5. Adding soft insulating bricks for inside walls and chimney.

6. Removing the wooden support from the kiln.

7. A thin layer of insulating fiber is placed over the soft bricks prior to adding a hard brick shell. Burner ports are left open.

8. Finished gas-fired kiln.

Try It Investigate and write a summary of what is needed to set up your own clay studio and market your work. Include the room size and ventilation requirements, utilities, materials and supplies list. Consider rent and location. Research how clay artworks are marketed in your area.

Variables in Firing

The type of kiln or fire used is only one aspect of the firing process that potters consider. Throughout history, potters have tried to control firing temperatures and gases. The more accurately potters monitored the heat in their kilns, the better they could gauge how the firing would proceed, yielding fewer broken pots and more beautiful glazes. Potters who could expertly manipulate the amount of oxygen and other volatile gases during the firing process could create stunning effects that increased the quality and value of their work.

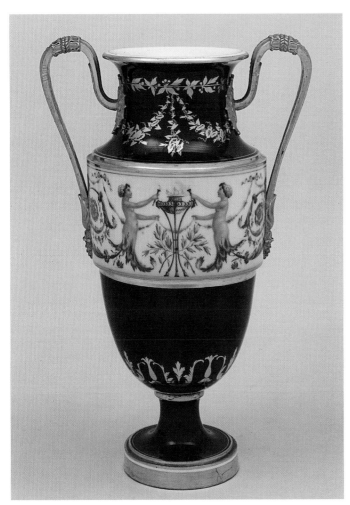

Note It Two variables—atmosphere (gases) and temperature—affect the final outcome of a firing. As you fire your pots, try experimenting. Keep a record of your results.

Atmosphere

Chapter 1 talks about the historical development of kilns and how the manipulation of firing **atmospheres**, or mixture of gases, can complete the finished product (pages 14–17). Today, a potter can create a variety of glaze effects by controlling the kiln's atmosphere.

When fired in an *oxidizing atmosphere* (in which oxygen is admitted into the firing chamber), a glaze reacts to the oxygen in the air and produces a clear, brilliant color. The fire burns brightly and the clay body maintains a subtle, clear color as well.

In a *reducing atmosphere*, most of the air is shut off and the open fire is moderately smothered, causing incomplete combustion. Because the air is restricted, oxygen needed to feed the fire has to come from elsewhere. Oxygen is drawn

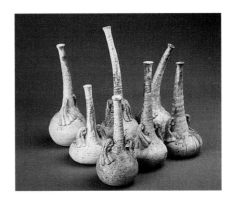

Fig. 6–9. In what ways are the pieces in this series alike? Does the title refer to function or form?

Gretel Walker, *Garlic*.

Wood-fired stoneware, 12" (30.5 cm) high (tallest). Stivers School for the Arts, Dayton, OH. Photo by Don Clark.

Fig. 6–10. The stirrup style of this vessel is pre-Columbian in origin. How is it similar to Fig. 1–9? How is it different? How do you think it was fired?
Edward Pina, *Untitled.*
Terracotta stirrup vessel, 14 x 9 x 7" (35.6 x 22.8 x 17.8 cm).
Illinois Mathematics and Science Academy, Aurora, IL.

from materials (oxides) in the glaze and clay body—this action completely changes the color of the clay and glaze. Reduction allows for multiple glaze effects from different metallic oxides in the glaze mix. Wood or gas kilns are best for reduction firings.

Note It You can control the amount of air present in a firing chamber by manipulating the damper on a gas or wood kiln. Open it to create an oxidizing atmosphere; close it to create a reducing atmosphere.

Fig. 6–11. The glaze applied to this sculpture before bisque firing is known as "secret sauce." After firing, the artist brought out the colors by applying additional heat with a gas torch.
Patrick F. Kipp, *Nogard*, 2001.
Glazed, cone 06, 16" (40.6 cm) long.
Shorewood High School, Shoreline, WA.
Photo by Sally Tonkin.

Elements of Design

Color

Color appears when our vision responds to different wavelengths of light. The color spectrum, seen when a ray of white light bends while passing through a glass prism, represents the brightest colors possible. Visual artists work with colors less pure than those found in white light.

Many factors come into play to determine the final color of a ceramic piece. Glazes undergo chemical reactions when they are fired, and kiln temperature and atmosphere can affect colors in dramatic ways. Because colors resulting from a glaze firing can "make or break" the success of your work, it is important to learn about glazes. For example, mixing a blue glaze and a yellow glaze does not necessarily result in green, as it would if you were mixing paint.

Fig. 6–12. Describe the glaze effects seen in this set of sculptural pieces. How did the artist achieve these colors?
Travis Highley, *Coral Vessels.*
Stoneware, cone 10 reduction, 6 x 12 x 10" (15.2 x 30.5 x 25.4 cm).
Stivers School for the Arts, Dayton, OH.

Temperature

Firing pots in a kiln is a little like baking cakes in an oven. But because of the intense heat generated in the firing chamber, you cannot open the door to check if the piece is done. Instead, potters use **pyrometers**—tools to gauge the firing temperature.

Note It Pyrometric cones are specially constructed ceramic pieces that show how much heat is absorbed in the clay body or glaze materials and thereby help measure the progress of the firing.

A pyrometer is a device specifically used to measure temperature. **Pyrometric cones** are made from a series of specially controlled ceramic formulas and are manufactured to soften and bend when a specific amount of heat has been absorbed. They are numbered to correspond to temperature and range from the lowest (cone 022) to the highest (cone 42).

Cone 017, for example, corresponds to a temperature of 1418°F (770°C). It will bend once that temperature is reached inside the kiln. Potters make a note of the temperature required to fire a certain clay or glaze. To tell when the temperature is at the right level, they look at the cone and see when it bends. Often, it's critical to turn the heat down or off once the target temperature has been reached. Without a cone, you won't know when to do this.

See the Appendix, page 188, for a chart of the cones that potters use, the temperatures they correspond to, and the type of clay or glaze that is best fired at that temperature.

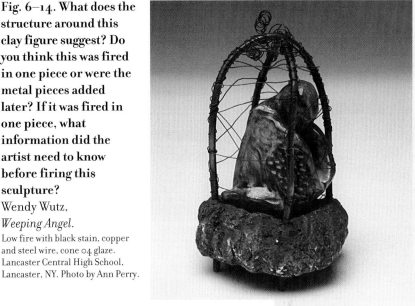

Fig. 6–14. What does the structure around this clay figure suggest? Do you think this was fired in one piece or were the metal pieces added later? If it was fired in one piece, what information did the artist need to know before firing this sculpture?
Wendy Wutz, *Weeping Angel.*
Low fire with black stain, copper and steel wire, cone 04 glaze. Lancaster Central High School, Lancaster, NY. Photo by Ann Perry.

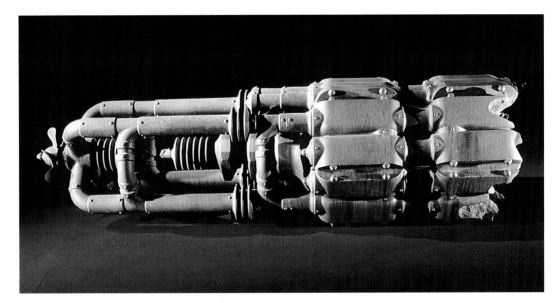

Fig. 6–13. Steven Montgomery combines hand-building, press-molding, and wheel-throwing in his sculptures of "fantasy machines." Why does firing at low temperatures best suit his work?
Steven Montgomery, *Partial Yield #3,* 1996.
Low-fired, painted, 19 x 71 x 21" (48.3 x 180.3 x 53.3 cm). Courtesy of O.K. Harris Works of Art.

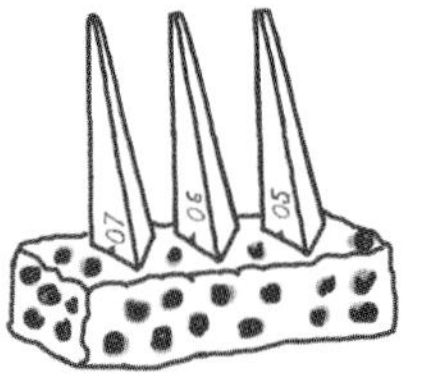

Fig. 6–15. Set cones in a "cone pack"—a wad of porous clay with holes poked in it to prevent cracking. Mount so that 2" (5 cm) of each cone is exposed above the clay, at an angle of 8°, and with enough space between them so they will not fall against each other.

Fig. 6–16. The guide cone has completely collapsed. The firing cone has bent to the correct curve. The guard cone remains in its original position. If the guard cone bends, you know you've fired too high.

Cones may be free-standing, or they may need to be propped in a cone pack (Fig. 6–15) to stand at the proper angle. Selection of cone numbers depends on the temperature needed to fire a certain clay body type (earthenware, stoneware, or porcelain) or glaze type (low or high fire). Three consecutively numbered cones are usually placed in the kiln opposite the

peephole so you can tell when the kiln has reached the necessary heat for bisque or glaze firing.

The cone group is comprised of the *guide cone* (one number cooler than the desired cone), the *firing cone* (the desired cone for the target tempera- ture), and the *guard cone* (one number hotter than the desired temperature). The firing cone should be placed in the middle between the guide cone and the guard cone.

Regularly check the cones as the firing progresses. When the guide cone begins to bend, indicating that you are close to the correct temperature, check the cones more frequently. When the firing cone bends, turn off the kiln and close all the peepholes (and close gas kiln dampers). If the guard cone bends, the kiln has been fired too high.

Safety Note Always protect your eyes with welding goggles or face shield when looking into a hot kiln. Sunglasses are not sufficient! Wear safety gloves when- ever you handle the peephole plug during firing.

Fig. 6–17. Brilliant metallic imprints contrast with subtle and intense random shades of color that float like clouds on the surface of this SA-KU fired pot. See more about this firing technique in the Studio Experience on page 178. Jerry Vaughan, *SA-KU Vessel*. SA-KU fired, 10" (25.4 cm) high, 8" (20.3 cm) diameter. Courtesy of the artist.

Fig. 6–18. Multiple firings at mid-range temperatures characterize Jean-Pierre Larocque's work. With each firing, the artist adds glaze and slip to achieve his desired effect.
Jean-Pierre Larocque, *Untitled (Horse)*, 2002.
Stoneware, 25½ x 27 x 11½" (65 x 68.6 x 29.2 cm). Courtesy of Dolphin Gallery, Kansas City.

Stages of Firing

A ceramic piece will usually be fired at least twice. The first time is the bisque firing. The second is known as the glaze, or *glost*, firing. Additional glaze firings are often done to achieve specific effects. Each type of firing has particular requirements from the beginning to the end of the process. Clay that has not been fired is known as greenware.

Note It When loading kilns, inspect the shelves for hairline cracks which can form over time due to stress. If you find one, put the shelf aside. Using a cracked shelf can result in extensive damage to pottery if it should break during the loading or firing.

Safety Note Always wear gloves when loading or unloading a kiln. Don't use your bare hands to brush a kiln shelf—sharp pieces of glaze adhering to the shelf can cut your fingers.

Bisque Firing

The bisque firing changes the chemical structure of clay and turns it to ceramic, but it also leaves the clay porous enough to soak up a liquid glaze. Moisture in greenware (unfired clay) causes the clay to expand when kiln temperatures are above the boiling point. This expansion sometimes results in explosions or cracking. For this reason, all greenware must be thoroughly dry before you load the kiln.

Fig. 6–19. Lisa Wolkow bisques her sculptures to cone o6, then applies white slip and refires to cone o6. She then applies glaze with a brush—a thin, even coat over the entire piece. The mottled results happen during the glaze firing, again at a temperature of cone o6.
Lisa Wolkow, *Guilford Seven #3*, 1999.
Earthenware, 16 x 5½ x 4" (40.6 x 14 x 10 cm). Courtesy of the artist.

Fig. 6–20. The three parts of this table were hand-built and fired as separate pieces. After decorating the bisqued pieces with airbrushed acrylic paints, the artist assembled the sections.
Maureen Mackey, *Tiger Table*, 1987.
Hand-built, fired to cone 04, 42" (107 cm) high. Courtesy of the artist.

Fig. 6–21. How did the artist use relief and texture to create an interesting surface? Name some low-fire techniques one could use to fire a piece such as this.
Lexy Durik, *Timberland Deity*.
Slab-built, relief and textured surface. Whitmer High School, Toledo, OH. Photo by Corey Gray.

Start the firing slowly. In fact, it helps to preheat the kiln on the lowest setting for several hours, leaving the lid or door open. Increase the temperature gradually each hour until the color of the interior of the kiln turns a dull red. Put on heavy gloves to protect your hands, and close the lid. At this point, the atmospheric water in the clay converts to steam (between 950°F and 1300°F). Water leaves the clay along with any gases that are produced by the burning of organic materials in the clay. The temperature then can be increased more rapidly to cone o6.

Loading the Kiln for Bisque Firing

Have your teacher or another experienced person load the kiln when you first start out. Pottery can be loosely stacked to allow for the slight expanding and contracting movements that occur during the firing. Smaller pieces can be placed inside or on top of stronger, larger ones. Bowls and plates can be boxed or stacked lip to lip, tiles can be fired in stacks, and lidded vessels should be fired as one piece with the lid in place.

The elements of an electric kiln or the burner flames of a gas kiln should never come into contact with your ware. Shapes that do not stack well should be set on shelves. Ceramic shelves and the posts that support them are known as *kiln furniture*.

Safety Note Check the area around the kiln for any combustible or flammable materials and move them well away. If you use a top-loading kiln, check the lid to be sure it is opened securely and locked in place. Test it every time you load or unload.

Loading requires a lot of bending, twisting, and lifting. Not only must you lift delicate ware into or out of the kiln, but you have to lift, fit, and stack the shelves in place as well. Follow these suggestions to reduce strain on your body:
• Bend your knees and keep your back straight when lifting objects.
• Lean against the edge of the kiln as you load or unload.
• Lift one leg as you lean over a top-loading kiln. This acts as a lever and helps you to balance.

Note It When you load a kiln, keep in mind that shelves and posts also absorb heat. Thick pieces, like sculpture, should be placed in the middle of the kiln shelf so they don't block smaller pieces from the radiating heat.

Fig. 6–22. Describe the steps you think the artist followed to construct these forms. How would you make the spouts?
Emily Collins, *Untitled.*
Stoneware, wheel-thrown and altered, cone 10 reduction, to 14" (35.6 cm) high. Stivers School for the Arts, Dayton, OH. Photo by Kim Megginson.

Glaze Firing

Once the pieces have been bisque-fired and glaze has been applied, they are ready for the glaze firing. It takes practice to become familiar with each kiln's peculiarities, especially for the glaze firing. Certain parts of the kiln can be hotter or cooler than other parts. Experience and observation help the potter to place pieces in compatible temperature zones. For example, round shapes can withstand higher temperatures, while shallow, wide vessels are likely to warp in the hot spots. Some glazes tend to overfire, while others can take stronger heat. Chemicals and temperatures affect color results.

Fig. 6–23. A textured stonelike low-temperature glaze containing trisodium phosphate (TSP) made the base for this spectacular surface design.
Jackson Medford, from *Desert Texture* series, 1985.
Incised design with brushed-on color (Mason stains in porcelain slip), cone 06, 24" (60.9 cm) high. Courtesy of the artist.

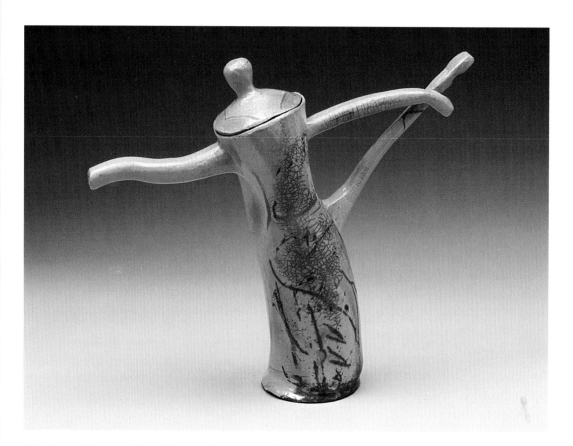

Fig. 6–24. How are shape, line, and space used to suggest rhythm and movement in this raku-fired teapot? What mood does it create?
Katy Vicory, *Untitled*.
Raku-fired, extruded, and hand-built teapot, 10½" x 13 x 3" (26.7 x 33 x 6.6 cm). Blue Valley High School, Stilwell, KS. Photo by Janet Ryan.

Preparing for Glaze Firings

Before loading the kiln, follow procedures that will protect your work and equipment. Glaze drips are difficult to remove from kiln shelves, but painting shelves with *kiln wash*—made from equal parts of kaolin and flint—will protect them from damage caused by melted glaze.

• Always inspect shelves for cracks before loading a kiln. Never use a cracked shelf in a setting.

• Mix dry kiln wash with water to the consistency of thin cream.

• Brush the shelf with water.

• Brush kiln wash on the shelf, keeping brushstrokes in one direction.

• Cover with two more coats of kiln wash, painting each coat in a different direction.

• Let the shelf dry slowly and completely before firing.

Loading the Kiln for Glaze Firing

Loading glazed pieces for firing takes special care, because glazes will fuse if the pieces touch one another. Pieces should be placed on shelves that have been painted with a thin coat of kiln wash.

Fig. 6–25. In raku firings unglazed surfaces will turn black from the carbon that forms when materials combust. What areas of this slab-built piece are unglazed?
William Penn, *Copper Pot*.
Raku, 5½" (13.9 cm) high, 8½" (21.6 cm) diameter. Stivers School for the Arts, Dayton, OH. Photo by Kim Megginson.

Pieces of approximately the same height should be placed together on a shelf with at least ⅜" (1 cm) between them. When the shelf is full, place supporting posts for the next level in the corners, and add another shelf on top of them. Continue adding levels until the kiln is full. Carefully place pyrometric cones on the shelves so that they are visible through the peepholes.

Cooling Down

Once the kiln reaches the correct temperature, it needs to be turned off. In fuel-burning kilns (like gas kilns), the dampers should remain open for a minute or two to allow any gases to escape, then closed tightly. The cooling-down period is very long. Don't remove pieces from the kiln until they are cooler than 130°F.

Note It It should take at least as long for the kiln to cool down as it does to heat up because chemical changes in glazes and clay continue to occur until cooler temperatures are reached.

Fig. 6–26. Describe the movement and rhythm in this group of teapots. How would it be different if you removed one teapot?
Diane Courington, *Teapot Series*.
Stoneware, hand-built with original press molding, cone 10 reduction. Stivers School for the Arts, Dayton, OH. Photo by Kim Megginson.

After the Glaze Firing

After unloading the kiln, follow these procedures to keep your studio well-organized.

- Scrape glaze drips off shelves using a putty knife. (Large glaze melts may have to be removed with a grinder or a chisel and hammer.)
- Repaint scraped areas with kiln wash.
- Stack shelves away from areas of traffic.
- Organize kiln furniture (stilts) according to size, and store on shelves.

Safety Note Always wear safety goggles when chipping glaze off shelves.

Movement and Rhythm

Movement is a design principle used by artists in many different ways. Some sculptors incorporate actual motion into their work—for example, in a mobile that moves when it catches air currents. Other artists create the illusion of motion, as in the student work on page 138 or Karen Brown's holographic mixed-media work on page 176. How can you incorporate movement into your own work?

Rhythm is a closely related principle—an ordered movement made by the repetition of visual elements. Guiding your eye through an artwork, rhythm can be smooth and flowing, or jagged and irregular. It can follow a definite pattern or be scattered haphazardly. Movement and rhythm can influence the viewer's mood and feelings.

Works in a Series

Clay artists, like other visual artists, often explore a "big idea," or theme, by creating a set of works that are connected in some way. A group of pots, forms, or figures that have a sense of continuity—whether in shape, color, topic, style, or design—is called a series. Although the pieces are similar, each member of a series is unique.

Discuss It Should creating thrown tableware be considered to be "working in a series"? Why or why not?

Fig. 6–27. Study the three works by Hirotsune Tashima. What do you think is the "big idea" behind his sculptural creations?
Hirotsune Tashima, *Tatami Series—Knitting*, 1999.
Multiple fired stoneware, 9 x 10 x 10" (23 x 25.4 x 25.4 cm). Courtesy of the artist.

Fig. 6–28. This artist also sculpts clay figures much larger than the examples shown here (life sized). Could a larger sculpture be a part of this series? Why or why not?
Hirotsune Tashima, *Tatami Series—Beetle Catching*, 1999.
Multiple fired stoneware, 9 x 10 x 10" (23 x 25.4 x 25.4 cm). Courtesy of the artist.

Fig. 6–29. Notice the similarities and differences between *Digital Grandchild, Beetle Catching,* and *Knitting.* If you could suggest to the artist a new sculpture for his series, what would it be?
Hirotsune Tashima, *Tatami Series—Digital Grandchild,* 1999.
Multiple fired stoneware, 7 x 13 x 10" (17.8 x 33 x 25.4 cm). Courtesy of the artist.

Fig. 6–30. What makes this work by Mary Kathryn Shields part of a series? Are there as many unifying factors in her series as there are in the work of Hirotsune Tashima?
Mary Kathryn Shields, *Tripod Series 3.*
Slab-built, low fire, 16" (40.6 cm) high. Spruce Creek High School, Port Orange, FL. Photo by Timothy Ludwig.

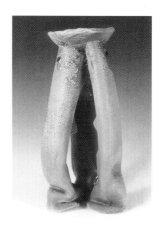

Fig. 6–31. Describe the surface treatment of this piece. How is it like the other two shown? How is it different?
Mary Kathryn Shields, *Tripod Series 1.*
Slab-built with extruded legs, low fire, 12" (30.5 cm) high. Spruce Creek High School, Port Orange, FL. Photo by Timothy Ludwig.

Fig. 6–32. Does this series have a theme, beyond the basic idea of the tripod form? If so, what might it be?
Mary Kathryn Shields, *Tripod Series 4.*
Slab-built, soda fired, cone 10, 12" (30.5 cm) high. Spruce Creek High School, Port Orange, FL. Photo by Timothy Ludwig.

Try It Select a form that you made in one of the earlier exercises using the pinch, coil, slab, or throw methods. It can be a successful piece or one that you feel could be improved. Think about a unifying factor to use in your series.

• Construct at least three more forms of similar shape and size using the earlier example as a guide. This group will be the basis for your series.

• Determine how to capture similarities among the pieces. Could it be through shape, texture, or color?

• Decide how to make each piece unique. Could it be by utilizing textural contrasts on the different surfaces or by forming outgrowths and protrusions on the body? Perhaps you could use a different design format with a unifying theme to decorate each piece using slip or glaze.

• Finish your pieces and be prepared to discuss how you achieved balance and unity within the series.

Finding Inspiration

How do clay artists come up with new ideas? Where do they get their inspiration? The process is different, of course, for each individual. Looking at natural shapes and forms—from a seashell to a mountain profile—can provide countless new ideas for designs and decorative treatments. Some artists are inspired by others' creations. Researching clay history sheds light on new areas to explore. Other crafts such as fabric design, jewelry, and metalwork are full of creative themes that you might adapt for clay. Books and magazines are also rich resources.

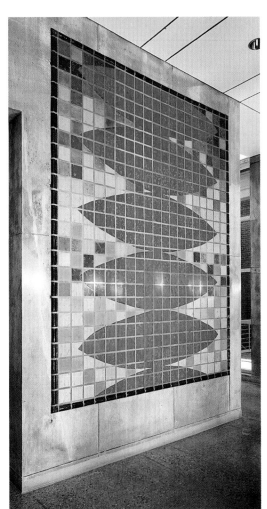

Fig. 6–33. Aurore Chabot created a series of tile installations for the University of Arizona at Tucson. She draws her inspiration from the earth's changing cycles and remnants of past eras that she finds in rocks and fossils. Viewed from a distance, one notices the large, contrasted forms of the designs and the pixel-like grid made by individual tiles.
Aurore Chabot, *Cellular Synchronicity*, 1997.
IEW-E Mural. Ceramic tile, 12.5 x 10' (3.8 x 3 m). Courtesy of the artist. Photo by Balfour Walker.

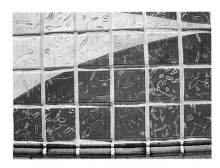

Fig. 6–34. Chabot's tile murals remind one of the layering process built into developing life forms—her use of inlays gives a rich textural surface to the tile face. A close-up view shows the inlaid images in each unique tile.
Aurore Chabot, *Cellular Synchronicity*, 1997 (detail).
ECW Mural, Marley Building. Courtesy of the artist. Photo by Balfour Walker.

Bring your
sketchbook
whenever you
visit a gallery,
sculpture park,
or museum.
When a specific
work draws your
attention, spend
some time with
the piece. Record
your observa-
tions and draw
specific features
of the work that
you'd like to
remember and
think about later.

Fig. 6–35. What famous work of art inspired this student?
Andrew Redd, *Tree*.
Coil and slab built. Bellarmine College Preparatory, San Diego, CA. Photo by Diane Levinson.

Fig. 6–36. What are some words you would use to describe the expressive qualities of this form? How does the title capture the artist's idea?
William Gregg, *Spirits of the Fire*.
Raku, slab construction, 10" (25.4 cm) high. Stivers School for the Arts, Dayton, OH. Photo by Kim Megginson.

Visit museums and galleries. Read artists' statements and analyze how they use imagery to express their ideas. Take time to sit, think, and notice what interests you. As always, carry your sketchbook to record your thoughts and impressions. You will soon discover that you have more ideas than you have time to carry out.

Once you've learned the basics and practiced various construction techniques and surface treatments, you may feel drawn to work in a particular style or technique. Some people prefer throwing tall, cylindrical objects, while others tend to like low bowls or platters. You might find that you most enjoy making hand-built forms.

Develop a series of pieces in an area that interests you. Explore all aspects of your chosen area. Research and try new techniques to simplify or enhance your creative process. When you have sufficiently explored your special area, gradually enlarge the scope of your work—begin to incorporate imagery, colors, and designs that have inspired you.

Fig. 6–37. What qualities make this series interesting? In what ways is each piece unique? How would you react if all the pieces were identical?
Ryan Thomas, *Wood Fired Bottles*.
Stoneware, wheel-thrown, wood fired, to 9" (22.8 cm) high. Stivers School for the Arts, Dayton, OH. Photo by Kim Megginson.

Peter Voulkos and the Birth of Ceramic Art

Bernard Leach, Shoji Hamada, and Peter Voulkos were notable clay artists whose lives intertwined and whose creative ideas led to contemporary trends in ceramic art. By the early 1900s, industrialization had taken over nearly all aspects of the production of useful ceramics. As a result, British potter Bernard Leach (1887–1979) pushed for the revival of clay as handcraft in the 1940s and 1950s through the Studio Potter movement. He had studied with clay masters in Japan and absorbed their aesthetics. In 1940 he published the acclaimed *A Potter's Book*, which rejected mass production and stressed the virtues of handmade pottery.

Leach set up a pottery studio at St. Ives with the help of Shoji Hamada, an accomplished young potter he had worked with in Japan who later achieved worldwide recognition. St. Ives became a place where potters were trained to produce simple, straightforward pots. Later Leach and Hamada traveled around the world teaching fundamental principles of clay design. American pottery in the 1950s was heavily influenced by the Leach and Hamada views.

Peter Voulkos, a gifted West Coast functional potter and teacher, met Leach and Hamada when they toured the United States in 1952. He was inspired to become part of the movement to establish ceramics as craft. In 1953 he met and was influenced by artists involved in the Avant-garde and Abstract Expressionist movements.

Fig. 6–38. Voulkos stretched perceptions of clay beyond the functional, where it was traditionally anchored in the handcraft category, thus opening doors to innovation and creativity for a whole new generation of clay artists.
Peter Voulkos, *Covered Jar*, 1956. Stoneware with glaze, gas-fired, 26½" high x 16½" diameter. Photo: Schopplein Studio. Collection of Scripps College, Claremont, California; the Marer Collection.

Over the next decades Voulkos built on this foundation, pushing the boundaries of functional clay beyond handcraft to art and setting the tone for a whole new generation of mid- to late-twentieth-century clay artists. Voulkos was likely also inspired by artists Joán Miró, Henri Matisse, and Pablo Picasso, by Asian philosophies, and by contemporary sculpture and jazz. His work shifted away from traditional pottery forms and he began to make large sculptural pieces. The function of these forms was to simply highlight the plastic energy within the clay.

The lines between craft and art had been considered separate until this point. Voulkos succeeded in blurring those boundaries with his Abstract Expressionist pots. As a result, a whole new concept—ceramic art—came into being. A clay object could now be valued solely for its sensory and aesthetic properties.

Firing Problems and Solutions

Sometimes, when your pots emerge from the kiln, you'll be delighted at the unexpected character of your finished pots. Other times, however, your finished product may be disappointing. This section describes some factors that can cause your final piece to be different from your expectations. Once you identify the cause of the problem, the solution is often quite simple.

Inadequate Venting

If the bisque ware looks too gray or glaze colors are dull, your kiln may not have adequate ventilation. A buildup of carbon monoxide and sulfur gases in the firing chamber can affect firing results and glaze colors. See if the kiln's vent system is functioning properly.

Firing Too Fast

A number of problems can result when pots are fired too quickly. If you experience any of the results below, you need to slow the firing rate for your pots.

• *Bloating* is when blisterlike areas form on a pot's surface. It occurs when gases that are trapped inside the clay expand.

• *Firecracking* can occur if the temperature increases too quickly. Water vapor turns to steam and can fracture the clay. Fine slips painted on the clay surface reduce the size of the pores through which water escapes, requiring slower heating. Thick-walled pieces also require slower heating.

• *Spalling* happens when moisture in the center of the clay wall expands and causes large pieces about half the thickness of the wall to separate away. This usually happens if the walls are thick and not dried completely before firing. This can be avoided by increasing the amount of time you take to preheat the ware.

• Gray/black patches occur in bisque ware when carbon materials remain in the clay

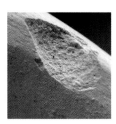

Fig. 6–39. Spalling can occur when clay is fired too fast.

body because not enough time was allowed in the firing to burn them all out. These patches weaken the piece, and glazes are more likely to craze, pit, blister, or bubble.

Overfiring

A variety of defects can result when pots are fired for too long at a high temperature. If you notice any of the following problems, monitor the temperature of the kiln carefully during future firings and shut it down as soon as it reaches the correct temperature.

• *Warping* is the distortion of a form caused by mild overfiring. (See the example on page 153.)

• *Squatting* happens when the clay body behaves like molten glass and begins to collapse.

• *Flowing* is the ultimate stage of overfiring when the clay completely fuses to the floor or shelves of the kiln.

Cooling Too Rapidly

Dunting cracks appear when a vessel is cooled very rapidly. Because heat is lost most quickly from the rim, the tension between the warmer and cooler parts of the vessel cause these cracks to occur at the rim. Prevent dunting cracks by allowing the fired ware to cool down slowly and completely before removing it from the kiln. Dunting can also occur if a clay body has been fired higher than its recommended temperature.

Fig. 6–40. Dunting can occur when fired clay is cooled too quickly.

Additional Firing Techniques

Firing in a ready-made kiln is the most common technique used in high-school ceramics studios. But, in traditional communities and in artists' studios around the world, many other firing techniques exist with numerous purposes and effects. As you develop your craft, you may want to explore other ways to fire pottery. Many of these techniques use relatively low-temperature firings and the pieces that result may not be suitable for holding food or liquid.

Fig. 6–41. At 1800°F, Menchhofer's large kiln is opened and the car is rolled to a post-reduction chamber. The chamber is then lowered to enclose the ware for the raku reduction process.
Courtesy of Paul Menchhofer.

Safety Note Do not attempt bonfire, pit, sawdust, wood, or raku firings without a knowledgeable adult present.

Fig. 6–42. This raku car-kiln was designed and built by Paul Menchhofer (see page 180), who uses it to fire his large-scale raku pieces.
Courtesy of Paul Menchhofer.

Fig. 6–43. A variation of the bonfire method is currently being used by potters of Mata Ortiz. (See page 26.)

Bonfire

A simple bonfire is the most ancient firing system, still used in many parts of the world. The process is relatively fast, because the combustibles used to fuel the fire burn quickly. Sometimes a fast firing can cause pots to break. Using grog, sand, or organic material in the clay can help reduce thermal shock and breakage.

Potters usually warm the ware to be fired in a bonfire by first burning straw inside the pots. They dry out any remaining water vapor in the pots by setting them upside down atop the embers of a wood fire. The thoroughly dried pots are then piled high on a bed of sticks, covered with shards (broken pottery fragments), and overlaid with sticks and more firewood. The lit fuel surrounds the pots with fire. More wood and grasses are added to increase the temperature of the fire. Grasses also insulate the pots from cold air, ensuring against breakage.

The pottery that emerges from the firing is naturally colored black where the carbon from the smoke has been trapped against the surface. Bonfire kilns generally reach earthenware temperatures of around 1290°F (700°C).

Safety Note Make sure the area is clear and safe from combustible materials and have a water hose handy just in case the fire gets out of hand.

Pit Firing

There are many ways to pit-fire ceramic ware. Firing pottery in a pit is more effective than the bonfire method, because the earth walls insulate the firing chamber and maintain its heat. The fire is easier to control and can reach higher temperatures than in a bonfire. A groggy clay body (such as one formulated for raku) is a good choice for this type of firing. Pieces should be bisqued at a low temperature (cone 018) before firing. There is less breakage with pit firing as opposed to using a bonfire because the firing is more even and the cooling process is slower.

Safety Note Make sure a knowledgeable adult is present. Keep fire hose and extinguishers handy and know how to use them.

Fig. 6–44. The artist made this wheel-thrown vessel while blindfolded. The work was then pit-fired.
Gretel Walker, *Blindfolded Vessel*.
Stoneware, 4" (10.2 cm) high, 4H" (11.4 cm) diameter. Stivers School for the Arts, Dayton, OH. Photo by Kim Megginson.

Fig. 6–45. Using sawdust is a popular pit-firing technique. If this piece had been fired with blue glaze instead, what kind of mood might it create? How would it be different?
Courtney Teschner, *Untitled*.
Coil-formed, sawdust fired, 12 x 24" (30.5 x 61 cm). Spruce Creek High School, Port Orange, FL.

Do a Pit Firing

Begin by digging a small hole in the ground about 2' deep and 2' (.6m) in diameter. Dry out the earthen walls by lighting a small fire in the hole. If you plan to use your pit kiln often, consider lining the walls with bricks or stones.

1 When the drying fire is extinguished and the pit is relatively cool, carefully place your dry, bisqued pots on a bed of combustible materials.

2 Lay an iron grill across the top of the pit and place twigs and sticks on top of the grill, or cover pots with pieces of wood and lay twigs over them.

3 Start a small fire. If you use a grill, gradually add larger pieces of wood until enough of the embers have filtered down through the grill to cover the pots and fill the pit. When the pots are covered with coals, the process is complete. Remove the pots after allowing them to cool thoroughly.

4 You can control the atmosphere of the pit firing by letting the fire burn out naturally (producing oxidation). Or you can produce a reduction atmosphere by adding more fuel and covering the pit to remove the oxygen and reduce (carbonize) the clay.

Tim Kapral laid his bisque-fired pots in a pit upon a layer of sawdust, and covered them with additional sawdust.

He covers the pots and sawdust with pieces of wood.

Kapral tops off the setting with dried branches.

Pieces of metal serve as a lid for the pit kiln.

Firing in the pit kiln.

Fig. 6–46. Some clay artists spend years developing ways to control pit-firing techniques. Jane Perryman is noted for refining the various effects of smoke on clay.
Jane Perryman, *Burnished Vessel*, 1999.
Coil-built with paper, clay, and wax resists; smoke fired with paper and sawdust, 11 x 9¾" (28 x 25 cm). From the collection of Attie Tordoir, Amsterdam. Photo courtesy of Graham Murrell.

Sawdust Firing

Sawdust can be used in a pit firing, as on page 173, or in a metal trash can. Burnishing and painting colored slips, oxides, or stains on the ware yields interesting results with this type of firing.

- Drill ½" (1.3 cm) diameter holes about 6" (15 cm) apart in the bottom, lid, and sides of the can to allow air to circulate. Raise the can off the ground by setting it on bricks.
- Place crumpled newspaper in the bottom of the can and cover with about 4" (10 cm) of sawdust.

- Spread a light layer of torn newspaper and twigs on top of the sawdust.
- Add sawdust-filled pots, leaving space between each pot, and between pots and metal walls. Lightly spread torn newspaper and twigs over the pots and heap another 4" (10 cm) layer of sawdust on top. Place a grill or iron rack atop the sawdust to hold a second layer of pots, if desired.
- Cover the top layer of pots with sawdust and three full sheets of newspaper. Make a paper log and place on top, then cover with a wire screen to prevent sparks from escaping. Light the paper at the top and the bottom with grill lighter torch. When (after about fifteen minutes) the sawdust catches, cover with a metal lid. The sawdust will burn very slowly.
- A sawdust firing can last from a few hours to several days. Wait until the smoking has stopped and the ware has completely cooled before removing the pottery from the can.
- Wipe the pots with a soft cloth. You can also apply shoe polish (neutral color) or oil-based furniture polish, and buff with a soft cloth to enrich the finish.

Wood Firing

At one time, most firings were fueled by wood. A number of special wood-burning kiln designs have evolved and been developed. In the Far East, multichambered wood-firing kilns have been built into hillsides. Western-style wood kilns usually have a single chamber with a chimney to draw the heat upward, thus ensuring even circulation of gases within the kiln. The kiln is fueled by burning wood from a fire beneath the chamber. For school studio use, electric and gas kilns are safer and more practical, and so they are more popular.

Controlling a wood firing is difficult—success relies upon an investment of

Fig. 6–47. How does the artist use repetition of basic thrown forms to create an interesting composition?

Canaan Good, *Wood Fired Service.*
Stoneware, wheel-thrown, wood fired, 14 x 7½ x 17½" (35.6 x 19 x 44.5 cm). Stivers School for the Arts, Dayton, OH. Photo by Kim Megginson.

time, skill, and hard work. A firing starts slowly and builds to intense heat. For at least one entire day, the potter must constantly watch the fire, stoke it, and keep it replenished with additional fuel (dry, seasoned wood). Stoking and manipulating the dampers scatter ash upon the ware and create flashings from the flames on the surface. The ash can create beautiful shades of orange and green on unglazed ware.

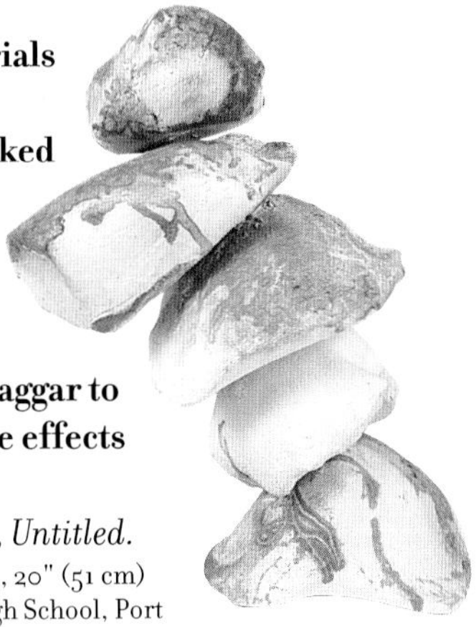

Fig. 6–48. Materials such as sawdust, rock salt, hay soaked in salt brine, wood chips, and a banana peel were enclosed in the saggar to create the surface effects seen here.

Leanne Siegfried, *Untitled.*
Coil-built, saggar fired, 20" (51 cm) high. Spruce Creek High School, Port Orange, FL. Photo by Timothy Ludwig.

Fig. 6–49. How would you describe the sensory and expressive qualities of this work?

Sherman Edwards, *Tornado Lidded Form.*
Slab-built, saggar fired with sawdust, 18" (46 cm) high. Spruce Creek High School, Port Orange, FL. Photo by Timothy Ludwig.

Saggar Firing

A **saggar** is a fire resistant container. It can be made of brick, a large pot that is turned upside down over what you're firing, or other fireproof material. This technique was originally developed by the Chinese during the Sung dynasty (tenth to thirteenth century AD) to shield porcelain ware from the ashes that accompany a wood firing.

Today, saggars serve an "opposite" purpose. Potters fill them with combustibles, metals, and chemicals to produce different and unusual surface effects on the clay. Some common materials used in saggars are plants, leaves, flowers, wire, steel wool, household cleansers, and metallic compounds. Saggar firings can be low or high temperature.

Karen Brown, *Faceted Biovoid with Layered Grid*, 1997.
Raku/holography, 12" (30.5 cm) high, 9" (22.9 cm) diameter. Photo by Robert Neroni. Courtesy of the artist.

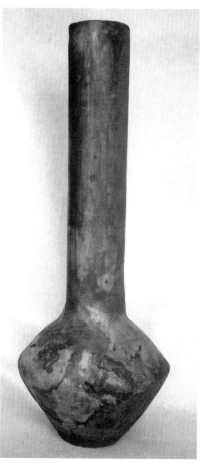

Fig. 6–51. A long narrow neck dominates the shape of this vessel. How is this contrasted by the bottom?
Teressa Riney, *Untitled*.
Raku, copper sand glaze, 25 x 10" (63.5 x 25.4 cm). Courtesy of the artist. Photo by Maureen Mackey.

Raku Firing

Raku firing is a fast-paced, fun process to witness or participate in. Previously bisqued and glazed pieces are fired quickly to a low heat that is sufficient to melt the glaze. Once the glaze matures (bubbles and melts to a smooth glassy surface), the potter pulls the piece from the kiln and places it in a receptacle containing organic materials such as leaves, paper, or wood shavings. By quickly setting a lid on top of the container, the potter smothers any flames and creates a reduction atmosphere. The carbon from the smoke permanently colors the clay body black. Once the pot has cooled, it can be removed from the container and washed to remove any firing residue. Glaze treatments produce crackled surfaces, metallic flashes, and other special effects that can occur between the pulling and the smoking parts of the process.

The raku-firing technique originated in Japan during the sixteenth century.

Fig. 6–52. Teacher Robert Putnam prepares a raku kiln for firing at Blue Valley High School, Stilwell, KS.
Photo by Kristen Holcomb.

Fig. 6–53. Glassy raku glazes get very bubbly as they melt. You can tell a piece is ready to pull when the glaze has melted into a smooth coating. The bottom of this piece was formed by slumping clay into a bowl; the rest of the piece was coil-built.
Dan daSilva, *The Herring Bone Incident*.
Raku fired with copper luster glaze. Bellarmine College Preparatory, San Jose, CA.

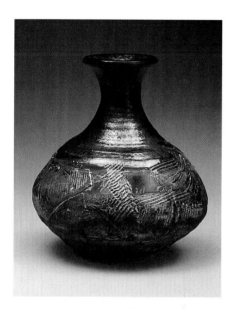

Fig. 6–54. What qualities immediately identify this as a raku piece? How does the texture enhance these qualities?
Kimberly Hardiman, *Untitled*.
Raku textured slab and thrown bottle, 7½ x 6 x 6" (19 x 15.2 x 15.2 cm). Blue Valley High School, Stilwell, KS. Photo by Janet Ryan.

Traditional raku firings used a small wood-burning kiln. Contemporary post firing and smoking techniques were developed in the twentieth century by American artists Hal Riegger, Paul Soldner, and others. Today, raku can be done in any kiln where the fuel and rate of firing can be readily controlled and there is easy access to the firing chamber.

Temperatures for raku firing range from 1481°F to 1904°F. Raku ware should be constructed from clay that contains a large amount of grog or sand, which helps it withstand extremes in temperature during the firing. You can buy commercially formulated raku clay or mix your own by combining equal parts fireclay, stoneware clay, ball clay, and grog. Supplies you need for raku firing:

- a welder's mask
- long, protective, heat-resistant gloves
- long-sleeved cotton shirt
- long pants
- tongs for drawing the ware out of the hot kiln
- organic material such as sawdust, wood shavings, paper, or leaves
- a trash can with lid

Safety Note When working with raku:
• keep a water hose handy for fire prevention.
• wear a welder's mask when removing ware from the kiln and placing it in the reduction chamber.
• wear heat-resistant gloves while unloading ware.
• wear heavy-duty shoes or boots to protect your feet from flames and red-hot ware should you accidentally drop it.
• keep the area around the kiln clear. All flammable materials should be kept in a covered container well away from the kiln.

Fig. 6–55. Molly Rodgreller dons leather apron, gloves, and a welder's mask to shield herself from the heat of the raku kiln.
Photo by Maureen Mackey.

Studio Experience:
SA-KU Firing

When you think of the thousands of years that people have been working with clay you would expect there were no new things to discover. Yet breakthroughs are still being made in technology and technique.

Clay artist Jerry Vaughan experiments with electric kiln firings using paperclay as a saggar shell. To achieve a new look on his finished pieces, he began linking saggar with a final raku firing. He calls this hybrid firing method *SA-KU*. Richly colored surfaces with flashing metallic highlights distinguish SA-KU ware. See page 160 for an example of Vaughan's work. You will fire one of your pieces using this method.

Before You Begin
- Throw or hand-build a vessel.
- Burnish when leather-hard.
- Bisque fire to cone 010. The lower temperature bisque works best with the saggar materials.
- Make paperclay. (See page 38.)
- Prepare a bucket of salt water (2 cups table salt, 3 gallons of water).

You will need:

- *cotton* cloth, large enough to cover the vessel
- copper wire or scrub pads, steel wool
- organic materials such as leaves, banana peels, flowers, seaweed
- cobalt sulfate and copper sulfate
- rubber gloves and mask
- masking tape
- spatula or trowel
- screwdriver or chisel
- steel brush
- scrub cloth
- cone 06 clear glaze
- paintbrush
- raku gloves, face shield, and tongs
- lidded trash can and shredded paper

Create It
Part I
1 Dip the cotton cloth in salt water and squeeze it out.
2 Place the damp cloth on a flat surface and layer pieces of copper wire and steel wool on it.
3 Add organic materials and random sprinkling of copper sulfate and cobalt sulfate.

Safety Note Wear rubber gloves and facemask when working with chemicals.

4 Wrap cloth with organic material, chemicals, and metals completely around the pot. Secure tightly with masking tape.
5 Using a spatula or trowel, cover the entire package (including the bottom) with a layer of paperclay about ⅜" (1 cm) thick. Your saggar is complete.

Fig. 6–56. Wrapped saggars coated with paperclay are loaded into kiln.
Photo by Randy O'Brien.

Part II
1 Fire to cone 06.

Safety Note Make sure the kiln is well ventilated or fire outdoors. Open the bottom peep until the smoking stops.

2 When kiln is cool, remove the package.
3 Separate the saggar from your piece using chisel or screwdriver.
4 Clean debris from the surface with a wire brush or sandpaper.

Fig. 6–57. Cassandra Smith removes the fired paperclay saggar with a screwdriver.
Photo by Randy O'Brien.

5 Cover the vessel with three coats of low-fire clear glaze.

Part III

1 Place the glazed piece in the kiln, close the lid, and fire to cone 04.

2 Shut off the kiln and remove your piece when it has reached temperature. Place it in a paper-filled trash can and close lid tightly.

Fig. 6–58. Placing ware into reduction atmosphere for raku stage of SA-KU firing. Photo by Maureen Mackey.

Safety Note Wear protective gear (raku gloves and face shield) when moving ware from the kiln.

3 When your piece has cooled, remove carbon residue with a scrub cloth.

Fig. 6–59. Kevan's finished SA-KU vessel displays the striking contrasts and unusual surface markings of this firing technique. Kevan Wildman, *SA-KU Covered Bowl*, 2002. 9½" (24.1 cm) high, 10" (25.4 cm) diameter. Photo by Randy O'Brien.

Check It Were you able to complete the firings successfully? Can you identify the sources for some of the surface results that materialized? Compare the way your piece looked after the saggar firing part of the exercise with the final SA-KU result. Describe the differences. What did you learn about firing?

Sketchbook Connection

Make sketches of the pots you fire and indicate the areas where the different chemicals and materials were used on them in the first step (saggar). Note firing temperatures and length of time for both saggar and raku firings. Evaluate and record the final results.

Rubric: Studio Assessment

4	3	2	1
Media Use • Creation and preparation of vessel and paperclay saggar • Raku firing • Final clean-up			
Vessel well constructed and appropriately prepared. Ample evidence of experimentation with materials used in saggar, paperclay well applied. Successful raku firing and post-firing cleanup results in vessel with exciting and unusual surface finish. Thorough process, experimental, exciting finish	Vessel well constructed and appropriately prepared. Sufficient evidence of experimentation with materials used in saggar. Most other steps successfully accomplished, resulting in vessel with intriguing surface finish. Full process, intriguing finish	Vessel preparation or some steps in coating, firing, or finishing process somewhat neglected or not completed; resulting in vessel with limited surface interest or incomplete effect. More care, attention indicated	Significant neglect or omission of important steps. Final product incomplete or unsuccessful in creating SA-KU-like results. Rudimentary difficulties
Work Process • Research on materials • Recording of results • Comparison of effects			
Thorough research and documentation; goes above and beyond assignment expectations. Thoughtful, thorough, independent	Sufficient research and documentation; meets assignment expectations. Meets expectations	Research and/or documentation is somewhat haphazard or incomplete. Incomplete, hit and miss	Research and documentation is minimal or very disorganized. Very incomplete

Career Profile:
Paul Menchhofer

Studio potter Paul Menchhofer earned his Master of Fine Arts degree from the University of Tennessee. He is also a Technical Associate at Oak Ridge National Laboratory in Tennessee. There, he is able to combine his creative work in ceramics with his interest in the scientific and technological possibilities of clay. Despite the technical aspect of his profession, Menchhofer is an artist first and foremost.

Describe some of your experiences working with clay.
Paul I started working with clay in elementary school and also at an art center in my hometown. Later, I was the apprentice

of American potter Charles Counts and then spent time in England, working with master potter Michael Cardew.

How did you become involved in industrial ceramics?
Paul I was teaching and was invited to visit the Oak Ridge lab. They were looking for a ceramist with hands-on experience and offered me a job. I began as a technician. I had always been interested in the technical side of ceramics, and this job has exposed me to many new areas of scientific research.

What are some scientific uses for ceramics?
Paul Cell phones, for example, have ceramic filters. Ceramic materials are also used in space probes, dental implants, as artificial bone materials, and for photovoltaic cells that allow people to generate electricity from sunlight. Ceramics are also important in superconductor technology, which we hope will someday save energy and change the world.

Has your technical career had an impact on your studio work?
Paul After working with such sophisticated equipment, I have simplified my pottery making. I have a very free approach; I'm not so conscious about the materials or techniques, but simply feel my way through the process. I use several wheels and a minimum of hand tools, mostly my fingers and hands to draw into the wet clay.

Where does your inspiration come from?
Paul The creative spring is within everyone; the more you use it, the better it flows. My ideas come to me in dreams, when I'm outside, and even when I'm doing something that isn't very "inspiring." You never know when the ideas will come. Just explore techniques and traditions and rely on them for inspiration.

Fig. 6–60. The artist states that "art and the process of creation fulfill daily human needs, as do food and sleep. It is through the elements of the earth—clay, water, and fire—that I define myself." Do you see evidence of these ideas in his work?
Paul A. Menchhofer, *New Start*, 2002.
Raku fired, multiple firings, 40" (101.6 cm) high. Courtesy of the artist.

Chapter Review

Recall What two variables affect the outcome of a firing?

Understand Explain why most ceramic pieces need to be fired more than once.

Apply Take two bisqued pieces of roughly the same size, shape, and clay type. Use the same glaze on each piece. Fire one in a reduction atmosphere, the other in an oxidation atmosphere. What differences do you notice in the finished pieces?

Analyze Examine the Sèvres vase shown in Fig. 6–8. What surface decoration techniques do you think were used? Estimate how many times this piece was fired.

Fig. 6–61. Only the coil edging and swirling relief decoration on the panels of this piece were glazed. How can you tell that this work was raku fired?
Maureen Mackey, *Untitled*, 2001.
Raku, 15" (38.1 cm) high, 11½" (29.2 cm) wide.

Synthesize How do kiln firings differ from traditional firings? Which firing allows you to better control the outcome? What are some reasons for choosing a firing whose outcome is less certain?

Evaluate Pieces that are porous are not suitable for holding food or liquid. Which firing techniques are best suited for creating functional ware? Why?

Writing about Art

You have had a chance to work with clay in several ways and have used a variety of processes. Carefully consider the materials, techniques, forms, and design elements with which you work best. Write a self-evaluation. What it is about these materials, forms, and techniques that draws you? Is there one particular form or theme that you favor, or several? What about materials and techniques? Have you worked in series? Do you lean toward particular elements or principles of design? Are there any environmental, cultural, or historical influences that you tend to incorporate into your work?

For Your Portfolio

Document various firing experiences with slides or photographs. Indicate title, date, and size of different pieces. Write a description of the SA-KU technique and include it with pictures of your SA-KU work.

Appendix

Ceramics Timeline

35000 — 6000 BC

- Earliest known pottery
- Fired clay figures and vessels

6000 — 5000 BC

- Unglazed earthenware
- Burnishing, slip coating, impressed designs, incised decoration (Mesopotamia)

5000 — 4000 BC

- Control of oxidation and reduction during firing (Mesopotamia)

4000 — 3000 BC

- Wheel throwing
- Egyptian paste (glaze ingredients mixed with clay, developed in Egypt; considered the earliest known glaze)
- Earthenware molds

3000 — 2000 BC

- Painted decoration (Indus River Valley)
- Neolithic Period—red, brown, and black swirling patterns painted on urns (China)
- Painting style based on nature. Octopus painting Minoan culture (Crete)
- Earliest pottery discovered (Ecuador)
- Jomon style coil-built urns (Japan)

2000 — 1000 BC

- Glass making (Mesopotamia)
- Wheel throwing (Egypt)
- Highly refined ware. (Mycenaean)
- Greek influence (Spain)
- Formative Period, domestic pots, slip decorated, burnished, incised (Central America)

1000 — 500 BC

- Tin-lead glazes, decorated tiles, ritual vessels (Near and Middle East)
- Unglazed stoneware, Shang dynasty (China)
- Ash glazed pots, Chou dynasty (China)
- Bronze Age influence (China)
- Classical Greek ware. Geometric style, black-and-red style figure painting.
- Wheel introduced, lead glazing (Europe)
- Life-sized terra cotta figures (Italy)
- Chavin style. Molds, stirrup handles, incised decoration. (Northern Andes, Peru)
- Olmec culture. Molded clay figures (Central America)

500 BC — AD 100

- Life-sized army figures and horses, Qin dynasty (China)
- Lead glazing, Han dynasty (China)
- Roman Empire, mass production of wares, terra sigillata, Arrentine ware. (Italy)
- Kilns, wheels and lead glazes introduced throughout Europe during Roman occupation.
- Moche culture. Mold made ware with rich decoration in narrative style (South America)
- Nok culture, life-sized terracotta figures (Africa)

100 — 200

- Turquoise Alkaline glazes (Middle East)
- Feldspathic glazes, Glazed stoneware (China)
- Use of the wheel (Japan)
- Silla dynasty Chinese influence, ash and lead glazes (Korea)
- Mayan polychrome style (Central America)
- Nazca culture (Southern Andes)
- Hohokam culture coiled vessels, southwestern U.S.

200 — 300

- Haniwa tomb figures (Japan)

300 — 400

- Wheel throwing (Japan)
- Classic Period, fresco technique. Mayan culture (Central America)

400 — 500

- Byzantine influence
- Kiln improvement extends stoneware range (China, Korea, Japan)

500 — 700

- First porcelain (China)
- Middle Eastern contacts introduce polychrome glazes; lead glazed ware with splash decoration. Tang dynasty (China)
- Lead glazed domestic ware.
- Higher firing techniques developed (Germany)
- Mayan Classic Period continues (Central America)

700 — 1000

- Islamic style: oxide painting on lead and tin glazes, luster glazes
- Sung dynasty (China) high temperature glazes developed, Ting ware and Tzu-chou ware.
- Koryo dynasty (Korea) slip inlay decoration, Mishima
- Fine Islamic pottery imported.
- Technical improvements imported from Germany, wheels, kilns, lead glaze (Great Britain)
- Mayan Post Classic Period, terracotta figures (Central America)
- Chimu pottery Peru (South America)

1000 — 1400

- Use of oxides for underglaze painting, lusterware, enamel glaze Persian style wares: Kashan, Ravy, Seljuq (Near East)
- Classic Period Sung celadons, Chun ware, Tzu Chou ware (China)
- Fine porcelain and stoneware, Koryo dynasty (Korea)
- Early stoneware (Germany)
- Hispano-Moresque ware, luster glazing (Spain)
- Maiolica ware (Italy)
- Aztec, ritual vessels (Central America)

1400 — 1700

- Isnik wares (Turkey)
- Blue-and-white ware, Gombroon ware (Middle East)
- Ming Dynasty. Blue-and-white stoneware and porcelain, copper-reds, enamel decoration (China)
- Ponchiong ware inlay decoration on stoneware, Choson dynasty (Korea)
- Raku ware tea ceramics, Imari, Arita, and Kakimon ware, porcelain exports (Japan)
- Salt glazing (Germany)
- Faience (tin-glazed earthenware) (France)
- Delftware (Netherlands)
- Soft paste porcelain (Europe)
- Slipware (England)

1700 — 1900

- First hard paste porcelain factory established 1710 (Germany)
- Industrialization and mass production, Josiah Wedgewood (Great Britain)
- Arts and Crafts Movement 1850, country potter tradition (Great Britain)
- Arts and Crafts Movement 1880 (United States)
- Art Nouveau 1895 (France)
- Revival Pueblo pottery 1890 (United States)

1900 — 1950

- Bauhaus influence (Germany) ceramic factories established in Germany and Finland.
- Studio Potters, Shoji Hamada (Japan), Bernard Leach (England), Michael Cardew (Nigeria)
- Modern Movement, Lucie Rie and Hans Coper (England)
- Nonfunctional ceramics, Pablo Picasso 1946–1953 (France)

continued on page 184

The New American Ceramics

1950 – 1960

- Abstract Expressionism—blurs the lines between craft and art—Peter Voulkos (California)

- Utilitarian wares with expressive character, Robert Turner (New York)

- Sculptural works with abstract expressive qualities, Ken Price

- Luster glazes on narrative vessels, Beatrice Wood

- Monumental sculptural forms, Jerry Rothman

- Volcanic glazes, Gertrude and Otto Natzler

- Salt glazing, Karen Karnes

1960 – 1970

- New techniques within traditional raku, Paul Soldner

- Funk Art—satirical response to popular culture—Robert Arneson and David Gilhooly

- Fake Art, Super Object, or trompe l'oeil technique, Marilyn Levine

- Workshops in Native American hand-building, decorating, and firing techniques, Maria Martinez and her son Popovi Da

1970 – 2000s

- New perspectives on the vessel: the vessel as an assembly of shards, Rick Dillingham; the vessel as contemporary art sculpture, Betty Woodman

- Monumental sculpture: geometric designs on giant dome-shaped figures, Jun Kaneko; imposing ten-foot-high figures, Viola Frey; enormous slab-built vases, Rudi Autio

- Decorative Innovations: fresco-like surfaces on hand-built pots, Lidya Buzio; exotic natural environments colored with china paints on classic shapes, Kurt Weiser

- Continuation of Studio Potter tradition: handcrafted functional ware, John Glick

Repairing Cracks and Breaks

It's a fact of life: ceramics will break or crack sometimes during the firing process. As a potter, you'll become adept at repairing the minor cracks and breaks that occur from time to time. You can repair the piece before or after it is fired. Before you throw a cracked or broken piece away, try to repair it with one of these methods.

Repairing Greenware

Different potters have their own preferred recipes for repairing broken pieces or cracks. They involve applying a bonding material to the broken pieces. A bonding mix usually contains a clay slip made from the same type of clay body as the broken piece, blended with something that increases molecular attraction between the two surfaces. Vinegar, epsom salts dissolved in a small amount of water, honey, and liquid glaze are substances that help increase the sticking power of the clay. (The glaze mix works with heat during the firing by fusing the clay together as it melts and vitrifies.)

Follow these steps to repair a break:

• Select one of the above bonding agents and mix it with crumbled damp clay to form a smooth slip.
• Use a wet paintbrush to dampen the edges of the pieces you're joining.
• Score the edges.
• Paint the edges with the slip mixture you have prepared.
• Press the slipped edges together and hold them tightly in place while they bond.
• Paint the repair with liquid wax to slow the drying action.
• Sand the rough surface after it has dried and before you fire it.

Follow these steps to repair a crack:

• Using a knife or sharp tool, carefully widen the crack by opening it in a V shape.
• Roll out a small coil from the same clay body as the piece.
• Dampen the V by painting it with a wet paintbrush.
• Dip the coil in water.
• Lay the wet coil into the V and press to fill the opening.

• Smooth the edges of the coil over the edges of the V.
• Paint the repair with liquid wax to slow down the drying action.
• Sand the rough edges of the surface after it has dried.

Note: Paperclay slip is excellent for repairing greenware. Commercial products can also be purchased to repair both broken greenware and bisqued pieces. Follow the instructions on the package.

Repairing Glazeware

Sometimes a repair will work well and survive firing to the higher glaze temperatures, but other times the defect reappears. If this happens, you can use an epoxy adhesive to repair the piece after firing. Epoxy bonds readily to ceramics and can be colored with any pigment such as tempera powder, ceramic stains, or oxides to blend in with the original glaze color. Follow the directions on the package to properly prepare and apply the epoxy.

Clay Body Types

Vitreous Clays

Vitreous clays become a hard, non-porous material, whose particles meld together and become like glass when fired to high temperatures. Glazing is mainly used for aesthetic and hygienic qualities. Some high temperature clays are:

Stoneware—Used for functional ware and sculpture. May be gray, beige, or brown.
Porcelain—A fine quality white clay; can be translucent after firing if the walls are thin enough.
Bone China—A hard, translucent white clay body.

Porous Clays

Earthenware is very plastic and good for throwing. It can be used for glazed functional ware, and glazed or unglazed sculptures. If functional ware is desired, earthenware must be glazed to make it non-porous. **Terracotta** (from the Italian, meaning "baked earth") is a reddish-brown low-fire porous earthenware that is very strong after firing because of its high iron content. It is commonly used for pottery, sculpture, and architecture, as well as for roofing tiles, pipes, and flower pots.

Other Clay Types

Air-dry clays can be shaped on the wheel or by hand. They self-harden within several days and when bone dry, may be decorated with oil, tempera, or enamel paints. **Oven-baked clays** harden within an hour in a 350°F oven. After baking they can be decorated with acrylic paints, tempera, or watercolor. **Precious metal clays** contain silver, gold, or other precious metals. When fired the precious metal rises to the surface and requires polishing to bring out its unique qualities. These clays are very expensive, have a high shrinkage rate, and are primarily used to make jewelry.

Determining Shrinkage Rate

All clay bodies shrink when fired. The degree of shrinkage depends on the composition of the clay body. To find out how much a clay body will shrink, make a cylinder 5" tall and 5" in diameter with walls 1/2" thick. Do this for each clay body. Measure the wet piece:

- Place the cylinder on a page in your sketchbook and trace around its base. Measure and record the diameter.
- Measure the exact height of the piece and the exact thickness of the wall and record that information.
- After firing place the base of your cylinder inside the original circle and trace around it again. Remeasure the height and thickness of the cylinder and note the results.

Compute the rate of shrinkage by subtracting the fired measurement from the original wet measurement. Divide the difference by the original wet measurement. The result is the percentage of shrinkage. Do this for the diameter, height, and thickness. The results should be the same.

Example: If the shrinkage rate is 10% then the final glaze-fired pieces of any object made from that clay body will be only 90% of the original wet clay size.

Clay Combinations

Other materials mixed with clay types will change or improve certain characteristics to help make the clay more workable. They can make it more or less plastic; reduce or increase the rate it shrinks; and lower or increase firing temperatures.

Calcium carbonate, or **whiting**, is found naturally in a variety of forms such as limestone, chalk, and marble. This material is also present in seashells and pieces of coral. It acts as a flux (lowers glass forming temperatures) and has a high melting point. It is used in many parts of the world as temper (a material to increase the consistency and toughness of the clay) for cooking ware.

Grog, crushed bisque-fired clay, is a human-made material. It is usually ground to coarse, medium, or fine-grained texture. Because the grog has already been fired it acts as a stabilizer in the new clay body and does not change when it is fired again. It helps the clay to dry more uniformly and reduces shrinkage and plasticity. Pottery damaged during the firing process can be crushed and recycled for use as an additive, rather than becoming a waste product.

Organics are very fine organic materials like plant remains, algae, and bacteria, that help make clay more plastic. On the other hand, if clay is too plastic, coarse organic materials such as chopped straw, shredded paper, or sawdust improve its workability. Shrinkage is reduced when the organic materials burn out during the firing and tiny gaps are left in the clay. These spaces help to reduce thermal stress in cooking vessels when temperature changes cause them to expand and contract.

Silica helps to reduce the plasticity of a clay body. It also limits shrinkage during the firing process. Silica also increases the thermal expansion of the clay mixture once it is fired.

Tip: How to Take the Heat

Raku Body

Make pieces out of coarse and porous clay bisqued at low temperatures.

Ovenware and Flameproof Bodies

Earthenware pots should use coarse-grained underfired clay that will stand the shock of alternating heating and cooling. Stoneware can be used in the oven if it is glazed with a cone 10 glaze. The clay body should contain feldspar and as little silica as possible. Make sure the walls of your pot have an even thickness.

Slip, Glaze, and Terra Sigillata Recipes

Oxides and Carbonates

Add 1 rounded teaspoon of color into $1/2$ cup water, add a pinch of bentonite, and mix well.

Note: The concentration of the oxide, type of glaze, firing temperature, and atmosphere of the kiln all contribute to the final result.

Black iron oxide: shades of brown, black results when mixed with manganese dioxide and cobalt oxide.

Chrome oxide: bright green (low fire), bright to olive green (high fire).

Cobalt carbonate: different shades of blue depending on how concentrated it is—can turn black when applied thickly.

Cobalt oxide: shades of blue or black when mixed with black iron and manganese.

Copper carbonate: light green–blue green over a glaze in oxidation, red in reduction.

Iron oxide: colors range from tan to red-brown to dark brown. Too much iron can cause a glaze to run in high firing.

Manganese dioxide: browns, black when mixed with black iron oxide and cobalt oxide.

Rutile: soft yellow for low fire and luminous blue when high fired.

Basic Slip Formula (Cone 06 to 10)
The following formulas are calculated in grams.

Mix equal parts

Kaolin 25g	Feldspar 25g
Ball clay 25g	Silica 25g

Colored slips:

Red iron oxide	3–10%	*light to dark brown*
Rutile	4–8%	*tans*
Copper oxide	2–5%	*light to dark green*
Chrome oxide	1–7%	*pale to dark green*
Cobalt carbonate	.5–5%	*light to dark blue*

Combinations of

Red iron oxide 2% + Cobalt oxide 1% + Manganese dioxide 3% = black

Chrome oxide 1–4% + Cobalt carbonate .5–3% = light blue-green to dark blue-green

Note: The color of the slip will vary from bright to dull depending on the amount of iron in the clay body. The type of glaze you use on top of the slip also affects color.

Note: **For a Basic Slip Glaze** Replace Feldspar with Lithium carb.

Naomi Keller's Slip for Superhero Narratives

Red clay 70g	Cobalt dioxide 15g
Manganese dioxide 15g	

Terra Sigillata

Ball clay 1000g	Water (hot) $9^{1}/3$c
Calgon 5g	
(or 2.5g Sodium silicate and 2.5g Soda ash)	

Dissolve Calgon in water, add clay, and mix thoroughly. Let the slip settle for a day or two. Do not move or shake it during this time. When the heavy particles have settled to the bottom siphon off the thin mixture from the top. (The thicker remaining sediment can be discarded.)

To color pour slip into separate containers and add a different pinch of color (oxides) to each one. Apply a thin coat of terra sigillata to dry greenware. If you do more than one coat wait for each layer to dry before adding another. Terra sigillata must be polished while it is still wet. Use a chamois or a piece of plastic wrapped around your fingers.

Secret Sauce Glaze

Apply to your piece, bisque fire, and finish with propane torch to bring out metallic color. (Developed by Tad Riste.)

Colemanite 40g	Copper carbonate 60g

PV Glaze Base

This is a simple formula that has a firing range from Cone 06 to 10.

Plastic Vitrox clay 50g	Zircopax 10g
Gerstley borate 45g	

For color add:

Pale Turquoise Copper carbonate 2g
Glossy White Tin oxide 7g
Blue Cobalt oxide 2g

Clear Crackle Raku

Gerstley borate 80g	Nepheline syenite 20g

Cone Temperatures

Examples of temperature equivalents °F

Cones only measure the amount of heat in the kiln. Because temperature and time affect heat absorption, faster firings require higher temperatures. The chart below shows the difference in the amount of heat required for fast and slow firings with regular cones. *Note: This table is a guide. Actual bending temperature of the cone depends on firing conditions. Information in the last two columns is approximate.*

Color	Cone #	Temp. Increase 270° / hr.	Temp. Increase 108° / hr.	Firing stages	Ware types and Glazes
Very dull red	022	N/A	N/A	Dehydration begins	
	021	N/A	N/A		
	020	N/A	N/A		
	019	1279	1249		Enamels Overglaze colors
	018	1350	1314		
	017	1402	1357		
Dull red	016	1461	1416	Organic matter burns out	
	015	1501	1450		Chrome red glazes
	014	1537	1485		
Cherry red	013	1578	1539		Luster glazes
	012	1616	1576		
	011	1638	1603		
Orange	010	1675	1648		
	09	1702	1683		Low-fire lead glazes
	08	1749	1728		
	07	1805	1783		Low-fire earthenware
	06	1852	1823	Red clays mature	
Yellow	05.5	1873	1854		
	05	1905	1886		
	04	1958	1940		
	03	2014	1987		
	02	2048	2014	Buff clays mature	Earthenware
	01	2079	2043		
White	1	2109	2077		
	2	2124	2088	Soft stoneware	
	3	2134	2106		
	4	2158	2120		China glazes
	5	2201	2163		
	5.5	2233	2194		
	6	2266	2228		Feldspar glazes
	7	2291	2259		
	8	2316	2277	Stoneware matures	Salt glazes
	9	2332	2295		Stoneware glazes
	10	2377	2340	Hard stoneware	
	11	2394	2359	Porcelain	Porcelain glazes
	12	2415	2379		

Note: This chart refers to Orton Regular Standard Cones.

To convert Fahrenheit to Centigrade, subtract 32 from the temperature given, multiply by 5, and divide by 9.

Bibliography

Birks, Tony. *The Complete Potter's Companion*. New Jersey: Little-Brown & Company, 1997.

Branfman, Steven. *The Potter's Professional Handbook*. Iola, Wisconsin: Krause Publications, 1999.

Branfman, Steven. *Raku, A Practical Approach*, 2nd Edition. Iola, Wisconsin: Krause Publications, 2001.

Brodie, Regis C. *The Energy Efficient Potter*. New York: Watson-Guptill, 1982.

Buckley, Cheryl. *Potters and Paintresses; Women Designers 1870–1990*. London: Women's Press, 1995.

Burleson, Mark. *The Ceramic Glaze Handbook*. New York: Sterling, 2001.

Cahill, Rick. *The Story of Casas Grandes Pottery*. Arizona: Western Imports Publishing & Trading Company, 1991.

Cardew, Michael. *Pioneer Pottery*. Westerville, OH: American Ceramic Society, 2002.

Clark, Kenneth. *The Potter's Manual*. London: Chartwell Books, Inc., 1986.

Cooper, Emmanuel. *Ten Thousand Years of Pottery*. Philadelphia: University of Pennsylvania Press, 2000.

Dormer, Peter. *The New Ceramics: Trends and Traditions*. Rev. ed. London: Thames and Hudson, Ltd. 1994.

Fournier, Robert. *Illustrated Dictionary of Practical Pottery*. Iola, WI: Krause, 2000.

Hessenberg, Karin. *Sawdust Firing*. Philadelphia: University of Pennsylvania Press, 1994.

Kong, Ellen. *The Great Clay Adventure: Creative Handbuilding for Young Adults*. Worcester, MA: Davis Publications, 1999.

Leach, Bernard. *Hamada, Potter*. New York: Kodansha, 1997.

Nigrosh, Leon. *Claywork: Form and Idea in Ceramic Design*. Worcester, MA: Davis Publications, 1995.

Nigrosh, Leon. *Low Fire: Other Ways to Work in Clay*. Worcester, MA: Davis Publications, 1982.

Nigrosh, Leon. *Sculpting Clay*. Worcester, MA: Davis Publications, 1991.

Olsen, Frederick L. *The Kiln Book*. Iola, WI: Krause Publications, 2001.

Parks, Walter P. *The Miracle of Mata Ortiz, Juan Quezada and the Potters of Northern Chihuahua*. California: The Coulter Press, 1994.

Perryman, Jane. *Smoke Fired Pottery*. London: A & C Black, 1995.

Perryman, Jane. *Traditional Pottery of India*. London: A & C Black, 2000.

Peterson, Susan. *The Living Tradition of Maria Martinez*. New York: Kodansha, 1990.

Pitelka, Vince. *Clay, A Studio Handbook*. Westerville, OH: American Ceramic Society, 2001.

Scott, Paul. *Ceramics and Print*. Philadelphia: University of Pennsylvania Press, 2001.

Wallner, Linde. *An Introduction to Pottery*. New Jersey: Chartwell Books, 1995.

Woody, Elsbeth S. *Pottery on the Wheel*. New York: Farrar, Strauss, & Giroux, 1988.

Woody, Elsbeth S. *Handbuilding Ceramic Forms*. New York: Farrar, Strauss, & Giroux, 1989.

Yanagi, Soetsu. *The Unknown Craftsman, A Japanese Insight into Beauty*. Tokyo, New York: Konansha, 1990.

Glossary

A

aesthetics The branch of philosophy that deals with issues of beauty such as what is considered to be beautiful and what is considered to be art.

airbrushing Applying liquid colorants and glazes with an atomizer that uses compressed air to propel the spray.

alkaline glaze The earliest glaze developed in the Near East in which alkalies (base compounds of sodium, potassium, and the alkaline earths) are the fluxes.

alumina A primary ingredient in clay and glazes. It strengthens the clay, adds cohesion to a glaze, and reduces gloss to produce a matte surface.

armature A support or frame used when sculpting clay; usually removed before firing.

ash A glaze made with by-products of burned wood or vegetation.

atmosphere The mixture of gases in a kiln environment.

B

ball clay A plastic secondary clay that can withstand high temperatures and fires to white or off-white, also used as an ingredient in high firing glazes.

banding wheel A wheel head mounted on a pedestal base and turned by hand, used in the formation and decoration of pots.

bat A base for throwing, hand-building, or drying; usually made of plastic, pressboard, plywood, or plaster.

biscuit See bisque.

bisque *(bisk)* Ceramic ware that has gone through the first firing at a relatively low temperature (generally cone 010 to 05) and still maintains its porous state.

blisters Surface bubbles in a glaze caused by the release of impurities or gases that result when the firing process is too fast.

bloating Increase in porosity and pore size in a ceramic body that has been overfired.

bone dry Stage of drying when moisture in the clay body has evaporated so the clay surface no longer feels cold.

burnishing Polishing the surface of a leather-hard pot to compact it and produce and maintain a sheen at low firing temperatures. Objects such as a smooth stone or the back of a spoon are good burnishing tools.

C

calipers A hinged tool used for measuring diameters on the inside or outside of a three-dimensional form.

carbonates A compound containing carbon and other elements, used in making and coloring glazes or clay bodies.

celadon *(se-la-dän)* A category of green, gray, or blue-gray glazes for stoneware and porcelain; developed in China and Korea.

centering The process of applying pressure to a lump of clay on a spinning wheel head to position it for even rotation.

centrifugal force The tendency of matter to "flee from the center" when spun. Faster rotation creates stronger centrifugal force.

ceramics Objects made from clay that permanently retain their shape after they have been heated to specific temperatures.

chamber The enclosed portion of a kiln where pottery pieces are placed for firing.

chamois A very soft, pliant leather; used when wet to smooth the surface of wet clay.

chuck A clay shape used to secure leather-hard pieces in place for trimming on the wheel.

clay body A mixture of clay, minerals, and other ingredients that make up the composition of a clay type.

CMC gum An organic cellulose gum—carboxymethylcellulose—used as a thickener, suspending agent, glue, and binder.

cobalt carbonate A compound used as a blue colorant for slips and glazes.

cobalt oxide A very strong oxide used to produce blue in slips and glazes.

coiling Attaching rolls of clay together to form pottery.

collaring Squeezing the upper part of a thrown form as it rotates on the wheel, in order to decrease the size of its diameter.

colorant An element or compound that contributes color to a slip, glaze, or ceramic surface.

cone An object made of ceramic materials with a specific melting point, used to show the temperature in a kiln during the firing.

coning Part of the centering process; raising clay to form a cone as it spins on the wheel head.

copper A soft, common element known for its high conductivity and often used for green coloration.

crackle A type of glaze that incorporates crazing for decorative effect.

crawling A condition where molten glaze pulls away from portions of the surface to leave areas unglazed. This can be caused by grease or dust on the bisque ware.

crazing A network of fine lines in a glaze caused during cooling when tension between the clay body and glaze is uneven.

D

deflocculant A substance such as sodium silicate or sodium carbonate that causes the clay platelets to separate and remain in suspension when it is added with water to the clay.

dipping A method of applying glaze or slip to a piece by immersing it and quickly shaking off the excess liquid.

dome The result of successfully centering clay on the wheel. An opened dome is necessary to begin throwing vessels, pots, and plates.

downdraft kiln A kiln where the heat and flames are drawn downward and out through openings at the base of the kiln.

drape mold A support that holds a clay slab in a certain shape until it stiffens.

drying The elimination of water from clay pieces before firing.

dunting Types of cracking caused by cooling vessels too rapidly after firing.

E

earthenware Glazed pottery that remains porous when fired at low temperatures (below cone 2).

enamels Prepared low-firing colors, usually painted over higher fired glazed surfaces.

engobe A prepared slip usually containing colorants.

extruding The process of shaping moist clay by forcing it through a die.

F

faience (*fe-äns*) Term for low-fired pottery decorated with colored glazes over an opaque base glaze.

fettling knife A long tapered knife used for cutting and trimming clay.

firebox The enclosed section of a kiln where fuel is burned.

fireclay Clay that withstands high temperatures.

firecracking A network of fine cracks on the surface of an unglazed vessel caused by firing too fast.

firing Heating pottery or clay sculpture to a temperature high enough to render it hard and durable.

firing cone Pyrometric cone that will bend at the desired firing temperature.

flange A clay ridge that holds the lid of a pot, allowing it to rest securely. It can either be on the pot or the lid.

flue An opening within a kiln through which hot gases pass from the chamber to the chimney.

flux A material that promotes melting or increases the glass-making qualities of a glaze.

foot The base of a pot upon which it can stand.

frit A mixture of materials that has been fused by heating, reground into a fine powder, and used as an ingredient in a glaze.

G

glaze A coating of glass that is fused to the surface of a ceramic piece.

glost Glaze; also another term for glaze firing.

greenware Unfired pottery or sculpture.

grog Crushed fired clay used as an additive to clay body to reduce shrinkage.

guard cone Pyrometric cone one number hotter than the target firing temperature.

guide cone Pyrometric cone one number cooler than the target firing temperature.

H

hand-building Making clay forms by a non-mechanical process, such as pinching, coiling, and slab building.

high-fire Clay or glazes that are fired from cone 8 to cone 12.

hump mold Any object (plaster, foam, crumpled newspaper, etc.) over which a slab of clay can be laid to stiffen in that shape.

I

incise To remove clay by carving.

inclusion Any part of a fired clay piece, such as plant remains, rock fragments, and temper, that was not originally a clay mineral.

inlay To fill an incised or impressed area with contrasting colored clay.

K

kaolin (kay-a-lin) A pure clay used in white clay bodies such as porcelain. Sometimes called china clay.

kick wheel A wheel powered by the potter's foot rather than by electricity.

kiln A structure built to fire clay at high temperatures.

kiln furniture Heat resistant shelves and posts used to hold ware during firing.

kiln wash A mixture of kaolin and flint used to coat kiln shelves to protect them during firing.

kneading The process of mixing plastic clay to distribute minerals, organic materials, and water evenly throughout the body and to eliminate air bubbles.

L

leather-hard The stage between plastic and bone dry when clay has dried, but may still be carved or joined to other pieces.

levigation A method of refining clay in water where the heavy particles sink to the bottom and smaller particles are skimmed off the top.

lip The rim opening of a pot.

low-fire Clays or glazes that are fired within the kiln temperature range of cone 015 to cone 02.

low-mid fire Clay or glazes fired within the kiln temperature range of cone 01 to cone 3.

lug Handle-like projection on the side of pot.

luster A type of decoration made when metallic salts fired at low temperatures give a metallic sheen to a body or glaze surface.

M

majolica (ma-yä-li-ka) Earthenware covered with a tin glaze and painted with oxides. Also known as maiolica, faience, and delftware.

maquette (ma-ket) Small, quick preliminary sculptural "sketches" in clay.

matte or matt Dull surface, not shiny.

maturing temperature The temperature at which the clay body reaches the desired hardness or when a glaze fuses into the clay body.

melting point When a clay fuses and turns to a fluid glasslike substance during the firing.

mid fire Clay or glazes fired within the kiln temperature range of cone 4 to cone 7.

mishima A surface decoration technique whereby an impressed design is filled with a different colored clay slip.

mixed media Artwork made with a combination of materials or techniques.

mold Any form used to shape clay.

muffle The kiln chamber or wall that protects the pottery from the flame when being fired.

N

neck The part of a vessel between lip and shoulder.

negative space Areas of empty space defined by surrounding material; important in an overall design.

O

opacifier A chemical used to make a glaze non-transparent. Tin oxide is a common opacifier.

opening the dome Making a hollow in centered clay on the wheel, then creating a base and shaping the clay into its intended basic form (cylinder, bowl, etc.).

organic A shape or form that is curved or irregular, not geometric.

organic material Vegetable or animal material present in natural clay.

overfiring Increasing the temperature or length of firing beyond the ideal for a particular clay body or glaze.

overglaze A glaze designed to be applied and fired at a lower temperature after the first glaze firing.

oxidation Firing when the amount of oxygen present is more than is necessary to combust the fuel.

oxide A compound containing oxygen and other elements, used in making and coloring glazes or clay bodies.

P

paddling Beating clay with a flat stick to strengthen joints, thin walls, alter shape, or create texture.

paperclay Mix of clay, paper pulp, and water that is very strong and flexible and has an extremely low shrinkage rate.

peephole A hole in the door of the kiln through which the potter can view the progress of the firing.

pigment A mixture of minerals painted on clay ware before or after firing to produce color.

pinching A hand-building technique that involves squeezing the clay, usually between fingers and thumb.

pit firing A pre-industrial method of firing, still used, in which greenware is surrounded by combustible material and fired in a pit or on the ground.

plastic/plasticity The property of clay that allows it to change shape without tearing or breaking.

polymer clay A synthetic version of organic clay that is manufactured in various colors and baked in an oven rather than fired. It has only been in existence for a few decades.

porcelain A white high-firing clay body that is usually translucent.

porosity The amount of empty space in the structure of the fired clay that makes it capable of absorbing liquids.

preheating Heating ware prior to firing to remove traces of moisture.

press molding Making shapes by pressing clay slabs into or onto molds.

primary clay Clay that is of the same composition as the parent rock from which it was formed. Kaolin is a primary clay.

pulling Stroking plastic clay with the hand to shape handles for a pot.

pyrometer An instrument that measures the temperature of a kiln.

pyrometric cones Manufactured objects—made of ceramic materials and enclosed in a kiln during firing—that bend when specified temperatures are achieved.

R

raku *(rah-KOO)* A firing process in which porous or grogged ware is taken from the kiln when red hot (1470–1830°F). The ware is immediately placed in water or combustible material for reduction.

raw clay Unfired clay.

raw glazing Applying glaze to an unfired piece, then firing clay and glaze together.

reduction A firing in which there is insufficient air in the kiln for complete combustion. The metal oxides in the clay body and glaze release oxygen because there is not enough present in the atmosphere. This changes the color of the clay body and glaze.

refractory The quality of being able to withstand high temperatures without melting.

relief Sculptural or decorative forms that project from a flat background.

rib A flat curved tool made of wood, metal, or plastic used to refine shapes.

S

saggar A container made from fireproof material that protects ware from combustion gases during firing. It is also used to hold ware and fuming materials for separate reduction during firing.

salt glaze A glaze created by throwing salt into a kiln at stoneware temperatures. Vaporized sodium combines with silica in the clay body to form a sodium silicate glaze on the clay surface. Harmful vapors are also generated by this technique; soda glaze is recommended as a substitute.

scoring Scratching the edges of clay before joining them together.

secondary clay Clay that has moved from its original place of formation by erosion. It has combined with minerals and organic materials over time.

setting Arranging ware in a kiln for firing.

sgraffito *(sgrah FEE toe)* A decorating technique where a layer of slip applied to a clay body is scratched through to reveal the clay color.

shard A fragment of pottery.

shivering A glaze flaw; sections of glaze lift off a piece.

short clay Clay that is not plastic.

shrinkage The reduction in size of the clay mass that occurs when water in the clay evaporates during drying and firing.

silica A white or colorless crystalline compound occurring abundantly as quartz, sand, flint, agate, and many other minerals. It is the sparkly material in sand.

silk screen Fabric (often nylon) mesh used for printing an image onto a surface. Ink is forced through the screen with a squeegee.

slabbing Hand-building technique that involves shaping clay into a broad, flat, thick piece.

slab roller A mechanical device used to prepare clay slabs.

slip A fluid suspension of clay in water used in joining clay pieces and for surface decoration.

slip glaze A glaze that contains a high percentage of clay.

slip trailer A device, such as a rubber syringe or tube, used to apply lines of slip on clay as decoration.

slurry Clay that is like paste in consistency.

soaking The stage of firing when the temperature is kept steady for some time allowing the clay body and glazes to mature.

soda glaze A glaze created by spraying a solution containing sodium carbonate (soda ash) or sodium bicarbonate (baking soda) into the kiln while firing ware. Soda vapors react with the clay surface to form a glaze.

spray booth An enclosure with a vent that collects glaze vapors when a spray gun is in use.

spray gun A device that uses compressed air to vaporize liquid glaze. This tool is used to apply a fine, even coating of glaze.

sprig A decoration in relief, attached to greenware with slip.

stacking Loading a kiln efficiently for best use of space.

stains Commercial pigments used directly on clay bodies or for coloring glazes.

stoneware Dense, non-porous, hard pottery that matures from cone 5–11 (2200–2400°F).

T

template A pattern used to shape the profile of a piece.

terracotta An iron-bearing earthenware clay that fires to an earth red color.

terra sigillata (*TER-ra sij-jil-AH-tah*) A fine slip surface treatment used as a coating for burnishing or decoration.

throwing The process of shaping plastic clay on the potter's wheel.

toxic Any material that is poisonous or injurious to the health.

traditional pottery Hand-built ceramics, decorated with natural pigments and fired with organic fuel.

trailing Using a tube or slip trailer to squeeze lines of slip or glaze onto clay for decoration.

translucency A glaze quality that allows the passage of diffused light.

transparent glaze A clear glaze.

trimming The process of refining a leather-hard shape with cutting tools.

U

underfired A clay or glaze fired below its maturation point.

underglaze Any coloring element, such as oxides or commercial colorants, applied prior to glaze application.

updraft kiln A type of kiln where the heat is drawn through the kiln and exits through the top.

V

vitrification The stage during firing when a clay or glaze loses its porosity and transforms into a hard, nonabsorbent, glasslike state.

volatilize To change under heat from a solid through liquid to a gaseous state.

W

ware A term for any ceramic.

warping Changes in a clay form usually resulting from uneven thickness of the walls, uneven drying, or stresses during firing caused by poor support or uneven heat.

water smoking The first part of the firing cycle when water is driven from the clay.

wax resist A decorative technique where liquid wax is applied to a fired or unfired clay body. The waxed portion resists the surface treatment (slip, stain, or glaze) leaving the raw clay exposed.

wedging A way of improving the workability of clay by reforming the mixture to make it homogeneous and even in texture while eliminating air bubbles.

wheelhead The flat circular revolving plate of the potter's wheel upon which the pot is formed.

Index

A

additives, 25–27
adobe, 15
aesthetics, 22, 33–37, 51, 190
Africa, ceramics of, 16–17
aging and clay, 8
airbrush technique, 145, 146, 190
alkaline glazes, 13, 137, 138, 190
alumina, 137, 190
American Art Pottery movement, 95
American Ceramic Society, 116, 180
Americas, ceramics of, 16–17, 127, 139
Anasazi, ceramics of, 26
anchoring, 97
appliqué, 122
architectural style, 38
armature, 77, 190
artists-in-residence, 40, 150
ash glazes, 13, 139, 190
assessment
    and studio experiences, 19, 39, 81,
        115, 149, 179
asymmetry, 54, 94
atmosphere, 15, 152, 157–158, 173, 190
attaching handles, 111

B

balance, 36, 94
ball clay, 24, 190
banding wheel, 49, 52, 190
base, 53, 55
bat, 52, 87, 88, 190
Belize, ceramics of, 18–19
biscuit, 190
bisque firing, 161–163, 190
    and paperclay, 39
    and tiles, 73
bisque ware, 118, 128, 129, 131, 143
black iron oxide, 187
blistering, 147, 190
bloating, 170, 190
blue-and-white pottery, 127, 151
Blue Willow, 127, 151
bonding mix, 185
bone china, 185
bone dry clay, 12, 190
bonfires, 171–172
borax, 138
borders, 74–75
bottom, 91, 102
bowls, 98–100
box, clay, 68–70
braces, 76–77
Brazil, ceramics of, 6
breaks, 185

Britain. *See* England
Bronze Age, 16–17
brushes, 129, 130, 145
burnishing, 11, 12, 99, 123, 133, 190

C

calcium carbonate, 186
calipers, 104, 105, 190
canvas, 59–60, 72
carbon, 11, 125
carbonates, 118, 125–126, 186, 190
career exploration, 151
carving tool, 122
Casas Grandes, ceramics of, 26
casseroles, 94, 110
celadon, 13, 190
centering, 84, 86, 89–90, 190
centrifugal force, 84, 190
ceramic art, 169
ceramics
    definition of, 3, 190
    new American, 184
    origins of, 5–6
    timeline of, 182–184
Chabot, Aurore, iv, 167
chamber, 190
chamois, 100, 190
chemistry, 125–126, 165
China
    and blue-and-white ware, 6–7, 127
    ceramics of, 9–10, 79, 154
    and glazes, 13, 139, 147
    kilns of, 15
    and molded clay, 62
    and porcelain ware, 141
    and saggar firing, 175
    and tea, 51
    terracotta art of, 17
china paints, 141
chrome, 125
chrome oxide, 187
chuck, 190
clay
    body, 37, 190
    box, 68–70
    chemistry of, 4
    clay stamps, 121
    and color, 124
    combinations of, 186
    dust, 28, 48, 57, 91
    and firing temperature, 160
    forming of, 9–10
    preparation of, 28–32
    properties of, 23–28
    studio, 156
    tablets, 6
    types of, 23 *See also* clay body
cleaning and spraying, 146
    See also safety
CMC gum, 142, 190

coarse clay, 27
cobalt, 124, 127
cobalt carbonate, 187, 191
cobalt oxide, 187, 191
coil
    as brace, 76
    definition of, 9, 42, 191
    as foot, 48, 63
    as handles, 109
    and joining, 47
    method, 43, 52–58
collaring, 84, 92–93, 107, 191
color, 124–135
    and aesthetics, 35
    and decoration, 119–120
    and design, 158
    and glazes, 125–126
    of tea ware, 51
    techniques for, 128–133
    and texture, 126
colorants, 11, 120, 139, 191
colored clay, 124–125
colored slips, 126, 128
combinations of clay, 186
combing, 11, 132
commissions, 82
compressing, 57, 99, 101
computer-generated decal transfers, 135
cones, 152, 159–160, 188, 191, 193
coning, 88–89
consistency, 87
contrast, 12, 126
cooking vessels, 9, 14
cooling, 165, 170
copper, 124, 125, 191
copper carbonate, 187
crackle, 191
crackle glazes, 147, 187
cracks, 170, 185, 191
crawling, 147, 191
crazing, 147, 191
criticism, art, 34
crystalline glazes, 141
cuneiform script, 6
cutting, 77, 121–122
    See also incising
cylinders, 92–93

D

Daly, Matthew, 95
dampers, 155, 158
de-airing clay, 28
decal transfers, 135
decoration
    and aesthetics, 37
    classical style of, 18–19
    surface, 119–151
    techniques of, 11–12, 52
defects, glaze, 147
deflocculant, 191

dehydrate, 27
design
    assessment of, 39, 81, 115, 149
    elements of, 10, 25, 78, 112, 123, 158
    principles of, 12, 29, 74, 94, 134, 165
    and teapots, 112
    and tiles, 72–73
design-transfer method, 127
dipping glazes, 143, 191
dome, 84, 89–91, 191
dome lid, 105–106
Dominguez, Eddie, 40
dowel, 48–49
downdraft kiln, 15, 191
drape mold, 64, 191
drawings
    and design, 148
    and planning, 111–112
    and relief panels, 74
    and sculpture, 114, 115
    See also sketches
drinking point, 51
drums, 53
drying, 10–11, 21, 25, 191
dryness
    managing, 68
    and plasticity, 11
dunting cracks, 170, 185, 191
dust, clay, 28, 48, 57, 91
Dutch East India Company, 127

E

earthenware, 24, 185, 191
effigies, 5
Egypt, ceramics of, 2, 138
electric kilns, 154–155
electric wheel, 86
emphasis, 29, 36
enamels, 141, 191
England
    and blue-and-white pottery, 127
    ceramics of, 88
    and slip trailing, 131
    teacups of, 83
    and transfer printing, 133–134
engobe, 191
epoxy, 185
Europe, ceramics of, 13, 127, 157
evaluation, self, 181
    See also assessment
explosion and firing, 77
expressive qualities, 37
extruding, 42, 54, 191

F

faience, 127, 191
feathering, 132
feldspar, 4
fettling knife, 191
figurative art, 16–19
figurines, Stone Age, 5

Finland, ceramics of, 127
firebox, 15, 191
fireclay, 191
firecracking, 170, 191
fires and safety, 171, 172
firing
    and aesthetics, 37
    atmosphere, 15
    cones, 160, 191
    early techniques of, 14–17
    open, 14
    problems with, 170
    process of, 153–181
    saggar, 76
    sawdust, 174
    stages of, 161–164
    temperatures, 151, 156
    variables in, 153, 156–160
    wood, 174–175
fit and lids, 105
flameproof bodies, 186
flanges, 103, 106, 191
flaring, 100
flowing, 170
flue, 191
flux, 118, 128, 36, 186, 192
foot
    and clay boxes, 70
    coils as, 63
    definition of, 192
    of pinched pot, 46
    technique for, 48
    and trimming, 99
form, 10, 35
formal qualities, 36–37
forming methods, 76
France, ceramics of, 127, 157
frit, 192
Fry, Laura, 95
fuels and firing, 14
fumes, 39, 141, 178
functional
    bowls, 98–99
    lids, 103
    ware, 137

G

gases
    and firing, 156
gas kilns, 155
geology, 4
geometric forms, 38
Germany
    ceramics of, 71, 127
    and glazes, 13, 140
glazes, 2, 12–13, 136–148
    alkaline, 13
    applying, 142–147
    and brushing, 145
    Chinese crackle, 147

colors, 125–126
and decoration, 119
definition of, 192
early, 13
and firing, 163–165
and functional ware, 137
ingredients of, 136–137
qualities of, 51
recipes for, 187
and Rookwood Pottery, 95
and safety, 138
slip, 140, 187
and temperature, 158, 160
thickness of, 143
transparent, 126
types of, 13, 137–142
and vapors, 145
glossiness, 141
glost firing, 161, 192
granite, 4
Greece, ceramics of, 15–19, 133
greenware, 118, 128, 161
    definition of, 192
    and glaze, 128, 129
    repairing, 185
    and slip, 149
    and terra sigillata, 133
grog, 22, 27, 80, 171, 172, 186, 192
Grygutis, Barbara, 82
guard cones, 160, 192
Guatemala, ceramics of, 18–19
guide cones, 160, 192
guide sticks and slab construction, 60

H

Hamada, Shoji, 88, 169
hand-building, 32, 43–83, 192
hand dipping, 143
handles, 109–111, 113
haniwa sculptures, 79
heat. See temperature
high-fire
    definition of, 192
    glazes, 13, 136, 139–141
Hohokam, ceramics of, 26
Holland, ceramics of, 71, 127
hollow sphere, 49–50
hump mold, 192

I

idea communication, 19, 39, 81
ideals, 37
igneous rock, 4
impressing, 11, 51, 121, 125
incising, 121–122, 125
    as decorative technique, 18–19
    definition of, 11, 192
    and mishima, 132
    and sgraffito, 149
    and studio experience, 148–149
India, ceramics of, 5

industrial ceramics, 180
Indus Valley, ceramics of, 38
inlay, 125, 132, 192
inspiration, sources of, 167–168, 180
interior form, 51
Iran, ceramics of, 7, 23, 71
iron, 11, 124, 125
iron oxide, 187
Islamic pottery, 15
Italy, ceramics of, 71

J

Japan
    and blue-and-white pottery, 127
    ceramics of, 44, 58, 79, 88
    and glazes, 13, 139
    kilns of, 15
    and mishima, 148
    and porcelain ware, 141
    and raku firing, 176
    and tea, 51
    techniques of, 125
joining
    and appliqué, 122
    and coils, 55, 63
    and pinch technique, 50
    and sculpture, 81
    and spouts, 107
    technique for, 47
Jomon ware, 58

K

Kaneko, Jun, 152
kaolin, 192
kick wheels, 86, 192
kilns, 2, 153
    building, 156
    definition of, 14, 192
    downdraft, 15
    electric, 154–155
    furniture for, 163, 192
    loading, 161–165
    and safety, 154, 160, 163
    types of, 15–17, 154–156
    updraft, 15
kiln wash, 164, 192
kneading, 22, 28–30, 192
knobs, 70, 104–105
Korea
    and blue-and-white pottery, 127
    ceramics of, 13, 29, 134
    and mishima, 148

L

Leach, Bernard, 88, 169
lead, 13, 138
leather-hard clay
    and box construction, 70
    and coil method, 57
    definition of, 11, 192
    and joining, 47
    and stiff slabs, 67

and trimming, 96
and wax resist, 131
Lee, Heeseung, 150
levigation, 7, 192
Levinson, Diane, 20
Liberia, ceramics of, 9–10
lids
    and clay boxes, 69
    and teapots, 113
    technique for, 103–105
line, 35, 112
lip, 49, 192
low-fire, 133, 138–139, 141, 145, 192
low-mid fire, 192
low-temperature firing, 141, 171
low-temperature glazes and flux, 136
lug handles, 110, 192
lusters, 141, 192

M

maebyong, 134
majolica, 127, 142, 192
manganese, 11, 125
manganese dioxide, 187
maquettes, 67, 80, 192
marketing, research on, 156
Martinez, Maria, 123
masking, 130
masks, 66–67, 144
Mata Ortiz pottery, 26, 171
matte, 141, 192
maturing temperature, 192
Mayan culture, ceramics of, 17–19, 50
media use
    assessment of, 9, 39, 81, 115, 149, 179
Mediterranean, kilns of, 15
melting point, 192
Menchhofer, Paul, 171, 180
Mesopotamia, ceramics of, 6, 38
metallic lusters, 141
Mexico
    and Casas Grandes pottery, 26
    ceramics of, 12, 71, 127
    Mayan art of, 17, 50
    Zapotec art of, 76
Middle East
    and blue-and-white pottery, 127
mid fire, 193
Minton, Thomas, 127
mishima, 132, 148–149, 193
miter cut, 68
mixed-media sculpture, 78, 114–115, 193
Moche, ceramics of, 8, 16–19, 62
models, 67, 82
Mogollon, ceramics of, 26
Mohammedan Blue, 127
moisture, 4, 10–11, 23, 27
molding, 9–10
molds, 42, 61–64, 193
monochrome, 35

monoprints, 134–135
mood, 37
Morris, William, 95
movement, 36, 165
muffle, 193
murals, 72–73, 167

N

narrative art, 16, 18–19
National Council on Education for the
    Ceramic Arts, 20
neck, 49, 193
needle tools, 100
negative space, 35, 193
neriage, 125
New Mexico, and public art, 82
New York State College of Ceramics, 40
Nichols, Maria Longworth, 95
Nigeria, ceramics of, 42
nonfunctional
    bowls, 98–99
    lids, 103
non-representational sculpture, 76

O

opacifiers, 125, 193
open firing, 14, 153
opening the dome, 101, 193
organic
    materials, 121, 186, 193
    shapes, 44, 57
Ottoman Empire, ceramics of, 71
outside form of tea ware, 51
ovenware, 186
overfiring, 170, 193
overglazes, 141–142, 193
oxidation, 173, 193
oxides, 118, 124–126, 187, 193
oxidizing atmosphere, 157–158
oxygen
    and kilns, 155
    See also atmosphere

P

paddling, 46, 193
paint, 141–142
painterly effects and glaze, 128
Pakistan, ceramics of, 5
paperclay
    definition of, 38, 193
    and repairs, 185
    and saggar, 178
    structures, 41
    and transfer printing, 134
paper resist, 130
pattern, 36–37, 134
peephole, 193
Persia, ceramics of, 71, 137
perspective, 56
Peru
    ceramics of, 8, 11, 18–19
    and molded clay, 62

narrative art of, 16–17
photocopy, 134–135
photo emulsions, 135
physical qualities of tea ware, 51
piercing, 122–123
pigment, 193
Pima, ceramics of, 52
pinching, 9, 42, 43–52, 193
pinholes, 147
pit firing, 14, 123, 133, 172, 173, 193
planning
   and sketches, 18, 38
   and teapots, 111–112
plasticity, 2, 4, 8, 23, 193
platelets, 4, 59
plates, 100–103
platters, 62–63
Poland, blue-and-white pottery, 127
polychrome, 35
porcelain, 4, 139, 141, 185, 193
porosity, 193
porous clays, 185
portfolio
   electronic, 83
   and studio experiences, 41, 81, 117, 151, 181
   uses of, 21
Portugal, ceramics of, 71
potassium, 138
pouring
   glazes, 144
   lips, 106–107
pre-Columbian ceramics, 12
preheating, 193
premixed clay, 29
preparation
   of clay, 28–32
   early techniques for, 7–8
press mold, 64
primary clay, 193
printing techniques, 133–135
problems
   firing, 170
   glazing, 147
properties of clay, 23–28, 41
proportion, 36
public art, 82
pulled handles, 109–110
pulling, 107, 193
pyrometers, 159–160
pyrometric cones, 152, 159–160, 188, 193

Q
Qin dynasty, 79
Quezada, Juan, 26

R
raku, 49, 139, 145, 152, 164, 176–179, 186, 194
Ram's Head Spiral, 32
rattle, 50–52

raw clay, 194
raw glazing, 194
recipes, 187
recycling clay, 28
red-figure style, 16–17
reduction atmosphere, 157–158, 173, 176, 179, 194
refractory, 194
rehydrating clay, 7, 27
reinforcement, 69
relief, 74–75, 83, 194
religious uses of ceramics, 6
repair of cracks and breaks, 185
representational sculpture, 76
residency programs, 40, 150
resist, 130–131
rhythm, 36, 165
rib tool, 44, 53, 93, 194
rims, 51, 91, 93, 102, 106
rolling tools, 59–60
Rome, ceramics of, 15, 133
Rookwood Pottery, 95
Roswell Museum and Art Center, 40
rough surface, 147
running, 147
rutile, 125, 187

S
safety
   and acrylic spray, 135
   and ash glazes, 139
   and back muscles, 91
   and chipping glazes, 165
   and clay dust, 28, 48, 57
   and cutting, 61
   and ergonomics, 31
   and fires, 171, 172
   and fumes, 141, 145
   and glazing, 126, 138
   and kilns, 160
   and paint, 142
   and photo chemicals, 135
   and raku firing, 177, 179
   and respirators, 143
   and tool use, 68, 73
   and ventilation, 39, 141, 154, 178
saggar, 76, 152, 175, 178–179, 194
SA-KU technique, 178–179, 181
salt glazes, 13, 140, 194
sawdust firing, 174
Sax, Sarah, 95
scanning, aesthetic, 35–37
Schein-Joseph International Museum of Ceramic Art, 40
scientific use of ceramics, 180
score, 47, 48, 53, 68, 194
sculpture, 76–81, 114–115
sealer and paint, 142
secondary clay, 194
secret sauce glaze, 187

self-evaluation, 181
   See also assessment
sense of touch, 97
sensory qualities, 35
series, 166–167
setting, 194
Sèvres vase, 157, 181
sgraffito, 132, 148–149, 194
Shang dynasty, ceramics of, 9, 79
shape, 10, 35
shard, 194
Shirayamadani, Kataro, 95
shivering, 194
short clay, 194
shrinkage, 23–25, 71, 186, 194
silica, 136, 186, 194
Silk Route, 127
silk screen, 194
size, 36
sketchbook
   and aesthetics, 37
   and clay relief, 74
   and design, 148
   and kiln structure, 15
   and museums, 168
   and paperclay structure, 39
   and SA-KU firing, 179
   and sculpture, 81, 115
   and sgraffito, 149
   and silhouettes, 53
   as tool, 33
   uses of, 19
sketches
   and coil method, 52
   and planning, 18, 38
   and SA-KU, 179
   and sculpture, 80
   and tile design, 72
   use of, 67
   See also drawings
slabs
   and casserole, 94
   definition of, 9–10, 42, 59, 194
   and roller, 194
   soft, 59, 61
   stiff, 59, 67–70
   technique for, 43, 59–75
slaked, 7
slicing, 61
sling mold, 62–63
slip glaze, 194
slips, 2
   and box construction, 68
   colored, 126, 128
   as decoration, 18–19
   definition of, 7, 194
   glazes of, 140, 187
   and handles, 111
   and joining, 47, 48

slips, *continued*
    technique for, 128
      and trailing, 131–132, 194, 195
slump mold, 64
slurry, 194
Smith, Charles, 116
soaking, 194
soda glazes, 140, 194
soft slabs, 59, 61
Soldner, Paul, 139
solid structures, 77
source of clay, 61
space, 35, 78
Spain, ceramics of, 71, 127
spalling, 170
spattering, 129
sphere, hollow, 49–50
Spiral, 31
sponging, 129
spouts, 103–108, 113, 117
spraying, 145–146, 194
sprigging, 118, 122, 194
squatting, 170
stabilizing materials, 8
stacking, 195
Staffordshire, 127
stains, 195
stamps, clay, 121
stencils, 72, 73, 130
stiff slabs, 59, 67–70
    See also slabs
Stone Age, ceramics of, 5–6
stoneware, 185
    definition of, 195
    and flux, 136
    and high-fire glazes, 139
storage containers, 9, 14, 58, 83
studio artist, career as, 116
studio assessment. *See* assessment
studio potter, career profile of, 180
Studio Potter movement, 169
style, 115
supports, 56, 76–77, 81
surface decoration, 119–151
symbols, 6, 120, 127
symmetry, 28, 44, 54, 94
Syria, ceramics of, 5, 71

T
tableware, thrown, 98–102
Tang dynasty, ceramics of, 79, 154
teapots, 107, 111–113
tea ware, 51
technical careers, 180
technical qualities, 37
techniques
    coil, 43, 52–58
    collaring, 92–93
    color, 128–133
    early, 6–17

    and firing, 153–181
    and glazing, 142–147
    incising, 121–122, 125, 148–149
    kneading, 30
    and molds, 42, 61–64
    monoprint, 134–135
    for pinch pots, 45–46
    resist, 130–131
    and rims, 91
    and slabs, 59–75
    and teapots, 111–113
    trimming, 96–98
    wedging, 18, 29, 31–32
    wheel, 86–98
temperature
    and color, 124, 158
    and cones, 188
    control of, 15
    and firing, 14, 21
    and flux, 136
    and glaze, 13, 138–139, 159–160
    and overglazes, 141
    and raku firing, 177
    regulating kiln, 162–163
    zones, 163
    See also firing; pyrometers
template, 195
terracotta, 16–17, 79, 195
terra sigillata, 133, 187, 195
test tiles, 147
texture
    and aesthetics, 35
    and clay type, 23, 25–27
    and color, 126
    and decoration, 119–124
    and slab construction, 61
    tools for, 120
Thailand, ceramics of, 13
theme, 115
thermal factors, 51
thickness, glaze, 143
throwing
    definition of, 195
    and forms, 84–117
    and handles, 111
    and tableware, 98–102
    tools for, 87
tiles, 71–73, 83, 167
timeline, ceramics, 182–184
tin, 138
tools
    carving, 122
    paddle, 46
    physical, 32–33
    for sgraffito, 132
    and spraying, 145
    and texture, 120
    and throwing, 87
    trimming, 96

    verbal, 33–37
    and wheels, 87
touch, sense of, 97
toxic, 195
    See also safety
tracing, 72
traditional pottery, 22, 26, 195
trailing, 131–132, 194, 195
transfer printing, 133–135
translucency, 195
transparent glazes, 126, 195
trimming, 84, 96–98, 100, 102, 195
Turkey, ceramics of, 71
Turner, Thomas, 127
turntable, 49
types of clay, 23, 185

U–Z
Uganda, ceramics of, 33
undercutting, 89, 101
underfired, 195
underglazes, 13, 124, 128, 195
unity, 36, 74
updraft kilns, 15, 195
Valentien, A.R., 95
value, 123
ventilation
    and electric kilns, 155
    problems with, 170
    See also safety
vessels, 9, 14
visual appearance, 51
vitreous clays, 185
vitrification, 195
volatilize, 195
volcanic rock, 4
Voulkos, Peter, 169
ware, definition of, 195
ware board, 80
warping, 71, 170, 195
waterproofing, 11
water smoking, 195
wax and glazing, 142
wax resist, 131, 195
web links, 20, 40, 82, 116, 180
wedging, 8, 22, 28, 29, 31–32, 195
Weiser, Kurt, 118
wheel, 84, 86–98
wheelhead, 195
whiting, 186
willow ware, 127
wire tool, 93, 100
wood-burning kiln, 177
wood firing, 139, 174–175
work process. *See* assessment
writing about art, 21, 41, 83, 117, 151, 181
Zapotec, ceramics of, 76